Justice for All

A Novel

Also by Phyllis Greenbach

The Blessing and the Curse

JUSTICE FOR ALL

Phyllis Greenbach

Justice for All references:
social justice, immigration, family, education, fiction

1st edition

Library of Congress Control Number: 2022906502

ISBN 978-0-578-28346-3 (paperback)

Cover design by Sissy Kaplan

Phyllis Greenbach, Palm Desert, CA

Printed in the United States of America

Dedication

*For my children, grandchildren, great-grandchildren
. . . and for all those yearning to breathe free.*

Disclaimer

The first duty of society is justice.

Alexander Hamilton

Justice will not be served until those who are unaffected
are as outraged as those who are.

Benjamin Franklin

Contents

The Lopez Family

Chapter 1

Mauricio Lopez

Quezaltepeque, El Salvador
Friday, April 22, 1983

SEÑOR GARZA the luxurious resort's general manager, hung around the lobby waiting for the evening security guard to arrive. He had something urgent to tell him. As Mauricio slipped through the side entrance, Señor Garza glanced at his watch, noting that Mauricio had seven minutes to spare before he began his evening shift.

Without so much as a smile, the general manager greeted him. "*Buenas tardes,* Mauricio. Tonight, when your shift ends, stop by my office. We must talk. It's important."

"Yes. Yes, of course," Mauricio said, puzzling over the request.

From four-to-midnight Mauricio followed his normal routine. He walked the grounds and checked the resort's corridors, the restaurant, and the banquet rooms, always searching for someone or something out of the ordinary. Over the years, he had developed a keen eye, noticing everything, from a burned-out light bulb to a misplaced chaise lounge. He often picked up miscellaneous items that were out of place, like scattered pool towels or cocktail glasses that needed to be returned to the bar.

As Mauricio moved from one area to the next, random thoughts zig-zagged through his head like a kite caught in the wind. A special meeting with Señor Garza struck him as odd. The resort manager usually ducked out long before Mauricio's shift ended. When he wanted to talk to the staff, he scheduled a general meeting. To be called in for a private meeting whet Mauricio's curiosity. *Perhaps tonight I will be offered a raise, maybe even a promotion.*

One desk clerk and the head housekeeper had been terminated earlier in the week. Mauricio speculated that might provide an opportunity for him to move up. While making the rounds, he thought about his family—his wife Rosa and their boys, Santiago and Javier. But most of all he thought of himself and what he would do with the extra money. Lately, his feet were burning by the time his shift ended. So, the first thing he envisioned, was a new pair of shoes.

Exactly at midnight, Mauricio entered the resort manager's windowless office. With a trained eye, he noticed that Señor Garza's usual keepsakes were gone from the top of his desk and the certificates of merit had been removed from the turquoise walls.

Señor Garza folded the newspaper he had been reading and without thinking, left it on top of his desk. Then he grabbed the manila folder from the credenza behind his desk. "Mauricio, come in. Please sit down."

Mauricio was more than willing to get off his aching feet. As he took one of the two wicker barrel chairs in front of the resort manager's desk, he crossed one leg over the other and noticed the worn spot on the sole of his right shoe. As he looked up, he caught the headlines of the folded newspaper, *Diario Co Latino,* that had been set to one side on the manager's desk.

PRESIDENT REAGAN PROVIDING $42.5 MILLION FOR
THE EL SALVADOR GOVERNMENT TO BUY MORE ARMS

Withering from the news, Mauricio lost his composure. "Why does the U.S. keep selling our government guns? Every day the soldiers murder innocent people."

"I don't know. I don't know," the resort manager lamented, scratching his forehead in frustration. "But what can we do? They claim we're all communists."

"Communists! *No comprendo.* I don't understand. The government taxes us to death. All we want is to farm our own land."

"Mauricio, this civil war has been going on for years. And our troubles keep getting worse. How long have we worked together?"

"Thirteen, maybe fourteen years."

"It has been a long, long time." The resort manager knew what he had to do, but it was disheartening. He had been doing the same thing all day. He leaned forward, anchoring both elbows on his desk and nervously entwines his fingers. Stalling for time, he cleared his throat, then looked directly at Mauricio. "I can't tell you how much I've appreciated your years of service. You've been a hard worker. A loyal employee. A good man."

Mauricio leaned back, pleased with what he heard. Then the mountain came tumbling down.

"But I'm afraid I've got some very bad news. It's difficult for me to say this, but I must. The resort is closing. It's over. We're finished. You, me, everybody."

In an instant Mauricio's life changed, and he suspected not for the better. In disbelief, he prodded the resort manager. "I don't understand. No more work?"

"*Nada.* None. You saw the headlines. *The Norte Americanos,* they have stopped coming. The *touristas* claim it's too dangerous. They won't be back until the blood stops flowing in the streets."

Almost as if he needed to hear it again, Mauricio questioned him. "For good? The resort is closing for good?"

"Yes, Mauricio, for good. I'm sorry. There's nothing I can

do. With all the violence, tourism has drizzled down to nothing. Señor Gutierrez, the owner of the resort, is an honorable man. He kept the place open, hoping that business would improve. But now he claims he's losing more money every day. Believe me when I tell you, he's just as sad as we are."

"But my family . . ." Mauricio's hands began to shake. "How will I provide for my family? I have two growing boys."

"Truthfully, I don't know." Señor Garza paused for a moment before admitting, "I worry about it for you . . . for me, for all the employees."

With his head exploding with unanswered questions, Mauricio stumbled out of the resort for the last time. He had done nothing wrong. For all his loyalty, for all the years of getting to work on time and doing his job without complaining, a swelling anger began to fester inside him. Sometimes after work he would stop off at his favorite cantina for a shot of *mezcal*. But this night was different. Mauricio needed more than a single shot. Life was closing in. In his gut, he knew how hard it would be to find another job.

Sometime after three in the morning, a waning moon provided barely enough light for Mauricio to stagger home. He emptied his pockets and laid his loose change on top of the pine bureau in the tiny bedroom. He dropped one shoe after the other onto the floor, each making a loud clunking noise. His head pounded and his feet still throbbed. It had only been a few hours since he lost his job, but already he felt worthless. Mauricio longed for the comfort and closeness of his wife Rosa. He climbed into bed naked, ready to make love. He spooned against his wife's backside, sliding his hand around to cup her breast.

Rosa barely opened her eyes. Without turning over, she rejected him. "Move away. Your breath stinks. You've been drinking again, haven't you?"

"Rosa, listen," he growled. "Tonight's different. I drink for a reason."

"Always, you find a reason to drink."

"Rosa, listen to me. The resort is closing. I lost my job."

"You'll find a job somewhere else," she snapped. "Now leave me alone and go to sleep."

Chapter 2

The Family

ROSA ALWAYS WOKE UP before the rest of the family to prepare breakfast. After the early morning meal—eggs, tortillas, and fresh fruit juice—her sons left for school. Just before they walked out the door, she warned them to be careful. "You boys, stay out of trouble . . . and mind your business."

Javier, a sharp-tongued seventeen-year-old, was growing more independent and difficult with each passing year. "Jeez, do we have to hear the same thing every day?"

"Yes! And show some respect. And Santiago, you be a good boy. Remember, no soccer until you come home and change your clothes."

As she hand-washed her sons extra jeans on a scrub-board in a galvanized tub behind the house, Rosa smiled inwardly. *Javier and Santiago are growing up so fast.*

On most days, Rosa brought in a few extra *cólones* selling flowers at a small stall between the park and the church. That morning, before leaving for the flower market, she prodded Mauricio, "What are you doing today?"

"Looking for work. What else?"

But every day Mauricio lingered longer and longer over his strong black coffee and absent-mindedly watched the macaws fly in-and-out of the cherimoya tree. Weeks went by, and as hard as he tried, he couldn't find work. With no job, he eventually began to spend his afternoons with a small group of laid-off men. They drank and cursed the fourteen wealthy families who controlled the country and the military that did their dirty work.

When at home, Mauricio groused, "Rosa, I need more food. All the time my stomach makes noise. It's empty."

"Well, if you didn't drink, we'd have more to eat. I do what I can, but the money is running out."

With no control over his life, Mauricio began to grow more hostile and belligerent, blaming everyone for his troubles. Even though he claimed to love his family, sometimes his temper flared out-of-control. He became unduly aggressive, frequently disparaging Rosa, and at times smacking Santiago and Javier for minor infractions.

At twelve years old, Santiago loved soccer. His soccer ball would forever remain his prized possession. Like most boys in Central America, the sport coursed through his veins like blood. He worshipped Pelé and dreamed of becoming a professional soccer player. Most days he couldn't wait for school to end. Only then did he feel free. Every day as the class waited by the door for the final bell, he reminded Francisco, his best friend, to wait for him in the alley behind the stores. "I need to go home first. Get my soccer ball and . . ."

Before finishing his sentence, Francisco invariably teased, "I know. Don't tell me. Your mother wants you to change clothes."

Santiago would shrug his shoulders and give a shy, embarrassed smile. But he did what his mother told him.

One afternoon while the boys were playing soccer in the alley, they heard a steady stream of gunfire coming from a low-flying helicopter. "Run," Francisco screamed. "The doorway! Get in the doorway." With their backs slammed against the door, and their hearts thumping, the boys froze. Time stood still. When there was nothing left but the desperate moans of those left in the street to die, Francisco whispered to his friend, "You okay?" Traumatized, Santiago didn't answer. Francisco repeated it. "Santiago, are you okay? Are you okay?"

In shock, Santiago was unable to speak until Francisco threw his arm over his shoulder and reassured him the worst was over.

The traumatized boys had just experienced El Salvador's insanity first-hand.

The ruthless military, who did the bidding for the corrupt government, had stepped up their brutality. They deliberately left a few dead and dying bodies on the street as a warning: *Don't mess with us*. On that day Santiago lost his innocence. From then on, every time he left home, even to go to school, the raw fear of death loomed just below the surface. Priests, nuns, and anyone who spoke against the regime were targeted. He had heard a grisly rumor that soldiers sometimes killed teachers right in front of their students.

Another event happened just five months later. On a sweltering Saturday—when the late afternoon temperature rose to 98 degrees with suffocating humidity—Santiago and Francisco were on a crowded bus riding home after watching a soccer match in San Marcos. When the bus pulled alongside the edge of the road to let several passengers out, a military truck filled with soldiers in green and brown fatigues blocked it. A gruff looking soldier, with a week-old beard and a black hole where a tooth should have been, pushed his way onto the bus. With his finger on the trigger of an AR-15 assault weapon, he screamed, "Out! Get the fuck out! Quick! Quick! Move quick!"

Santiago and Francisco, who had been sitting towards the back, followed the others who shuffled out single file. With his head down, Santiago felt his heart beating so hard he thought it was pounding inside his head. Trembling, he dared not look the soldier in the eye, for fear that he'd be shot on the spot. A cluster of soldiers stood by with fiendish smiles, enjoying the sight of the submissive and fearful group stepping down off the bus. Just in case anyone resisted, they too had their fingers strategically placed on their assault rifles. Another soldier, with a thick, black mustache and scruffy beard, held the head of a teacher on a stick, as if it were a cherished trophy. The soldiers forced the captives to file by and look at it.

About to vomit, Santiago turned his head away. But an ill-tempered soldier with sausage-like fingers grabbed him by the chin. "Look at him. Take a good look. This is what happens to those who fight against us."

Trembling, Santiago stared at the grotesque head with the vacant eyes.

A few weeks later, Santiago hustled home from school. As he neared the front door, he overheard his mother and father arguing. Fearing to go in, he stood outside and listened.

"Boarders? NO! Rosa, *no* boarders. Not under my roof."

"Listen to me," Rosa pleaded, "They'll pay us rent. You're always complaining there isn't enough to eat. With boarders, you will have more to eat. Besides, you are gone half the time. What difference would two boarders make?"

In the end, Mauricio was forced to share their humble home with an older couple who were barely squeezing by on what they earned doing odd jobs. They too were just trying to survive. With the boarders, Rosa's whole family slept together in a single room. A couple of old sheets hung from a rope that separated Mauricio and Rosa's space from their two sons.

Outdoors, a lattice structure, partially covered by corrugated tin, served as Rosa's kitchen. She managed to cook on a black metal grill supported by cinder blocks. Without an indoor kitchen, Santiago's family and the boarders ate all their meals at a weathered picnic table partially shaded by a large cherimoya tree. A hardscrabble of chickens gathered around and squawked as they scratched at the dirt in the dusty front yard searching for scraps of food.

Mauricio's mood worsened. Along with a warren of unemployed and disillusioned men, he drank and cursed the military for destroying their lives and ruining the country. When he wandered home drunk from these gatherings, his family tried to stay out of his way. It wasn't easy in such small quarters. Small irritants and tensions often boiled over.

By contrast, Rosa tried to maintain a calm and positive atmosphere for the sake of their boys. Every morning she woke up earlier than the rest of the family to prepare breakfast. And each day she smiled cheerfully and parroted the same kind words, "I make breakfast for my men."

One Thursday evening after another meager supper, Mauricio once again announced that he would be out for the evening.

"We hardly see you anymore. All the time you leave us. Where to this time?"

"The university. I'm taking a class."

"Don't lie! You've never been interested in school. Something's going on?"

"Rosa," he said sharply, "it's better you don't know. Believe me, nothing good can come of it."

Their conversation didn't end well as he slammed the door and walked out.

At dinner the following Thursday, Mauricio admonished Javier for challenging him when he spoke. "Shut your goddamn mouth. Hear me? Someday it's going to get you in a heap of trouble."

After he had eaten, Mauricio grabbed the only book in the house and announced he was going to his class at the university. Still fuming over his oldest son's belligerent attitude, Mauricio started the two-and-a-half-kilometer trek to the university. His routine went well enough until several soldiers patrolling the area in a muddy, beat-up Dodge Ram rounded a corner and pulled alongside him. "Hey, you. Stop!" the driver bellowed through the open window and quickly slid out of the truck.

Mauricio fought with himself to act calm. He knew if he ran, he'd be shot in the back.

Both soldiers, wearing dirty fatigues, confronted him. The taller one with a jagged scar running across his cheek took charge. "Where you headed this time of night?"

Mauricio stammered, "Well . . . uh, I'm taking a history class at the university."

"History?" the short, stocky one mocked. "Who takes history classes?" He grabbed the book out of Mauricio's hands and held it up, glancing at the title. "Look at this," he scoffed, *Mayan Civilization*. Then his mood turned suspicious. He glared at Mauricio for what seemed like an inordinate amount of time. Not sure what to do next, he turned toward the other soldier.

Not wanting to bother, the other soldier shrugged, "Aw, let 'em go."

After the two soldiers drove away, Mauricio thought about his close encounter and began to tremble. His heart was still racing when he reached the university library. Nevertheless, he repeated his usual routine, pretending to search for a rare, infrequently used book on Mayan agriculture. The complicit librarian, a young man with slicked back hair and furtive eyes, directed him down a flight of narrow stairs that led into a musty smelling, poorly lighted basement. Mauricio wandered through a labyrinth of large rooms with stacks of rarely used old books. He glanced around to make sure no one was there, then slipped into a windowless storeroom where two other men waited.

Fifteen minutes later, the librarian directed a scholarly professor, who taught classes on Aztec and Mayan history, downstairs on another pretext. The professor, whose black horn-rimmed glasses magnified his eyes and made him look owlish, refused to say how or where he got his information. But he would update the few trusted men on the insurgents' latest resistance tactics. At the end of their illicit meeting, the professor's eyes grew more intense, as he whispered the same challenging phrases each week: "No more exploitation! No more deaths! The spiral of violence must be stopped."

Chapter 3

Mauricio Arrested

MAURICIO LOPEZ was a righteous man. The continuing brutality against ordinary citizens and the church repulsed him. He could never reconcile the recent abduction, rape, and murder of four nuns by armed men in uniform. He thought it an unpardonable sin. In incremental steps, he had joined the rebels and periodically disappeared for several days and nights. When he returned home, unshaven and scruffy, his clothes covered in dirt, he refused to discuss his whereabouts.

For his compatriots, a sympathetic cantina owner provided a secret meeting place in his small warehouse, located in an industrial part of town. Away from the watchful eyes of the soldiers, the disgruntled men sat on gray metal folding chairs surrounded by unopened cases of liquor and relived their narrow escapes. While drinking *mezcal*—tequila made from agave—they plotted future moves against the government.

One Friday night, shortly after ten o'clock, a series of black clouds eclipsed a fingernail moon. Several two-and-a-half-ton

U.S. military trucks—their markings obliterated—with canvas cargo holds came to a halt fifteen meters from the warehouse. In a practiced drill, the company of soldiers in brown-black military fatigues hopped from the beds of the trucks on cats' feet. Their orders were specific: *If possible, capture the insurgents alive.*

They quickly surrounded the warehouse. When the leader raised his arm and swung it forward, two soldiers with a battering ram smashed the heavy, fortified entry. In less than a minute they ripped the door off its hinges and the soldiers flooded in.

"Run," one of the insurgents screamed.

Pandemonium ensued.

The panicked rebels scrambled in all directions. It proved chaotic as folding chairs clamored to the floor. In their haste to escape, a few of the insurgents collided right into the arms of the soldiers. Mauricio, a little too drunk to move fast, was immediately captured by a bulky soldier with a vise-like grip.

"Resist and you'll die!" the soldier snarled. Another, smelling of stale tobacco, helped cinch Mauricio's hands behind his back with thick jute rope.

"Blindfold him and throw him in one of the trucks."

A soldier threw an abrasive gunny sack over Mauricio's head. He struggled to break free but was no match for the soldiers who dragged him outside and tossed him onto the metal bed of the first truck. With no way to protect himself, he landed hard on his right shoulder and the side of his head. Despite the intense pain, he tried to steady his breathing and racing heart.

Depending on how they landed, other insurgents whimpered or howled as they were pitched into the bed of the truck. Mauricio heard one man pleading to be free. "Let me go! It's all a mistake! Where, where you taking us?"

"Shut up!" one of the soldiers screamed. "I'll kill the next one who opens his fuckin' mouth." After that, no one said a word. The rebels' bravado quickly disappeared.

Mauricio couldn't be sure how much time elapsed. His shoulder and head throbbed, but his ears perked up as both trucks pulled away. His body jostled this way and that as the truck rolled up and down the hillsides on pitted, dirt roads. His panicky thoughts collided with each other. *Why did I get involved? If I die, what will happen to Rosa? To my boys?* He prayed, *Jesus, have mercy on me.*

Eventually the two trucks turned onto a steep gravel path. They stopped abruptly in a gulch, hidden behind a copse of eucalyptus trees. An elongated wooden storage facility—once used to dry coffee beans—stood isolated, kilometers away from another living soul. With cool efficiency, the death squad separated the rebels and herded them in for interrogation. Two soldiers flanked Mauricio, one on either side. They pinched his shoulder blades so hard that arrows of pain shot up his neck and into his head, amplifying the pain he was already feeling. His legs buckled and he stumbled.

"Walk, coward. Stand up and walk!" one of the soldiers growled.

Once inside, they dragged Maricio into a makeshift partition, no bigger than a horse's stall. An interrogator with cold, calculating eyes sat behind a makeshift table that held a single notebook, a pen, and a handgun. "And who've we got here?" he snarled with more than a touch of sarcasm. "Name? What's your name?"

Gasping for air, Mauricio mumbled, "I can't breathe. If you take this blindfold off, I'll tell you."

"You. You're a fuckin' traitor to this country! And I don't negotiate with traitors. So, let's start over. Your name? Give me your name."

"Take this damn blindfold off," Mauricio sputtered between coughs, ". . . and I'll tell you."

"You misunderstand. I've no patience. And I don't play games. Now, I'll ask you one more time. Your name?"

At that moment, Mauricio heard the pathetic wails of agony coming from another partition. Then a shrill scream. The putrid odor of excrement assaulted him. Disoriented and fearful for his life, he couldn't be sure whether it was coming from him or from someone else. With the suffocating hood over his face, an ungodly panic coursed through every corpuscle in his body.

"Okay. Okay. *Me llamo es Mauricio Gonzales Lopez.*"

"Good. Now your address."

"No. You'll never get my address. Not now, not ever."

"Very well. Kill the little bastard."

"No! No! Wait! Please." Fearing for his life, Mauricio sobbed as he gave up his address.

"Okay, Mauricio, now we're getting somewhere. Before I take the hood off, I want the names and ages of your family. Everyone."

"No! No! You'll kill me. Then you'll kill them! Cowards. You're nothing but a bunch of cowards."

"Okay. Have it your way." The interrogator signaled for one of his henchmen to cut off his air.

With his hands still bound behind him, Mauricio was helpless. He couldn't stop the soldier who was squeezing his windpipe with his bare hands. Gasping for air, he begged, "Please. Please stop! I can't breathe! Let go!" His voice tapered off and his legs fell out from under him.

The sadistic interrogator took glee watching Mauricio struggle. He did not speak again until Mauricio was halfway to the floor. "Enough. Let him breathe. Maybe he's got a change of heart."

The soldier that almost killed him, let go and forced Mauricio to an upright position.

"One last chance. The names of your family. Tell me and I'll remove the shroud. Otherwise, I'll kill you."

With his heart pounding like a Taiko drum, Mauricio struggled for more air. His head buzzed, and he could barely think. At this, the weakest moment of his life, he provided the interrogator with the names of his family.

"Okay. Good. You see. If you cooperate, I'm not such a bad guy. Go ahead. Take off the head covering."

Mauricio blinked and blinked, his eyes trying to adjust to the solitary light bulb that hung from a wire overhead.

And then the interrogator began again in earnest. "What were you and the others planning?"

"Nothing."

The interrogator pounded the table hard with a closed fist. "Nothing! Nothing! Don't tell me NOTHING! The truth. I want the truth!"

Mauricio heard the piercing screams again, penetrating the thin, makeshift partitions.

The interrogator smirked. "Tell me, what you were planning?"

"I told you . . . we were just drinking." Mauricio was no fool. Judging from all he knew about the death squads that controlled El Salvador—and all that was taking place here—he realized he was about to die, no matter what he said or did. There were no second chances. No forgiveness. No way out. Knowing that nothing would change the outcome, his fear vanished, replaced with a rush of bravado and pure hatred. The only thing separating him from his interrogator was the truth. His truth.

With his adrenaline pumping, he did the only thing he could do. He bellowed, "You will all go to Hell! You and your henchmen are nothing. *Putas!* Whores! Lackeys with guns." With that, he spat on the ground. "The rich, they count their money and laugh. You, all you and your men do is destroy families. Ruin our country. In the end, there will be nothing. For you, for me, for anybody but the wealthy."

Chapter 4

Flight

THE FOLLOWING DAY a truck rumbled over the dirt road and stopped in front of their house. Rosa awakened to the unfamiliar noise and vibrations. She thought it peculiar. No large trucks ever rumbled by. Except for a few scattered houses and wild fields, there was nothing beyond. She wanted Mauricio to check it out. She looked over to see if Mauricio had come home in the middle of the night like he often did, but he wasn't there. Rosa started to curse him when she heard a loud *THUNK!* The chickens began to squaw incessantly. In her bare feet, she shuffled out to see what was going on. Although the dawn light was still soft and mellow, she caught sight of her husband's body splayed in the dirt. A wretched wailing, like the pathetic howl of a wounded animal, filled the morning quiet. Then Rosa screamed over and over. *"Oh, Dios mío! Oh, Dios mío!* Oh, my God! Oh, my God!"

The chickens were pecking away at Mauricio's face and uncovered arms. Still howling, she crouched alongside him and tenderly caressed his head, matted with barely dried blood. The old couple, with whom they shared the house, heard Rosa's anguished cries and dashed outside. Santiago, who had been in a deep sleep, awoke slowly to the unusual commotion coming from the front of the house. With his eyelids still half-closed, he shouted, *"Qué pasa?"* Curious to find out what happened, he slid out of his bed roll and headed towards the opened door.

His brother Javier had arrived moments before. "Stay back!" he ordered. "Don't come out!"

"Why? What's happening?"

As Santiago headed to the front door, Javier—older and much stronger—slammed him against the wall. "Stupid, for once do what I say."

"Get out of my way," Santiago yelled as he twisted and broke his brother's grip.

A moment later he caught sight of his father's mutilated and bloodied body. Mauricio's eyes were open but glazed over, his jaw contorted as if still grimacing in pain. Three fingers were gone from his right hand. Then Santiago saw the nearby plastic bag that held the missing fingers along with a small piece of paper.

"Our names are there, on that paper," his brother Javier whispered, fear radiating from his deep brownish-black eyes. "It's a warning; we could be next."

Santiago flung one hand over his mouth. With the other hand, he grabbed his brother's shoulder and tried to steady himself as his legs weakened. Then he vomited.

"I told you not to come out here. You wouldn't be puking right now if you listened to me." Taking stock of his younger brother, Javier shouted, "I tried to warn you."

Between Santiago throwing up, his father's mutilated body lying in the dirt, his mother's wailing, and the chicken's squawking, complete pandemonium engulfed the scene. The boarders that shared their house tried their best to calm Rosa. They pulled her limp body away from Mauricio and dragged her to one of the wooden benches. Then the man ran over to keep the chickens from pecking at Mauricio's remains.

Raising her face to the sky, Rosa shrieked, "Mother of God, this can't be true."

Even though they all tried to avert their eyes from the corpse, it would forever be etched in their minds. While Javier remained frozen, not knowing what to do, the woman boarder yelled towards him. "Javier, get some water. Quick. Your mama needs water."

In the small, close-knit community, bad news traveled fast. Several neighbors and a few members of the church arrived. After the women forced Rosa inside, two men lifted Mauricio's body and placed it on the outdoor picnic table, away from the pecking chickens. Santiago overheard bits and pieces of conversation as the men whispered among themselves.

". . . missing three fingers."

". . . a priest. Find the priest."

". . . a coffin."

Santiago, traumatized and frightened, could not bear to look at his father's disfigured body. But thinking of his father stuffed inside a coffin and forever buried in the dirt terrified him even more. While he tried to grapple with the reality of his dead father, he was virtually left on his own. He received a few perfunctory pats on the back, but no one came forth to comfort him. Left alone to mourn, he tried to forget the beatings born out of his father's frustration and concentrate on happier times.

In a flood of memories, Santiago recalled one joyful incident. It happened before his father lost his job. Mauricio had tried to teach him to whistle. And they had laughed together when Santiago puckered his lips and blew, but nothing but a weird noise and a steady stream of air emerged.

Hours later, a familiar parish priest arrived with additional men and a simple pine casket. It was then that Rosa grasped the finality of her husband's death. She also understood the veiled threat left in the plastic bag with her name and that of her boys. Her father, who joined her as soon as he heard the news, wrapped an arm around Rosa, as a river of tears continued to flow.

Two neighborhood women, using a tin bucket full of water and a clean cloth wiped the caked blood and dirt from Mauricio's face and hands. Afterwards, two men lifted his limp body and gently placed it in the pine coffin. On the far edge of those that gathered round, Santiago stood alone, frightened, and bewildered. More than anything else, he needed reassurance and comfort. Every so often, he slid over and touched his mother's shoulder, as if she could make this nightmare go away. As the sun set and daylight faded, the local priest led a prayer vigil. A memorial of white candles glowed brightly against the black sky, offering a sliver of solace.

On the day of Mauricio's funeral, a suffocating humidity wrapped itself like a wet towel around the somber mourners. The small amount of security Santiago had felt growing up suddenly evaporated. In an attempt at bravery, he swiped the tears from his eyes with the side of his arm as he watched three solidly built men slide the plain pine coffin into the back of the small pick-up truck.

Rosa, in a black dress, and the two boys in their Sunday best, led the cortege of mourners. No one spoke as they walked somberly behind the old pick-up truck that slowly made its way to the familiar cemetery alongside the church. Keeping his head bowed and his eyes fixed to the ground, Santiago gripped one of his mother's hands for reassurance. Javier, his older brother, held his mother's other hand, but his mind sought revenge. *Someday I'm going to find a way to kill the bastards that murdered my father.*

At the foot of the church steps, the familiar priest clutched a well-worn Bible and greeted the mourners. He touched Rosa's shoulder gently and whispered, "Everything will be okay. Jesus will protect you."

Friends and neighbors—some holding flowers—gathered around the coffin at the cemetery. Supported on each side by Santiago and Javier, Rosa wept as the soft-spoken, sympathetic Roman Catholic priest—who unfortunately had buried more than his share of insurgents—led them in prayer:

"O my Jesus, forgive us our sins,
save us from the fires of hell,
lead all souls to Heaven,
especially those most in need
of thy Mercy."

Somber looking men carefully lowered Mauricio's coffin into the open grave. As they shoveled dirt over his father, Santiago's whole body winced with each hollow THUD. On his way out of the cemetery, he turned his head for one final look. The few bunches of marigolds and white lilies had already started to wilt. In the end, all that remained of his father's life was a homemade wooden cross and memories.

In nineteen years of marriage, Mauricio insisted on making every decision. With her husband gone, Rosa grappled with all the well-meaning advice. Like most widows, she was stuck between courage and insecurity. More than anything, she needed to learn how to think for herself. *I'm the only one responsible for Javier and Santiago. What should I do? How will we survive?*

During the traditional eight days of mourning, indecision swirled around Rosa's head. *Shall I do this? Should I do that?* Despite the hardships, she felt that Mauricio had once anchored her life. Now everything felt tenuous. With no direction, she felt as if she were about to plunge into a deep, black abyss. Her father reminded her that the death squads did not hold back. They were in grave danger and needed to flee El Salvador . . . the sooner the better. But she was drowning in a tide of indecision.

Rosa's father worried constantly about the safety of his daughter and grandsons. He began to carry the gun he usually hid under the counter at his *cantina*. He shadowed Rosa protectively. One afternoon while they sat at the sunbaked picnic table, he couldn't help noticing Rosa's sorrowful, swollen eyes. "I don't have to remind you of the threat," he said, gently wrapping his arm around his daughter's back. "This is no life. To be safe, you and the boys must get away from the long reach of the soldiers."

"I know, *Papá,* but where? Where should we go?"

"I've been thinking about it a lot. Make your way north. You'll be safe there."

"No! No! Somewhere else. The United States is too far away. Besides, I don't speak their language."

"You'll learn. You'll see. Life will be easier."

"I have too little money. Remember . . . Mauricio was out of work for so long."

Rosa's father owned an unpretentious *cantina.* In the late afternoon, some of the telephone company's workmen stopped in for a cold bottle of beer or a shot of tequila before going home. In the evenings, locals stopped by. Over the years, Rosa's father had squirreled away a modest sum, hoping it would sustain him in his old age. But after Mauricio's murder, things changed abruptly. He not only offered Rosa his blessings, but the better part of his little nest egg. "I've got money."

"No. I won't take it."

"Rosa, listen. Stop and listen to me. When I sell your house, I'll recoup the money. Besides, I don't need much. You've got the boys to worry about. They'll have opportunities you never dreamed of."

"Papá, only if you go with us."

"I'm too old. I'd just be a burden. Besides, I can't sell the cantina so fast. You must go now. Not in a month, not in a year. But NOW!"

For days they argued over the money, but in the end, Rosa accepted his offer, even though her plans were still muddled.

Rosa's cousin, whom she had not seen in years, rode two buses to offer her condolences. She had always held her eldest cousin in high esteem. As they sat together at the picnic table sipping black coffee, Rosa admitted her deepest fears about heading north.

"Ah, don't you worry, Rosa," her cousin said while patting her hand. "Remember Nacho, my oldest son?"

"Of course."

"For ten years he lives in California. He's got a good job. Sends money home. I know my son. If you reach California, he'll help you. I'm sure of that."

"Oh, I don't know," Rosa replied, wringing her hands together. "I can't impose."

"Don't be crazy," her cousin said, patting Rosa's hands. "I'll call him first thing tomorrow. Then you can talk to him yourself. You'll see, he's a good boy."

That was the tipping point. Rosa's indecision gave way to a vague plan. But other arrangements needed to be made. Her father offered to pay for the use of a neighbor's telephone. The next day, Rosa and her father placed three separate long-distance calls.

The first was to Nacho, her cousin's son, who lived in a small town in southern California. As she began to explain her dire situation, Nacho interrupted "I've already spoken to my mother. She explained everything. Look, I can't help you to cross the border. You've got to do that on your own. But I'll do whatever I can, once you're here." Nacho told her where he lived and spoke about his family. With his assurance, Rosa's plan was beginning to seem real.

"I'm going to call Eduardo," her father insisted. "He's an old friend. Your bus ride will be long, and you'll be tired. I'm going to ask him to put you up for a day or two. Give you and the boys a place to rest."

Not used to being so forward, Rosa felt uncomfortable asking strangers for favors. But things were different now. Since Mauricio was murdered, she had no choice. Her father placed the call from the neighbor's house as his daughter stood next to him, listening to every word.

"Yes, Eduardo, I'm fine. My good friend, I'm calling for my daughter. I was wondering if you would do me a favor." After apologizing profusely, he recapped what had happened. "Yes, the three of them will be heading north. As you know, the bus ride is endless. I was hoping that they could stay with you . . . for a few days. Simply to rest."

Eduardo and Delores had set out for *el norte* twenty years earlier, during another El Salvador uprising. But they only got as far as Durango, Mexico. Once there, they hired on as ranch hands, raised a family, and made a life for themselves.

Tension mounted as Rosa made the final phone call to a friend of a friend. Josefina and her family lived in Tijuana. Always a soft-hearted woman, she was most sympathetic as Rosa explained her situation.

"*Pobrecita!* I'm so sorry. For years, we've heard ugly stories coming out of El Salvador. Yes, of course, come. *Mi casa es su casa.*"

That evening when the house had quieted down, Rosa sat Santiago and Javier down for a serious talk. "I have something important to tell you," she said with newly found resolve. "You know what happened to your father. At any time, the soldiers could come for us. We must leave El Salvador. We'll head north to California."

Both boys looked at her with blank expressions. Despite the uprising, they had never thought of living anywhere else. This was their home. This is where their friends were. This was all they knew.

Javier, her rebellious son, immediately protested. "Not me. I'm not going. I'm staying here. I'm going to kill those bastards that murdered *Papá.*"

"No! No!" Rosa screamed. "Don't be crazy. They'll kill you first. There are too many of them. Javier, for once, don't argue with me. Just do what I say. I need you right now. At seventeen, you're the man-of-the-house."

Javier mulled it over in his mind but didn't share his thoughts of getting even.

Santiago, insecure and needy, stood by and listened.

With no more than a whisper of hope for a better life and the promises of help, Rosa jumped into the abyss. She bought the least expensive bus tickets she could find heading north. Fearing for their lives, she packed a few belongings hurriedly. At the last minute, she wrapped a small ceramic statue of the Virgin Mary in a white embroidered blouse and tucked it in her big straw bag. Rosa, trying to keep her emotions in check, oversaw what her boys would take as well.

When Santiago grabbed his soccer ball, Rosa shook her head vigorously. "No. *Mi hijo*. No soccer ball! It's too big . . . too bulky!"

"I'll keep it in the net. I can carry it with one finger."

"No! I know you want to, but it's a long journey. We can't take everything."

"I'll carry it. I promise. Please . . ." Santiago begged. "Please."

She knew the soccer ball meant the world to him. Taking everything into account, she rubbed the stress from the back of her neck and weakened. "Okay, take the soccer ball, but you're the one that has to hold it."

The most difficult part was saying good-bye to their neighbors and extended family, warm people that had been so good and caring. Francisco, Santiago's best friend, came over with his mother to wish them well. He brought his beloved soccer jersey, the one with Pelé's number 10 on the back. Francisco's mother said, "Francisco has something for you."

"Here. Take this shirt with you," he said shyly, looking down at the ground so no one would notice the tears in his eyes. "You know, to remember me."

"Go on. Take it," Francisco's mother insisted. "He wants you to keep it."

Santiago looked at his mother for direction.

"It's okay. Go ahead. Take it. I can squeeze one more shirt in." Santiago's face lit up.

While they waited at the small, weathered bus terminal, Rosa's father wrapped his arms around his grandsons and daughter one last time. Tears stung his eyes. "Have you got everything? Remember to write. Let me know where you are. That you and the boys are safe." He knew—but wasn't saying—the journey was laden with danger. In the cantina, he had heard heart-breaking stories about predators preying on the innocent. But thought, *what choice do they have? If they stay, the military will surely kill them.*

The rickety bus finally arrived. Somewhat in a daze, the three of them climbed aboard along with two other passengers.

Rosa's father stood alongside the bus. "May God be with you."

But they couldn't hear him as they juggled their belongings and concentrated on finding seats. Expelling black fumes, the bus pulled back onto the road. Like so many before her, Rosa had turned her back on the repressive political regime.

Chapter 5

Long Bus Ride

WHEN ROSA AND HER BOYS arrived in San Salvador, the capital, they bought other tickets and transferred to another bus. This one slogged through the highlands and lush rain forests, stopping in Candelara de la Frontera. At the open-air terminal, Rosa, Javier, and Santiago waited with all their earthly belongings for nearly three hours for yet another bus that would take them across the border to their next destination, Guatemala City. Like her father, Rosa had heard stories about the bandits, and she could ill afford any setbacks. In case they were robbed, she had stashed most of her money in her bra, praying it wouldn't be discovered.

As they were about to cross the border the following morning, four *banditos* stood in the middle of the road, demanding the bus driver pull over and stop.

The bearded one cursed and pounded on the closed bus doors, "Open the fuckin' door!" He climbed aboard the hot, stuffy bus carrying his assault rifle. "Out!" he screamed. "All of you! *Vámonos!* And take your things with you."

Rosa, who had been holding her rosary, grasped it even tighter. Without consciously thinking, she began the rotation of prayers, beginning with the Apostle's Creed:

I believe in God, the Father Almighty, Creator of heaven and earth . . .

Santiago and Javier, who were sitting across the aisle, looked at their mother for guidance.

"Everything *es* all right. Just do what he says."

With no other choice, the fearful passengers shuffled off without pushing or shoving. The other bandits, also carrying assault rifles, herded the group into a semi-circle, three-deep, surrounding the head *honcho*. He made his demands clear. "If you plan to get back on that bus, it'll cost you twenty thousand *cólones* each or you walk."

Without uniforms, no one could be sure if they were soldiers, policemen, or gang members. No one knew if they were from Guatemala or El Salvador. It simply didn't matter. Extortion was extortion. Javier, who fought the urge to fight back, and Santiago, full of fear, flanked Rosa. They watched helplessly as she threw her rosary back into her straw bag. With shaking hands, she dug around, searching for the small brown pouch that carried her money. She was forced to fork over sixty thousand *cólones* a substantial amount from her meager reserve.

From then on, life grew sparse.

At each terminal, vendors hawked cheap sunglasses, gum, or simple foods. Afraid that her money would run out, Rosa hardly ate, surviving on mangoes and water until supper. By late afternoon her stomach was growling, and her head ached from hunger. But she was intent on making sure there was enough money to feed her growing boys. They only got off the bus to use the bathroom, stretch their legs, fill their *bota* bags with water, or wait at a crowded bus terminal for a transfer.

Time passed slowly. Santiago grew restless, constantly badgering his mother, "How much longer 'til we get there?"

"Soon. We stop soon," she repeated. *"Mi hijo,* you must be patient." As bedraggled as she felt, she convinced herself that every mile they traveled would lead them closer to *el norte.*

The rhythmic motion and constant droning of the bus hypnotized Santiago and often lulled him to sleep. Overcome with more stress than he could handle, he took to biting his nails and nervously picking at the skin around them. Despite the open windows on the bus, the sweltering heat and humidity made for an unpleasant journey. The boys only treat was the sweet, juicy mangoes their mother could buy for pennies that quenched their constant thirst.

As brothers do, Santiago and Javier began to haggle over their seating arrangement. Javier tormented his brother. "It's your turn to sit by the window."

"No, I'm not sitting there. I'm not moving. How come you only want to trade when the sun's shining in your eyes?" Santiago was ashamed to tell his brother the truth. When he sat next to the window, it gave him the creeps. In addition to the forests and fields, and the little clusters of shacks along the side of the road, he imagined his father's body floating alongside the bus. And that image flooded his mind with gruesome memories.

Santiago yelled at Javier. "Stop it! Stop pinching me."

"I'll stop when you do what I say. Trade seats, stupid. Sitting here is getting to me, okay?"

"Okay, okay! I'll sit by the window . . . but just for an hour."

Even though they squabbled, Santiago looked up to Javier and tried to please him.

Black diesel exhaust spewed from the bus as it clawed its way up and down the steep mountains on narrow, winding roads. Kilometers of monotonous cornfields with tall green stalks or sugarcane spread across the lower elevations. From time to time their bus had to stop to allow slow moving animals to cross the dusty, rural roads. Often, sweaty, overheated passengers packed the aisles, some juggling sacks of vegetables or crates of live chickens.

For long, tedious hours, Rosa and the boys sat uncomfortably on the hard seats in abject silence. In their own way, each of them fought off the demons that paraded like soldiers inside their head. Rosa often cried silently, grieving over the uprising in her country and Mauricio's brutal murder. *If only he didn't get involved.* Sometimes she cried for herself, her unknown future, and all she had left behind, especially her father. Her rosary was her only consolation. Soundlessly, she fingered the beads as she recited the rotation of prayers. At night, numb from the monotonous bus ride, she attempted to sleep with her orange woolen shawl wrapped over her arms and shoulders, while her sons crunched up their sweat jackets and used them as pillows.

The next day their bus slowly tread its way along the pitted road towards the downtown terminal in Guatemala City, Santiago tapped his mother on her shoulder.

"When can we get off the bus?"

"Soon. We have to transfer to another bus that'll take us to Mexico."

As they approached the outskirts of the city, Rosa noticed houses with rolled barbed wire that stood atop high walls. And private guards with pump-action shotguns protecting shops from intruders. She surmised that the store owners were forced to hire their own security forces. *The police in both countries,* she thought, *only responded on behalf of the ruling class.*

It would be another three-hour wait to transfer buses at the terminal. Growing rambunctious, Santiago begged his brother to play soccer. They kicked the soccer ball around in the narrow alley alongside the terminal. Rosa observed her boys playing and smiled inwardly. *It's good to see them laughing again.*

Minutes later Santiago screamed at his brother. "Why'd you kick it so hard? You did that on purpose." The soccer ball had rolled under a two-toned Ford parked on the side of the narrow street. "Go get my ball!"

Javier folded one arm around the other. "Hey, it's your ball. If you want it, get it yourself."

Reluctantly Santiago crawled beneath the car to extricate the ball, soiling the front of his tee-shirt with grease.

Crossing into Tapachula, a notoriously lawless border town in Mexico, presented another fearful episode. Rosa had heard about the vicious gangs. Knowing the possible dangers after the first extortion episode, she had set aside some money for bribes, but once again hid the remainder in her bra. *I don't want to run out of money, or we'll be forced to beg on the streets.*

Everyone's nerves were on edge. Santiago and Javier had spent the last two days bickering.

Javier taunted his brother. "Go sit somewhere else. You smell like shit."

"You stink worse."

The squabbling continued.

Javier threatened his brother, "If you don't shut up, I'm gonna take your damn soccer ball and shove it out the window."

Always resolute and stoic, Rosa tried to keep the peace. "Schuss!" She nodded, indicating there were other people on the bus. "We're almost there. Calm down. Be quiet."

By the time they arrived in Mexico City, they were all exhausted. They barely had enough time to go to the bathroom, wash up and get something to eat before transferring to another bus that made its way to Durango.

Rosa's father's friend Eduardo and his wife Delores welcomed them as if they were family. For many years, they had worked on an isolated ranch. It was a joy to see faces from home. Delores, a short, stocky woman, whose wiry gray hair was pulled off her face with a simple orange headband, worked as a cook in the main house. Eduardo worked as a ranch-hand and jack-of-all-trades. With the help of others, they personally built a small house and raised their children there. Now in his late sixties, Eduardo had a touch of arthritis in his knees and hands, and walked with a slight limp, from an accident several years earlier.

"I apologize," Delores said. "Please forgive me. Our house is unusually crowded. I had no idea when you were coming. Two days ago, we had a big *fiesta* Eduardo and I celebrated our 45th anniversary. One of our sons and his wife and their four children are still here visiting. I'm embarrassed. We don't have any room for you to sleep. Our small place is bursting with people. But I have an idea that might work . . . We can put you up in the barn, on the haystacks. We'll slide the doors closed and give you lots of heavy blankets."

Rosa and the boys were too tired to care. They were simply grateful to get away from the bus fumes, the crowded terminals, and filthy washrooms. More than anything, they needed a place to rest, shower, and wash their clothes.

With the help of her daughter-in-law and Rosa—who was only too delighted to be in a real kitchen—Delores prepared a succulent cauldron of *caldillo duranguense,* a tender beef dish with ancho chilies, tomatillos, and garlic. Delores pulled out all the left-over food and dessert that remained from her party. With so many people to feed, they ate in shifts. She suspected her newly arrived guests were the hungriest and insisted on feeding them first. With a sense of satisfaction, she watched as the boys leaned over the bowls and quickly devoured the food.

"More?" she asked.

Santiago couldn't help himself. "Yes. Can I please have more?"

Delores faced Javier and asked him. He nodded his head, indicating he wanted more too. Pleased that they were enjoying her cooking, she dished out an even bigger portion for each.

Santiago would never forget the pungent aroma and the savory taste of her food. When dessert was offered, he scarfed down her rich custard and a large piece of the left-over cake. She offered him some fresh fruit and he gobbled that down too. And if given the opportunity, he would have eaten three more helpings of everything.

For the moment, the food and kindness revived the weary travelers' sagging spirits.

Rosa and her boys slept in the barn where much of the farm equipment was stored. Santiago, who had become accustomed to sleeping on hot, stuffy buses, nearly froze, when the night temperature dropped almost twenty degrees. In the morning, his dark skin grew discolored from the extreme temperatures and Rosa worried that he might be catching a cold.

When they left Durango, it was a long, hazardous bus ride up and down the curvy mountain roads and along Federal Highway 40 to the warmer climate on the Mazatlán coast. After hours of driving, Javier grew impatient. Since he was sitting in the row directly behind the bus driver, he began to badger him. "Hey man, we're crawling. Speed it up!"

The white-knuckled driver valued his own life as he faced a myriad of hairpin turns. With little patience for a loud-mouthed kid, the bus driver replied, "We're on *El Paso de la Muerte*, The Path of Death. One slip-up and boom, we're over the edge. Trust me. The authorities would leave the bus wherever it fell. Look down. Can you see the bottom?"

There was silence.

"It's too steep and rugged to pull anyone . . . or anything out. Do you really want me to go faster?"

Rosa, who was sitting across the aisle, reached over and grabbed Javier's arm and schussed him.

Terrified, Santiago, who happened to be sitting in the window seat near his mother, tried to look over the edge. He couldn't see the canyons below. *"Es hondo, hondo, hondo* . . . It's deep, deep, deep . . ."

"Don't be a 'fraidy cat," Javier taunted. "We'll all die soon enough."

"Stop it!" Santiago begged.

"Stop fighting. Settle down. We're almost there."

Javier mocked his mother. "We're almost there! We're almost there! I've been hearing that for days!"

Chapter 6

Josefina and the Coyote

Tijuana, Mexico

THE LAST FEW DAYS were agonizing. Rosa's body felt stiff after sitting on the bus for so many days and nights. Adding to her miseries, she had tripped on a stair getting off at the last bus station and her right knee, the one she fell on, still throbbed. Her patience with Javier and Santiago had worn thin; she was as tired and cranky as they were. She was more than grateful when they finally reached their last stop before crossing into the U.S.

In Tijuana—a border town separating Mexico and California—Josefina, Diego, and their three children scraped by in a modest two-bedroom home, originally painted a hot pink. It had long ago faded from the blazing sun. A television antenna protruded from the flat roof. Metal bars on the windows and a chain link fence protected their property. Their yard lay bare, except for the cacti under the living room window.

Weeks earlier, Josefina had received Rosa's desperate telephone call. A kind and gentle soul, Josefina sympathized with Rosa's frightful situation and immediately agreed to help, without first discussing it with Diego. On Friday afternoon, beat and bedraggled, Rosa and the boys appeared for the first time. Josefina and Diego extended a warm welcome to the exhausted travelers, although Diego was a little put out, wondering how long they would be staying.

Within the overcrowded house, Rosa and the boys slept in the tiny living room, the boys on the floor and Rosa on the dusty couch. First thing in the morning, the weary house guests piled their meager belongings along the wall. Rosa warned her sons to be as unobtrusive as possible and to be mindful not to inconvenience their gracious host and hostess.

On their first Sunday in Tijuana, both families strolled together to the nearby church. Later in the day, while the children played outside, Rosa reveled in the familiarity of being in the kitchen. She felt useful helping Josefina prepare for their early supper. The children ate first. Once Rosa, Josefina and Diego completed their meal, they lingered at the table. Even with all the doors and windows open, the air was hot and still. Diego, wearing a tank top and shorts, grabbed a cold beer from the refrigerator. "Want one?" he asked his wife and Rosa.

"No thank you," Rosa replied politely, trying hard not to be a burden.

"Rosa, how 'bout some coffee?" As Josefina started to rise from her chair, she said, "I'll brew us some."

"No, I'm fine, really. Don't get up." Rosa listened with fascination as Josefina rattled on about their life in Tijuana. "I'm curious," Rosa said, "You live on the border. Did you ever want to live in the U.S.?"

"No. Not really,' Diego said, shaking his head. "This is where we were born."

"Speaking for myself," Josefina added, "I couldn't take the pressure. We'd always be outsiders. You know, we've got family, friends, the church right here. For us, it's enough."

Rosa listened but knew in her heart she felt differently. After coming this far, she was determined to fulfill her father's dream. On the long, monotonous bus ride, she had nothing but time to think. Getting to California had become an obsession. She convinced herself it would be a refuge, a place of safety and opportunity. When she slept, she dreamt she was there; during the day, fantasies of a better life occupied her thoughts. "Well, I'm so grateful for your help. You're both a Godsend. But, frankly, I'm not sure what to do next. Exactly how do we cross the border?"

Diego put down his beer. "It's no secret. One way or another, people cross, more often than not, with the help of a *coyote*"

"A *coyote?*"

Diego chuckled, thinking Rosa way too innocent for her own good. "That's what we call a smuggler, someone who takes people across the border. It's their job. They know the ropes."

Just then one of his sons, who had been sitting on the front steps with his friend, started to blast his boom box. "Will you turn that damn thing down?" Diego hollered through the open door. "We're trying to talk in here." He paused and apologized to Rosa. "Damn kid, he doesn't know any better. Now, where was I?"

"The coyotes," Josefina reminded him. "You were talking about the coyotes."

"Oh, yeah. The coyotes. They can be helpful, but you must be careful. Some make outrageous promises, take your money, and disappear. Like everything else, some are better than others."

"I'm confused. How does that work? The coyotes, I mean."

"I'm no expert," Diego admitted. "But over the years, I've heard plenty. Some float you across the Río Bravo, the border between Mexico and the U.S., on inner tubes after dark."

Rosa twisted her paper napkin nervously and grimaced. "We can't swim. Suppose we fall in,"

"You didn't let me finish . . . besides, you'd probably wind up in Texas. And you told me you wanted to be in California. Right?"

"Right."

"Can I say something?" Josefina interjected, drumming her fingers on the table impatiently. "Some coyotes know where you can slip through a fence."

Diego shook his head. "That's mostly in the Arizona's desert. Then you'd have to outrun the Border Patrol. People get lost or separated. Too many die out there."

Still fingering the napkin, Rosa, who was listening intently, said, "Wait. Just so you know, my cousin's son said that if we cross the Tijuana border, he'd pick us up and drive us to his apartment."

"I get it," Josefina said. "so, here's another way . . ."

Rosa felt desperate when she nixed another one of Josefina's ideas. She couldn't see herself stowing away in the hidden compartment of a car or being stashed in the bed of a loaded truck. "Remember, there's three of us."

"Rosa, can I speak frankly?" Diego said, feeling like they were getting nowhere.

"Of course."

"One way or another, it's risky. The main thing is you must trust whoever you're dealing with. I've got an idea, but I make no guarantees. Over the years I've heard of a coyote, he's a legend around here. He simply drives people across the border using *green cards*. But he charges a fortune."

By her expression, it was apparent that Rosa didn't understand.

"I know it sounds weird, but the U.S. gives some newcomers green cards. It really has nothing to do with color. For some odd reason, that's just what they call them. It's basically a work permit."

Josefina added, "The thing is, if you've got a green card, you're not quite a citizen, but you're not considered illegal either. For the coyote, they're perfect. Someone who has a green card can go back and forth across the border without being hassled. It's like a winning ticket."

"We don't have green cards."

"But the coyote does. He's got a lot of them. I don't know how or where he gets them, but I hear he's got baskets full . . . for men and women."

"What about my boys? We're all going together."

"I think he's got green cards for all ages. But I really can't say for sure," Diego said, scratching an irritating flea bite on his neck. "Frankly, everything I know is second and third hand. But, Rosa, if that's the way you want to go, I know someone who works for the coyote. He could answer your questions better than me."

The day had come. After some digging, Rosa finally had a date to talk to the *coyote*. To reach the *zócalo,* the plaza, she cut through an area where American tourists shopped for souvenirs. A crowd of older, well-fed tourists were just stepping off a tour bus and congregating on the wooden sidewalk. The doors to the merchants' shops were open. Stores displayed leather goods, ponchos, guitars, and colorful embroidered skirts and blouses. The irony was not lost on Rosa. *If only we could sneak aboard that bus,* she thought to herself.

In making her arrangements over the telephone, Rosa was told to look for a thin, middle-aged man wearing a black cowboy hat, blue western shirt with white fringe, a silver eagle on his bolo tie, and black cowboy boots. "He'll be sitting on one of the benches feeding the birds." Rosa was nervous as she scrutinized the plaza. As she passed from one side of the gazebo to the other, she spotted him. He looked like a well-heeled merchant or rancher with deep, furrowed lines on his forehead and a ruddy complexion.

Rosa introduced herself.

"I'm Petro," he said, modestly.

For a few minutes they made small talk, but Rosa grew impatient. She had only one thing in mind. "How much do you charge to get across the border?"

"I work for *el hefe* the head honcho," Petro explained, trying to make the distinction clear. "*El hefe* charges by the person."

"There are three of us. My two boys and me." Her heart sank when she realized his fees were far steeper than she could imagine. Mentally and physically exhausted from the trauma of her husband's murder, the long arduous bus trip, keeping her boys together, and staying in someone else's home, she ached for permanence. Determined to reach California, she begged him to lower the price.

Petro held fast. "Sorry, but that's what he charges. I've got no control over his fees."

"Can I send him the rest when I get to California? I swear on my boys' life, I'll send him the money as soon as I get work."

"Afraid not. All money is up front . . . or there's no deal."

Without a meeting of the minds, their encounter was cut short. Thwarted by her lack of money, Rosa dragged herself back to the house. *What was I thinking? Maybe getting to the U.S. is just an unrealistic pipe dream.*

"How'd your meeting go?" Josefina asked, anticipating good news.

"Horrible." Tears welled up in Rosa's eyes. "The price . . . it's too much money. I don't have nearly enough." Then, with a sudden burst of resolve that originated from a hidden well of determination deep within, she readjusted her attitude. "I need more money. Can you help me get work?"

Josefina paused, not sure whether to encourage her or not. "I won't kid you. Jobs are hard to find. But I'll keep my ears open. I'll ask around."

After work a few days later, Josefina came home beaming. "Maybe I found a job for you. I heard about an American couple. Retired, I think. The wife fell and broke her hip. And her husband can't keep up with everything. They're looking for a housekeeper-caretaker."

At last, Rosa caught a break.

The old couple hired her. They were pleasant enough and Rosa found the job easy. But by her calculations, if she was ever going to get to California, she still needed more money. When she heard about a night job, even though it didn't pay well, she considered herself lucky. After a quick supper she worked with a few other women in a stuffy garage. They sat on high, wooden stools at a large table gluing colorful crepe paper onto piñatas.

She and the boys were forced to stay longer than she had planned. Since they were only guests—taken in by well-meaning friends of friends—she felt obligated to contribute a small sum for their room-and-board. Unfortunately, that set her back, but she persevered. Week-by-week, then month-by-month, Rosa socked away what was left into the worn leather pouch she used as her bank. Though exhausting, life settled into a routine: helping Josefina with the household chores, work, the church, and what little time she could spare with her sons. Diego wasn't happy about their long stay, but didn't want to fight with his wife.

Chapter 7

Javier

ROSA'S OLDEST SON, Javier, had always been difficult to raise, but she noticed ever since they arrived in Tijuana his behavior had grown worse. With so many other things to think about, she gave him free reign. She let him miss school. But Rosa insisted that Santiago, more docile and compliant, attend the local school even though it was temporary.

"Why do I have to go," Santiago whined, "if Javier doesn't go?"

"Because I said so. Maybe you'll make new friends."

Less than enthusiastic, Santiago attended class. He couldn't wait for the dismissal bell so he could play soccer with the boys in the neighborhood. For him, sleep became an issue. He couldn't shake the recurring nightmares of the chickens pecking at his father's body.

With so many unknowns, Rosa constantly prayed. She carried her rosary wherever she went. "No matter what else you do," she admonished her sons, "Sunday mornings we go to Mass together." Since Santiago and Javier were enjoying more freedom than they ever had in El Salvador, they were reluctant to deny her that single request.

Javier adapted quickly to life in Tijuana. With his days free, he stumbled onto a job at a car wash. For the first time in his life, he earned his own money. Thinking the small house too confining, and his mother too controlling, he spent his evenings hanging out with a rowdy, slightly older crowd. And he usually didn't return home until the wee hours, knowing everyone in the house would be asleep. Diego, who had keen hearing, woke up whenever Javier tip-toed back home, but shrugged it off, reasoning the boy was Rosa's problem. Not his.

At night, the *red-light* district bustled with possibilities. Street walkers lingered on the sidewalks near brightly lighted signs. Randy young men from Tijuana and college boys from southern California hung out in a myriad of cantinas listening to the loud, rhythmic music, smoking a little grass, and drinking. For Javier's eighteenth birthday, his new friends hooked him up with a beautiful, but loose woman.

One night, shortly after his first sexual encounter, the guys were harassing him when a half-looped blond kid—with a plastic shark tooth pendant dangling from a leather strap around his neck and a tee-shirt that read San Diego State—interrupted their revelry. "Hey, have you guys heard Carmen Ruiz?"

"No, should we?" Angel asked.

"Oh, yeah. Man, she's hot. A real babe! And when she sings, you'll squirm in your seat."

Not one to pass up opportunities, Javier, Angel, and three of their buddies grabbed their unfinished bottles of Corona and traipsed over to the other cantina. Javier thought the walk well worth the effort. In the back of the room, they crowded around the last table next to a group of giggling teenage girls. From the older guys, Javier had picked up the art of flirting. And immediately began to tease the girls, especially a spunky sixteen-year-old named Maria. Her flashes of wit and outgoing personality captivated him. That night, he walked her home and managed a good-night kiss. He never had a girlfriend before, and it didn't take long for him to fall in love. Being with Maria erased his insecurities and chased away his loneliness.

Weeks later, as was their ritual, Rosa and her sons strolled along the cracked, uneven sidewalks on their way to twelve o'clock Mass. An inversion layer of gritty smoke blocked the sun, irritating Rosa's eyes and throat. Javier stopped and turned to face Rosa. Not insensitive to his mother's wishes, he swallowed hard and looked down at his shoes "*Mamá*, stop. I've got something to say."

Rosa, puzzled by his request, stood waiting.

Then the words tumbled out of Javier's mouth. "I'm not going to California. I'm staying here, in Tijuana."

Rosa couldn't believe her ears. Santiago, her younger son, knew instantly they were heading for a family crisis. Adrenaline crawled into his stomach.

"What did you say?" Rosa asked.

"I'm staying here."

"No. Absolutely not! Your father . . . he was just murdered." Her voice caught, and her eyes flooded with tears. "No, Javier, you must go with us. I need you. Don't tell me you would leave me. What about your brother? You may never see us again. You would have no family. Listen to me. A beautiful life waits for us."

"But I'm happy here. You met Maria. She's beautiful. I don't want to leave her. *Mamá*, I love her."

"Maria is beautiful. *Sí*. But love . . . what do you know of love? You're not yet a man. You were cooped up on a bus for a long, long time. You wanted freedom . . . and I gave it to you. That I understand."

"That's not it. I love Maria. I love my life here."

Absorbing it all, Santiago started to pick at his nails. For the moment, he chose to set aside El Salvador's brutality. He yearned to recapture the time before his father's murder, when they were a family. It was hard enough to imagine life without his father, but he couldn't think about losing his brother, too.

"*Mi hijo,* my first born, you're the light of my life," Rosa said, with her sorrowful brown, eyes. "Take my word, this is your first girlfriend. You'll meet many more girls."

"No, *Mamá,* you're wrong. I want to be with her."

"Javier, stop and think. You're making a huge mistake."

"*Mamá,* stop crying."

"You're acting crazy. You'll regret it."

"No, I won't. Maria and I will be happy here."

Growing angry, Rosa tried to reason with him. "How will you support yourself? How will you support Maria? You can't stay at Josefina's forever."

"Maria's father . . . he promised to get me a good paying job at the Ford plant where he works. I'll make good money." Javier had multiple reasons for staying in Mexico. Besides falling for Maria, he sought revenge, imagining that someday he would return to El Salvador. In his quixotic fantasy, he planned to steal his grandfather's gun and kill the men that murdered his father.

For days Rosa begged, wrangled, and cajoled Javier, desperately trying to convince him to go with her. As adamant as he was in his refusal, she was equally inconsolable in her disappointment. The thought of leaving her oldest son behind blasted another huge hole in her already broken heart. She wanted nothing more than to give her boys a better life.

Rosa refused to let go of her son so easily. But Javier was unyielding. He flat out rejected the idea of traveling further. Then, taking his cue from his brother, Santiago too, begged his mother to stay in Mexico.

"Absolutely not." Her voice climbed to an angry pitch. "If your brother abandons us, that's up to him. But you, my precious one, are going with me. I need you. You're all I have left."

It took a long time for Rosa to realized that Javier wasn't backing down.

But if there are only two of us, she reasoned, maybe I've got enough money to pay the coyote to get Santiago and me into

California. She counted the money in her old, brown leather pouch one more time. Then counted it again, to make sure. Rosa contacted Petro and arranged another meeting in the *zócalo.*

They had no sooner greeted each other when Rosa spoke her mind. There was excitement in her voice when she asked, "You charge by the person, sí?"

"Sí, by the person."

For a moment, Rosa clammed up, too emotional to talk. What she was about to say, pained her deeply, and rivulets of tears slid down her face. "Things have changed. Only two of us are going. Javier, my oldest son . . . he's staying in Tijuana."

A brief conversation ensued. "No, it's his choice . . . No, it breaks my heart. But now, with only two, I think I've got enough money."

Not inclined to delve too deeply into family business, Petro simply remarked, "It's still the same price per person."

"Then we're ready to go."

"Not so fast. As I told you before, I need the money up-front. After I count it, I turn it over to *el hefe.* When he's comfortable, you go. But there are preparations. On the night we travel, you'll each get a *green card.* They're extremely valuable. Gives you permission to cross the border. But let's not get ahead of ourselves. On the night we cross, you're going to pretend to be Americanos, just returning from a visit with family. Rosa, you and your son can only carry what's in a duffel bag . . . as if you were just in Tijuana for a couple of nights. Everything, and I mean everything, must have an American label, including the duffel bags. Right down to your toothbrush and toothpaste. Your clothes don't have to be expensive, but something an American would wear. Your son's a teen-ager, right?"

"Right."

"Buy him American brands. Basketball shorts, tennis shoes, a sweat jacket, a few tee-shirts with English sayings on them. That's it. Wash the clothes a couple of times and remember to scuff up the tennis shoes so they don't look brand new."

"I'll need more time. Maybe a month, maybe more, to save money for the clothes.

Petro remained cool and business-like. As a *coyote* he had prepped many people before Rosa for the crossing. "Don't worry. When you're ready, bring the money. I'll take care of the rest."

Chapter 8

Making Plans

T HOUGH HER HEART wasn't in it, Rosa continued to hold down her day job working for the old American couple and her night job making piñatas. For three-and-a-half weeks, Petro's instructions reverberated in her head. She had finally purchased her last two items, Old Navy sweat jackets for her and Santiago. Although a bundle of nerves, she fought hard to keep it together as she once again contacted Petro.

For most people, the day was ordinary. But not for Rosa. Today she would finally set her dream into motion. She sauntered over to the park in front of the church to meet Petro. She had a sense of accomplishment knowing she had worked hard and finally saved enough money. But at the same time, she also had huge misgivings: *Can I trust Petro with my life savings? Can he really get us over the border like he claims? What if he just takes my money and dumps us off in the middle of nowhere? What happens if we get caught? If we get to California, will Nacho remember to pick us up? How will we survive?*

Petro was blunt. "Rosa, there's no sense beating around the bush. Do you have the money?"

For the moment she hesitated, thinking this whole thing was a huge leap of faith. But she had no choice. She had counted out the money twice the night before, just to make sure it was all there. Reluctantly she handed him her brown leather pouch.

He took the money and slipped it into a satchel. "When *el hefe* is convinced it's all there, I'll get back to you on the details."

"It's all there."

"I believe you. But he's a careful businessman. I'm just the go-between. Meet me here, same time tomorrow. If it's a go, I'll give you more information."

Rosa was an emotional wreck. She was terrified that she might never see the money or him again. When he got up and walked away with all the money she had scrimped and saved, she headed for the church. After lighting a candle, she slipped into one of the light oak pews that faced a marble statue of Jesus mounted on the front wall. Out came her rosary. For almost an hour she sat and prayed and thought and worried. Her emotions ran the gamut from fear to hope.

Later that night, when she returned from her job making piñatas, Diego, who had mixed emotions about his house guests, tried to reassure her that handing the coyote the money upfront was standard procedure. "That's how they all work. It'll be fine. Have faith."

"But suppose Petro doesn't show up tomorrow? Suppose he runs off with my money? I don't even know where he lives?"

"Rosa, you've got to believe. Now get some rest."

That night, she slept little, contemplating all the what ifs.

The following day, she could barely get through her house-keeping job. The old couple she worked for were kind but needy. And for whatever reason, that day she resented everything they asked her to do. It was if she had been bitten by the freedom bug. After she completed her day job, Rosa set off again to meet Petro.

Ugly, unsolicited scenarios clogged her mind. Fearful that he won't show, she was on high alert. Her eyes darted back and forth, scanning, and rescanning the zócalo. Several men in white coveralls were repainting the gazebo positioned exactly in the center of the park. Little boys were laughing and yelling while playing tag on the grass. Two young women were on a path pushing baby strollers, and a cluster of old men sat on a nearby bench. When she didn't spot Petro, her heart dropped. She knew she was early, but that did nothing to soothe her angst. Rosa started to berate herself for being taken for a fool. Fearing the worst, she tried playing mind games to regain her self-control. *Funny* she thought, *I never even noticed the cactus garden along-side the bench.* But as much as she tried to think of other things, her thoughts swiftly returned to Petro and her money. Without a watch, she really couldn't say whether he was on time or a few minutes late. Finally, she spotted a man with a blue shirt rounding the gazebo and heading in her direction. She smiled, never so glad to see anyone in her life.

As soon as Petro joined her on the bench, he patted Rosa's knee, "Good news. *El hefe's* satisfied with the money. Are you prepared to leave?"

No man had touched her since her husband's murder. Uncomfortable with his unfamiliar touch, Rosa pulled away, hoping he meant no harm. With so much at stake, she couldn't deal with romance or a sexual predator. She forced herself to refocus. She blurted out, "I bought our new clothes."

"Good, Rosa. All American brands, I hope. You look nice in these clothes."

She lowered her eyes and quickly changed the subject. "Petro, I need time . . . some time to tell them at work that I'm not coming back. That's only fair."

With more on his mind, he ignored her comment. He opened his satchel and handed her the empty leather pouch. Also, inside the satchel was a notebook, a calendar, and a pen. "Before you leave today, we'll set a firm date for your departure, and it must be on a Friday."

After all she had gone through to get to this point, Rosa hesitated.

In a way, she couldn't believe it was finally going to happen.

Petro understood her reluctance. He had seen it all before. So, he forced the issue. Pointing to a date a little more than two weeks hence, he wrote her name on the calendar. "Rosa, what's your address? Where will I pick you up?" He repeated the address back to her. Then he wrote the departure date on a slip of paper, ripped it out of the notebook, and handed it to her.

"That Friday I'll pick you up at seven sharp. Friday and Saturday night, you and your boy will sleep at the *rehearsal* house. Tell me his name again.

"Santiago."

"Right. Santiago. When you and Santiago settle in, we'll sort through baskets of *green cards*. You'll both get new identities. But remember, we won't leave for California until Sunday night. That's when the border's most crowded. Loads of people heading back from a weekend in Mexico.

Anxiety was written all over Rosa's face. "Will other people be there?"

"Where?"

"The rehearsal house."

"Yes. Probably a few more people. Don't worry about them. We'll rehearse your new identity over and over, until you'll know it by heart. I'll ask questions and you and Santiago will practice giving me the answers. By the time we leave, you'll have everything memorized."

"What about food? Should I bring some?"

"No. I've got it covered. But when I pick you up, be packed and ready to go. I expect you both to just hop in the car. No long good-byes. Oh, I almost forgot the most important thing. Remind your contact person to pick you up the next day. On Monday." In his little notebook, he wrote the address of the drop-off house across the border and handed it to Rosa. "Make sure you give him this address."

On her way back to Josefina's, Rosa passed street vendors selling fruits, sodas, candies, and cheap trinkets, but she was caught up in her own world. She made a mental note to call Nacho, her cousin's son. *I must tell him where and when to pick us up.* Then she prayed silently to the Virgin Mary that everything would go as planned. As her mind wandered, she tried to imagine what it would be like living in California.

Rosa had no way of knowing that a quarter million people pass through the Tijuana/San Diego border daily. It was one of the busiest border crossings in the world. The Border Patrol was well-aware of the brutal civil war in El Salvador. They knew that every day refugees risked their lives seeking safety in the U.S. and it was their job to hold the line, to stop them from entering. It was a cruel game of cat-and-mouse.

That night Petro was picking them up. Out of nerves, Rosa spent a portion of the day obsessively cleaning Josefina's house. Petro had advised her multiple times to travel light. Like a snake molting its outer skin, Rosa shed what little she had carried from El Salvador, except for her precious rosary. She was being forced to reinvent herself, giving birth to a new identity, a new life.

"Santiago, leave your soccer shirt here. Give it to one of Josefina's boys."

"NO! Francisco gave it to me."

"I know, but the shirt was made in El Salvador. When we cross the border, everything must have an American label. Remember, we're supposed to be down here visiting relatives for a few days."

"What about my soccer ball? Can I take it? Please."

She couldn't bear to take that away too. Santiago carried it all the way from El Salvador. The soccer ball was his security blanket, his anchor. He cherished it like a little child holding a teddy bear. Against Petro's instructions, she told him it was okay to bring it.

Just before supper, Rosa took a walk to shake-off the butterflies in her stomach. She had a few remaining pesos. Almost as an afterthought, she bought a couple of cans of guava juice and several bags of chili limón flavored tortilla chips from the nearby soda stand. While saving money, she had never allowed herself this pleasure. If stopped by the border patrol, she would tell them they were just a few things to nibble on before they got home.

Rosa barely ate the special supper Josefina had prepared. The hour before they were to be picked up, she spent quiet time with Javier. Holding his hands, she asked one last time, "Are you sure you want to stay here?"

"*Sí, Mamá.*" I'm happy here. I made friends. I have a girl. Promise of a good job. Don't worry. I'll be okay."

"*Mi hijo,* is there nothing I can do to change your mind?"

Javier sluffed off his guilt and responded. "I'll be fine. Don't worry."

"If you stay, promise me, no gangs. No trouble."

"I promise."

"Go to church. Pray for us and I'll pray for you. Know that I'll be thinking of you every day. Someday I'll come back to visit."

When Rosa and Javier embraced for the last time, it was as if a part of her was being ripped from her body.

At seven sharp, Petro rounded the corner. He pulled up to the house in a seven-year-old Chevy sedan with California license plates, a San Diego Chargers decal on the back window and a Reagan/Bush sticker affixed to the rear bumper. Despite Petro's warning, there was one last round of hugs. Javier tousled Santiago's hair and gave him a light punch on his arm. Josefina reached into her skirt pocket and gave Rosa a key ring with a miniature cross. Diego, glad to get rid of two house guests that lingered way too long, pressed a crumbled twenty-dollar bill into Rosa's hand. "Take this. You'll need it."

Diego, Josefina, and their children, along with Javier, stood outside waving until the car faded from view.

What Petro had called a rehearsal house was nothing more than a boarded-up mobile home on what was once a used car lot. Neither sordid nor luxurious, it stood on the edge of an isolated, industrial complex. Long-haul trucks were lined up in the nearby dirt lot. In the far distance, across a paved road, stood an abandoned PEMEX gas station.

Several men and another *coyote* were there for the same reason. That first night, Rosa feared she might be attacked by one of the men. She had heard so many stories about women heading north. But, fortunately, no one wanted trouble. Sleeping on the floor was nothing new. For Rosa and Santiago, it had become a way of life.

On Saturday Petro spent hours helping Rosa and Santiago thumb through baskets of *green cards*. They scanned the photos looking for people that resembled them. Petro thought Santiago's skin tone could be a problem, but he kept that doubt to himself. He was too dark to be taken for a Mexican. Dark skin tipped-off the Border Patrol that they were born further south. If caught, they wouldn't be tossed back across the border. They would be flown all the way back to El Salvador, where the death squads awaited them.

On Sunday evening the fateful crossing hour approached. Rosa, a bundle of nerves, and Santiago, who had little to say about anything, climbed into Petro's Chevy. Rosa sat in front on the passenger side of the car. Her heart was beating like a metronome as she fingered her rosary, hidden in a pocket of her Old Navy sweat jacket. Santiago sat alone in the back seat, with his sweat jacket thrown casually over his soccer ball.

"I want to remind you of a few things," Petro said. "When we near the border, I'll raise my right hand. From then on, don't say a word unless asked. Our conversation may be monitored. Unless an agent speaks directly to you, let me do the talking. But if the agent asks you a question, don't look away. Look him in the eye and answer. Don't worry. They speak Spanish. But stop and think before you say anything. It's better to hesitate than to say the wrong thing."

Rosa nodded. Santiago was too scared to say anything.

Petro continued. "Keep your green card within easy reach. Remember your *new* name and birthdate. We've rehearsed enough times. If they ask what you were doing in Tijuana, say you went to a birthday party. Santiago, if the border agent asks you, be sure to say it was your grandfather's 75th birthday. Got that? *Grandfather's* 75th.

Santiago shook his head. Then he repeated his carefully rehearsed line.

"That's right. Now try to look relaxed."

"Rosa, if asked, say it was your *father's* 75th birthday party. Are your clear on that?"

"*Sí,*"

Petro slipped an Olivia Newton John cassette into the slot. Coincidentally the song that popped up was *Let Me Be There.* Not understanding a word of English, the upbeat song meant nothing to Rosa or Santiago.

Petro looked as American as apple pie. He wore Levi's, a faded red polo shirt, and a black U.S.S. Enterprise baseball cap, his good luck charm. In Rosa's mind, she had spent a fortune trying to make Santiago look like an overindulged American kid. He wore baggy, silver basketball shorts, a black tee-shirt, and Adidas tennis shoes.

On Sunday nights, with tourists heading back to the U.S., the traffic was invariably brutal. That was precisely the point. Six lanes of cars slowly inching their way towards the Mexico—U.S. border. Stop and start. Stop and start. The exhaust fumes forced Petro to roll the window up. Street vendors, defying the traffic, darted across the lanes, looking to sell colorful souvenirs. A few men offered to clean their windshield for a few *centavos* but Petro waved them all off.

It took almost two hours in bumper-to-bumper traffic before Petro raised his hand indicating quiet. Not that any of them talked beforehand. As they closed in on the border, an aura of tension wrapped around Rosa like Christmas paper. Suddenly blinded by self-doubt, she wondered if she and Santiago should have stayed in Mexico like Javier. But now, at this moment, she had no choice but to trust Pedro.

When they finally approached the border, the first thing the Hispanic agent noted was the direction of Petro's headlights. If tilted upward, someone or something heavy might be hidden in the back. An old smugglers' trick.

"Good evening," the unsmiling agent said.

"Good evening," Petro responded, careful not to say anything more than necessary.

"Your driver's license and papers?"

Petro, who knew the routine well, had his wallet handy. Like an old pro, he handed the border agent his driver's license and green card.

"What about the other? Their papers, too."

"They're all here," Petro said, handing both their green cards to the agent.

The agent looked at them, then shone a flashlight into the car, studying Rosa and Santiago's face and clothing. Suspense lingered in the air like cigar smoke. Rosa hoped the agent wouldn't notice her chest rising as she sucked in the air. Santiago squinted and tilted his face away from the blinding flashlight. Thankfully, in the dark, it was impossible to tell the exact shade of his skin.

The whole procedure only took three0 or four minutes but felt like an eternity. Before the agent handed the green cards back through the driver's open window, he asked, "Your purpose in Mexico?"

"My father lives in Tijuana," Pedro explained. "This weekend we celebrated his 75th birthday. I drove my sister and nephew down for a big family party."

"I see. Where to?

"You mean now?"

"Yes,"

"First, I'm dropping my sister and nephew off in El Cajon. Then heading back to Solana Beach. I got to get to work early tomorrow."

"Where's work?"

"Encinitas . . . Marcos Nursery."

The no-nonsense border guard furled his forehead and scowled.

"Sir, step out of your vehicle and open your trunk."

Rosa and Santiago were both left to wrestle with their fear, as Petro slipped out of the car and did as he was told. Silently, Rosa felt her rosary and prayed. *"Oh, Mary, Mother of Jesus, please help us . . ."*

The border agent shone his flashlight inside the trunk and felt around the edges searching for contraband. Then he used a mirror attached to a long pole and his flashlight to peek under the car. Convinced there was nothing unusual, he said, "Sir, you may step back into your vehicle."

With an artificial air of nonchalance, Petro slipped back into the driver's seat.

Knowing there was a never-ending line of cars behind this one, the border agent said, "Have a good night," and waved them through.

As the car rolled forward, Petro calmly announced, "You're now in California."

Rosa wept with joy, thinking this was the pinnacle of her life. Her dream had come true. Feeling euphoric, she turned towards Santiago, who sat in the back seat. *"Mi hijo* just think, we made it. We're in California!"

Even though Santiago could now relax and breathe normally, a different kind of tension was building. *"Mamá,* what about Javier? Will we ever see him again?"

"Sí, someday we'll see him again. What's wrong? You look so sad?"

"I was just thinking, everyone except us speaks English here. I'm not going to know anything."

"Don't worry. You'll learn, like everyone else."

Petro, whose job it was to drive illegal immigrants over the border, was devoid of emotion. "You did good," is all he said in praise. As promised, he dropped Rosa and Santiago at an isolated house on the outskirts of Chula Vista. But before they got out of the car, he insisted they return the green cards.

The two-bedroom *stash* house was a dilapidated refuge for undocumented immigrants anxious to begin life anew. Seven other immigrants had been dropped off ahead of them by several other *coyotes* And a few more straggled in later. That night, with their few possessions piled against the wall, everyone slept on the filthy carpet smelling of urine. Men in one bedroom. Women and young children in the other. Because of his age, Santiago was forced to leave his mother's side. He slept in the living room along with two other teenage boys. Emotionally drained, Santiago fell asleep quickly.

The very first thing Santiago did when he awoke was check for his soccer ball. "It's gone!" He tried not to cry in front of the other boys, but rivulets of tears ran down his face. "Someone took it! Someone stole my soccer ball! ONE OF YOU TOOK IT, DIDN'T YOU?"

One of the boys, who was still half-asleep, hollered, "No, I didn't! And stop blaming me!"

The loud screams and scuffling woke everyone in the house. From the bedroom, Rosa recognized her son's voice and ran to see what was going on.

"SOMEONE STOLE MY SOCCER BALL!"

"Mi hijo, we'll find it, don't worry," she said, brushing a swatch of hair away from his eyes.

Angry and grief-stricken, he pushed her away.

Not wishing any confrontations, the weary immigrants in the crowded apartment lowered their eyes, afraid to move for fear of being accused. Rosa and Santiago searched everywhere and interrogated everyone, but they all proclaimed their innocence.

As they waited for Nacho, Rosa's nephew, to pick them up, Santiago remained inconsolable. A brooding teenager, he shrugged off any attempt at conversation. "Leave me alone," he sulked whenever his mother tried to console him. "I want to go back to Mexico. What was wrong with Mexico anyway?"

Rachel & Stuart Roth, & Banning

Chapter 9

New Job

Reno, Nevada

STUART ROTH felt the need to change jobs. He found his current boss, a wealthy developer, to be a penurious man, who would skimp on every project, then walk away and expect Stuart to work it through. Now, at the height of his career, Stuart was eager to move on. Today's interview held promise.

He readjusted the knot on his regimental tie as he emerged from the elevator at Mr. Banning's penthouse in the Atlas Towers. He was expecting a formal interview. When Mr. Banning opened one of the double doors to greet him, Stuart immediately wondered if he had the right place. Dressed in a creamy-colored velour warm-up suit, Mr. Banning, had an unkempt beard and was barefoot. The half-zippered jacket exposed the curly black hairs on his chest and a thick gold chain around his neck. With his vivid imagination, Stuart felt like he was about to enter the *Playboy* pad of Hugh Hefner, who was famous for greeting everyone while in his pajamas. Nevertheless, well-schooled in the formality of an interview, Stuart made eye contact and extended his hand.

"Glad to meet you, Mr. Banning."

"Oh Christ, can the Mister crap. Just call me Banning. Everyone does. We're pretty informal 'round here."

Within seconds Stuart sized the man up. *Somewhere in his forties and another eccentric developer.* He didn't mind. Stuart had an extremely high tolerance for characters. He was drawn to them like a magnet. His father and his father's cohorts were bigger than life. And as far as characters went, he wasn't too far off the mark himself. Besides, he had plenty of experience working for developers. They all came out of the same mold. They had a penchant for thinking outside the box. Pushy dreamers, they bull-dozed their way through every obstacle that crossed their path. As far as he was concerned, they were the doers, the movers and shakers of the world.

"Here. Grab a seat," Banning said, leading him to one of the two overstuffed frieze club chairs, knockoffs of chairs from the forties.

Stuart smiled inwardly. *My grandmother used to have chairs like these.* He glanced around the cavernous living room, accessing the artwork hanging on the stark white stucco walls. Cheap repros that could be purchased at any weekend art fair. Ocean scenes in gilded frames. A copy of Blue Boy and another framed piece of a naked lady reclining on a couch. Stuart couldn't place the artists, but he remembered seeing these paintings somewhere else. Ever observant, he did pick up the pungent smell of marijuana hanging in the air.

The penthouse had floor-to-ceiling glass walls with dramatic, unimpeded views. Banning sat on the couch and stretched his bare feet on the low-slung glass coffee table, almost knocking over a large orange ceramic ashtray. Stuart was repulsed by his yellowed toenails.

The first salvo of the interview started with an innocuous question. "You married?"

"Yes," Stuart replied with a source of pride, "for thirty-three years. Rachel, that's my wife, she's a teacher."

"Nice," Banning commented while fiddling absent-mindedly with his star sapphire pinkie ring. "Any kids?"

"Three. Two are married off. The last one is attending grad school in New York."

The two men waltzed around the usual generalities—about Stuart's family and experience. Eventually Banning stopped fiddling with his ring and got down to business. "I'm primarily a land developer. But I just bought the twenty-one-story hotel across the alley. I plan to time-share it. What'd you know about time-share?"

"Uh, nothing really." Stuart said, thinking that might be the kiss of death.

"Well, it's a pretty simple concept. I'm planning to remodel the hotel rooms. Convert every two rooms into a livable suite: a living room, bedroom, bathroom, and a small kitchenette. Once that's done, I'll turn around and sell the hell out of 'em . . . a week at a time. Instead of a hotel, I'll call it a *club*. Ultimately, it'll belong to the time-share owners. I'm looking for someone to help me rehab the building. Maybe put in a little restaurant. See that it runs right."

Stuart knew developers loved to paint grandiose pictures. "I'm curious about the remodeling . . . how much are you planning to do?" In the back of his mind, he remembered how cheap his last boss was. Everything Stuart wanted to do, his boss nixed, claiming it was too expensive.

Banning held the back of his hand up to his nose and sniffed. "I plan to gut the place. Look, . . ." and he fumbled for a name.

"Stuart, Stuart Roth," he interjected, helping Banning out of an awkward moment.

"Well, Stuart, I liked what I saw on your resume. Hotel, restaurant, and development experience. I'm looking for someone to oversee the whole project. From soup to nuts. I've got the sales side covered. A dynamite crew. We worked together in L.A. I'm gonna fly 'em up to sell the time-share units. Believe me, these guys are tops. They can sell snow to the Eskimos."

From the get-go, Stuart understood his vision.

At that moment, Banning's wife, in her early twenties, entered the living room. Stuart's eyes quickly changed direction. Dani greeted him casually and then snuggled-up next to Banning on the gold velvet couch. Her thick black hair hung below her shoulders. With deep olive skin, striking black eyes, and narrow hips, she looked exotic. Dani reminded Stuart of the tropical women in a Gauguin poster that hung in his family room. Dani wore nothing under her gauzy, transparent white blouse. Her uplifted boobs and commanding nipples—the size of porcini mushrooms—immediately grabbed Stuart's attention. He sized the situation up quickly. Striking. Sexy. And very distracting.

Stuart got the job.

Even though Banning lacked a formal education and couldn't compose a business letter if he had to, he had the uncanny ability to recognize a good deal. More importantly, he had the Midas touch. Be it luck or skill, he was extremely wealthy. To circumvent California's heavy tax burden, he had transferred his entire operation to Reno, Nevada, a state with few taxes.

In addition to his penthouse in the Atlas Towers—and a separate apartment on the eighth floor that he retained for his personal friends and partying—Banning also leased the entire second floor of the Atlas Towers for offices. It was all very convenient: his penthouse, the separate apartment for his lifestyle, and the business offices, everything located in one building, directly behind the hotel.

On the first day of his new job, Stuart found himself working in a corridor of glassed-in offices. The CPA—a classic bean counter who knew the ins and outs of the tax codes—worked in the first office nearest the counting room. A charming old-timer—with a gift of gab—who had a knack for working his way through the governmental regulations, held the second office. An IT expert handled the technical side and possessed the third office. The office next to Stuart's was a non-practicing attorney who specialized in real estate. The remainder of the floor space contained bookkeeper types. Mondays through Fridays they kept track of the bags of money—monthly payments—rolling in from Banning's land sales in Hawaii, California, Nevada, and Arizona.

From a previous marriage, Banning had an eighteen-year-old daughter, Hannah, but they were not particularly close. She lived with his ex-wife in Thousand Oaks, a suburb of Los Angeles. Banning—not exactly the ideal father—was never cut-out for mowing lawns or inviting his neighbors over for a barbecue. He relished a salacious lifestyle that included an entourage of party girls and *hanger-on-ers*. There was no doubt that he savored life. Sometimes with Dani, his second wife, and sometimes without her. But always with a steady rotation of sexy young women. Some just a trifle under-age.

As the sole owner of TRB World Holdings, he conducted business on his own time schedule. Most days he did not show up until noon or later. But when he finally appeared, like Neptune rising from the sea, he would summon his lieutenants to the conference room and delegate tasks. On his agenda, he checked off who he wanted to accomplish each item. When Banning assigned a job to Stuart, he simply drew a Jewish star next to the task. Stuart respected his new boss and simply overlooked his warped sense of humor.

Banning began his career as an encyclopedia salesman. He perfected the art of salesmanship by going door-to-door. Early on, he learned to have a ready response to overcome any obstacle a potential buyer could throw at him. It didn't take long before he made a stab at land sales, a much more profitable venue. With that success under his belt, he ventured out on his own, buying raw land in Antelope Valley and subdividing it. He sold home sites to dreamy-eyed servicemen and women who could only think of one thing: someday buying a plot of land, building a home, and watching their investment increase in value. It was all so simple. Banning appealed to their greed. Sight unseen, they plunked down $400 and made monthly payments of $30 until their lot was paid off many years later. A rumor floated in the air that Banning was good for forty-four million and that kind of cash had real clout in the 80's.

Although Stuart's primary job was to rehab the hotel and hire the staff, he soon found himself immersed in other real estate negotiations and ongoing projects. Banning grew to respect Stuart's organizational skills, quick mind, and tenacity. When Banning got an idea—and he usually had them late at night in his free-floating, drugged-out state—he knew if he passed it on to Stuart, it would get done. It was a perfect relationship. Banning the dreamer. Stuart the master of efficiency.

Chapter 10

Twin Palms Resort

SEVEN MONTHS after Stuart climbed aboard, Banning summoned him to his penthouse for a private meeting. "I'd like you to look at a couple of foreclosures I picked up from the bank. They're not far from Palm Springs. I want your feedback." He paused and sniffed. "I've got something in mind. If you're game, Willy can take us to the airport tomorrow morning. We'll take the Citation down to the desert before lunch, check things out, and be back in time for dinner."

Stuart's mind swirled with unanswered questions. But for the moment he let them go. "Sure, why not?"

"Great. I'll let the pilots know. We should be good to go by eight-thirty."

Stuart and Banning chatted in the backseat of the black Rolls Royce. The vehicle had dark tinted windows that offered full privacy. Willy, a well-groomed Jamaican with a slight build, doubled as a jack-of-all-trades. A quiet, unassuming man, he drove at a steady pace along South Rock Boulevard to the Reno airport. Familiar with the route, he pulled into the parking lot at Atlantic Aviation, a separate building used to accommodate passengers with private planes.

Stuart was duly impressed by the obsequious service extended to them inside the private terminal. They sat in a lounge with mahogany walls, tasteful art, and soft leather chairs, while the two pilots prepared the flight plan and readied the jet. Stuart knew his place. He understood that he was just along for the ride. The staff catered to Banning, trying to fulfill his every need. Stuart saw first-hand just how deferential people were to the wealthy. An old saying popped into his head and he smiled inwardly. *Them that haveth the gold, maketh the rules. No wonder the rich have such bloated egos.*

As they stepped into the Cessna Citation, Stuart admired the customized interior. As he sank into one of the eight rolled-leather white bucket seats, he commented. "You know, I've never flown on a plane where I could actually stretch out my legs. Nice."

During the take-off, Stuart watched the pilot and co-pilot manipulating the panel of instruments through the open cockpit door. Until the plane climbed through the cover of clouds, it was a bumpy ride. The small, private jet finally leveled off just above the snow-capped Sierra-Nevada Mountains and turned south. Not used to flying at such a low altitude, Stuart looked out the window and grimaced.

Banning faced Stuart. "How 'bout a drink? Booze, juice, Coke, coffee? Whatever you want."

"Nothing, thanks," Stuart replied.

"A sweet roll or bagel?"

"A Coke would be fine," Stuart said rather primly.

Banning unfastened his seat belt and walked to the back of the cabin. He made a Bloody Mary for himself and returned with a chilled Coke for Stuart. He could hardly wait to describe the resorts. "The small one's a real dog. Just an old rundown motel up on a hill," he said dismissively. "I'm not sure what to do with it. But the other one's got potential. Most of it was built during the 20's, sixteen old-fashioned motel-style units. Rock walls and Mexican tile roofs. Charming in a nostalgic sort-of-way. I'm not sure what it is, but I've got a good feeling about the property. Maybe it's the empty land, hot for development."

Stuart noticed Banning's frequent sniffles and asked if he was fighting a cold.

"No. Allergies," Banning explained. *Jeez, this guy's observant,* then lost his train of thought. "Okay, where was I?"

"You were describing the larger property. Telling me about the units."

"Oh, yeah. Anyway, there's another eight condominiums. Built, I'm guessing, around the mid-50's. The guy who built them started to add another eight units, but the poor bastard went belly-up. I heard he had problems with the IRS and took a powder. Anyway, the units sat there. Wide open. No windows. No roof. Just foundation and walls. Over the years, sand practically buried them."

Stuart got the picture.

Banning stopped talking just long enough to finish off the rest of his Bloody Mary. "Frankly, it's the bare land that intrigues me the most. Land's been damn good to me." Almost as an after-thought, he pivoted back to the resort. "I wanna know if we can resurrect those units . . . and build more, turn it into a real resort." He paused for a few seconds to let his thoughts sink in. Then he added, "Maybe we can even time-share the whole shebang."

The two men arrived at the Palm Springs airport mid-morning. The temperature had already risen to the high 80's. Obviously Banning knew what he was getting into. He had flown down in walking shorts and a faded Grateful Dead tee-shirt. On the tarmac, he pulled a pair of wrap-around Ray-Ban's with reflective lenses from a black leather man-bag. He placed a custom-made Panama hat on his head and turned the brim down low to shade his pasty face from the direct sun.

Twenty-five minutes later, they drove into Desert Oasis, a backwater town that did not keep up with the times. Stuart, who had a keen eye for details, noticed the large potholes in the streets. He thought the town a throw-back to the 20's and 30's. Lowrider houses—cheaply constructed and neglected—stood between huge patches of bare land. A Standard Station, Dunkin' Donuts, and an independent pizza parlor dominated the main drag. Sidewalks were sparse. At the shopping center—anchored by a Von's Supermarket—they turned right onto Twin Palms Drive and drove up to Miracle Hill.

"I'll show you the dump first. It'll only take a few minutes." As they pulled up to the curb, Banning readjusted his sunglasses. "This is it."

The unappealing Boyd Motel, with peeling pink paint and a flat roof topped with white rocks, had twenty guest rooms plus a manager's apartment. As they walked around, Stuart noticed a collection of windblown trash strewn along the perimeter of the buildings. A dinky, out-of-date pool in the courtyard was surrounded by sparse, mostly dead plants. No trees. No grass. No flowers. No redeeming features. He tagged it a white elephant in need of a good power washing. Nevertheless, he thought it prudent to keep his mouth shut.

As they entered the manager's office, Stuart, who didn't care much for cats, noticed a bowl of cat food on the floor next to the desk, and a mangy black cat coiled up, sunning itself on a wicker chair by the large plate glass windows that overlooked the small patio and pool.

The tour did not take long. Actually, there wasn't much to see.

As they pulled away from the curb, Banning begged the question. "Any thoughts on what to do with the place? Ya know, you won't offend me. Hell, I don't think the bank wanted it on their books. Probably they just threw it in. A giveaway."

"Before I answer," Stuart said, "could you turn on the air-conditioner. I'm sweltering. Thanks. For sure, it's a loser. Spruce it up. Maybe offer some of the employees cheap rent. Get rid of the manager. He hasn't done jackshit. Besides, no one in their right mind is going to come in off the street to rent a room."

As they drove back down the hill to the other property, they passed several more small, outdated motels with cracked and peeling stucco, all crying for a fresh coat of paint and some serious remodeling. New Age owners with trust funds, renamed these outdated motels *health spas.* On faded wooden signs, they advertised massages, colonics, and nutritional counseling. Some even claimed to be wellness centers. These strange businesses were surrounded by tired looking houses with white security bars on every window and dirt and weeds where lawns once grew.

"What the hell's a colonic?" Stuart asked innocently enough.

Banning roared with laughter. "Really, you don't know. It's an enema. You know, they shove water up your ass and claim it's healthy. Cleans you out."

"Now that I think about it, that's exactly what Miracle Hill needs. A good flushing out. Seriously, do people really pay for colonics?"

"You bet your sweet ass they do? You can't imagine what's going on around here. It's hippie heaven. There are crystals, rebirthing centers, chakras, or some damn thing, and so-called fields of energy. It's a different world from the one you and I know."

Stuart didn't want to appear stupid, so he let it go.

A few minutes later they arrived at Twin Palms Resort, with its expansive acreage. Banning suggested they walk the property. The terrain consisted of uneven sand dunes and clumps of wild grasses. The two hundred-and-twenty acres sloped downwards, in the direction of the I-10 Freeway, at least four miles away. Palm Springs was three miles beyond that, on the other side of the highway.

As they paraded through the desert, nothing surrounding them but wide-open spaces and absolute quiet. A vast emptiness. No houses, no telephone poles, no cars, no buses, no signs of humanity. Despite the dry, oppressive heat, Stuart felt a sense of serenity. There was nothing but a clear blue sky and sand. Always imaginative, he thought of Lawrence of Arabia. *All I need is a white robe and a camel. But right now, I'd settle for a pair of sunglasses and a baseball hat.*

"Whew, the sun's a killer."

A devilish smile crossed Banning's face. "People love it. They bask in it for hours, like desert rats."

Stuart slogged along in his casual clothes—a polo shirt and long khaki pants. *Damn, my shoes are filling with sand.* "Geez, it's only November. What's it like in August? There's not even a breeze."

"I probably should've warned you," Banning remarked casually. "You gotta dress for this kind of heat."

Now you tell me Stuart thought to himself. By the time they turned onto a hard-packed dirt path and headed towards a cluster of buildings three hundred yards away, his face felt flushed and his mouth dry.

Soaked in perspiration, the two men entered the resort's air-conditioned dining room. Every morning several carafes of ice water were placed on an antique sideboard just inside the doorway, a simple courtesy for the guests. Stuart grabbed one of the pitchers, poured himself a glass of water, and gulped it down so fast that part of it dribbled down his chin.

They settled down at the wooden table nearest the kitchen. Banning checked his watch. "Lunch won't be served for another twenty minutes. But I'll get you something to drink. What'd you want?"

He came back from the kitchen holding an ice-cold bottle of beer for himself and a chilled can of Coke for Stuart. "I haven't shown you the massage rooms. They're right beneath us. After lunch I'll give you a quick tour. A bunch of hippies who live around here give massages. They're pretty damn good at it, too." Banning gave a knowing wink. "I never fly back to Reno without getting one. Sunshine's my gal. The best. She kind of holds down the fort. Knows everybody. She's hung around here for years."

Neither hippies nor massages interested Stuart. He zeroed in on the practical. "Do the massage therapists have licenses? Knowing California, I think they'll need them.

Banning shrugged. "You're the man to make sure everything's on the up-and-up. I'm a developer. Running a resort's not my bailiwick."

As they sipped their drinks, Stuart, who always had food on his mind, pummeled Banning with questions. "Who runs the dining room?"

Banning lowered his voice almost to a whisper. "Pepper. He's an old friend of mine. We go way back. I've known him since I lived in L.A. He used to run a little health food joint off Melrose, near my offices. You know the kind of place. Alfalfa sprouts, sunflower seeds, stuff like that. His restaurant folded a few years back, but he and I remained buddies. Party pals. I felt sorry for the guy, so I put him to work."

"Pepper? Is that his real name?"

"I don't know. I never thought to ask."

"It's a great name for someone working around food."

Just then Pepper stepped out of the kitchen. At forty-two-years-old, with traces of gray in his curly black hair, he looked like a well-fed, but aging hippie. Wearing rumpled khaki shorts, a stained tee-shirt, and a leather necklace with a wooden peace pendant, he had an earthy look about him, as if he spent his later years in a co-op growing corn and tomatoes.

He stopped at their table to greet Banning, who in turn introduced him to Stuart. After chatting briefly, Pepper headed to the front porch. A shiny cow bell was mounted on one of the porch posts. He clanged it multiple times. "Lunch is ready!" he shouted. "Come and get it!"

Guests—for the most part couples—straggled in.

With a flair for the dramatic, Pepper and a young kitchen helper carried a plank with a smorgasbord of dishes into the dining room. The plank, actually an old door, was covered with a pink, blue, and red paisley cotton bedspread that substituted as a tablecloth. It was a poor imitation of a grand banquet, like something out of an Arabian Nights. The guests ran the gamut from vegetarians to carnivores. They picked up a plate and helped themselves to a New Age buffet.

Pepper had prepared chicken tandoori that smelled of garlic, onions, and unidentifiable seasonings. A ceramic bowl of quinoa salad and another made with unfamiliar grains accompanied the main dish. *Who eats this stuff?* Stuart wondered. He felt relieved when he recognized a tossed green salad. For some odd reason, the presentation reminded him of summer camp. Coming from a restaurant background, he knew instinctively that the food service was a little too hokey.

After lunch, he and Banning toured the spa. It was nothing more than a converted basement with a low ceiling, situated directly underneath the dining room. Stuart, who loved Broadway musicals, didn't like the New Age music, with the tinkling of bells and the sounds of falling rain. Pink ceiling lights—Banning's discovery—flattered the sharp edges in a warren of tiny massage rooms. Feeling claustrophobic, Stuart preferred wide open spaces, bright lights, and brassy show tunes. The spa was not his bailiwick. Nevertheless, he found himself inhaling deeper than usual.

"What's that smell?"

Banning shrugged. "I don't know. Ask Sunshine."

When she overheard her name, Sunshine took it as an invitation and walked away from the reception desk to join them. Stuart vaguely remembered Banning saying that she was his favorite massage therapist. Now he knew why. Sunshine stood several inches above him, with long, blondish-white hair and an olive complexion. *Maybe Scandinavian,* he thought.

She spoke in a whisper. "Doesn't that eucalyptus smell divine? I adore it."

Straining to hear her, Stuart commented. "Good stuff. Kinda makes you want to suck it in."

"That's the idea. It's an aromatic, homeopathic balm. Creates a sense of well-being."

Stuart, who had always thought of himself as a "with it" guy, didn't understand the New Age jargon. Neither *aromatic, homeopathic* nor *balm* rang a bell.

After touring the spa, the two men viewed several unoccupied condominium units. As they strolled through the property, the heat intensified. By the time they returned to the air-conditioned dining room, Banning barged into the kitchen to help himself to another ice-cold beer and brought out another Coke for Stuart.

"Well . . ." he said folding one arm across the other, "now that you've seen the operation, what'd you think? Your gut reaction?"

Stuart hesitated. He wasn't quite sure how to express his opinion without stepping on anyone's toes. "I see plenty of up-side. Good possibilities. But the place needs a transfusion . . . and deep pockets." He paused again, mentally prioritizing his talking points. "Number one, to make this into a *real* resort you'll definitely need more units. You've gotta remove the sand out of those unfinished units and finish them off. Add more units. If you want to raise the rates, you've gotta upgrade everything. Bring the rooms up to date. I think Pepper's doing a good job, but you need to add professional food service. A top-notch chef will draw in the right crowd."

A few days after they returned to Reno, Banning gave Stuart a new assignment. "I've been thinking. I like what I heard the other day. You're right on the money. I want you to fly down to the resort. Stay two or three days a week. And handle whatever needs to get done."

It wasn't all bad. Stuart thrived. Sometimes he flew on Banning's private jet. Other times he flew first-class from Reno to Los Angeles, racking up Frequent Flyer Miles and dreaming of places to travel with Rachel. The only bad part was the heart-stopping pencil thin, puddle-hopper from Los Angeles to Palm Springs. As it flew over the San Bernardino and San Jacinto Mountains, he could see every boulder and branch on the trees. Barely over the mountains, the plane would dive like a kamikaze down to the Palm Springs airport, only straightening out just before the wheels hit the tarmac.

Although Stuart continued to maintain his office in Reno, he commuted back and forth. One afternoon, after an executive staff meeting, Banning called Stuart aside and urged him to stay. "Let's head over to the café. I need to talk to you in private." The wind whipped up the dirt and dust as the two men sauntered across the alley that separated the Atlas Towers from the hotel/club. Once they were seated in the little café on the second floor, Banning got right to the point. "I've been thinking. Instead of commuting, how would you like to move down south . . . to the resort?"

"Permanently?"

"Yeah. You could live in one of the condominiums . . . or until you find your own place. Having you on the premises 24/7 would be a good thing. That way you could see exactly what needs to be done and it'll give you more time to do it."

Chapter 11

Moving

RACHEL WAS IN THE MIDDLE of dicing tomatoes for tacos when she heard Stuart burst through the front door singing *Happy Days Are Here Again*. As he entered the kitchen, Rachel said, "Well, don't you sound like a happy camper? What's up?"

"Guess what?" And before she had an opportunity to guess, he blurted it out. "Banning wants us to move down to the resort."

"Is this an April Fool's joke? Cause you better be kidding."

"No, I'm serious."

Rachel's response was not what he expected. "You better sit down," she said, putting down the paring knife and wiping her hands on the nearby dishtowel. She pulled up a kitchen chair across from him and cautioned herself to remain calm. "I want to say something. Get it off my chest. I've lost count of the number of moves we've made. I'm tired of it. And you're asking me to pick up and move again?"

"Well, this is a fantastic opportunity. Now's our inning."

"No way. N-O! It's not going to happen. Hear me out. On snowy nights, while you sat by the fire watching football, I drove clear across Reno on the icy roads. I devoted time and energy to getting my master's degree. For over a year, I've volunteered my time coordinating the adult education program at the middle school . . ." Rachel paused to take a breath, and then continued. "I'm on the fast track to become a school principal. And you want me to throw it all away. Guess what! I'm not doing it."

Stuart listened with half an ear. "But it's an opportunity of a lifetime."

"No. No, not for me, it isn't. For once, think of me. Look at it from my point of view," Rachel screamed, holding back tears of frustration. She got up and poured herself a glass of water. "I've gone half-way around the world for you and your jobs. It's my turn! This is my shot at success. A chance to put my ideas to work. What about what I want?"

For the moment, Stuart had no answer. "Half-way around the world? That's bullshit!"

"Yeah, half-way around the world. Hilton Head, San Diego, Hawaii . . ." and at that moment, she couldn't think of all the other places they'd moved. At this point, Rachel couldn't stop herself. "Besides, I can't pick up and leave just to make you happy. I'm committed to teach 'til the end of the year. The district would come unglued if I simply walked out. And what about the kids? Am I supposed to abandon my students just for you?"

Stuart brushed aside her concern. "Look, Rachel. Get real. You don't think a teacher's ever left in the middle of the school year? They can always hire another teacher to take your place."

"And what about the kids? Do I just walk out on them?"

"They're not your kids. For God's sakes, they'll live without you. And you, you'll live like a goddamn princess at the resort . . . and think of the money we'll be saving? You won't have to work if you don't want to. And you can enjoy all the amenities. Get spa treatments any damn time you please. Every day if you want. You'll never have to shop or cook. We can eat every meal in the dining room. Maid service every day. If you can honestly say you wouldn't like all that, I'll buy you a new hat!"

"That's all well and good, but who wants to live in Desert Oasis? Tell me that!"

"For chrissakes, stop with the *buts.* You're right on top of Palm Springs, the glamour capital of the world. Most people would give their right arm to be in your shoes."

Bickering. Brooding. Posturing. Pouting. The silent treatment. For well over two weeks Rachel and Stuart explored all the nuances of a serious argument. In the end, Stuart simply wore her down, like he always did.

Even though Rachel capitulated, she was stubborn enough to insist on the final word. "I guarantee you this will be my last move. If you think I'm going to move any more after this, you're wrong. You'll have to go without me. And I refuse to leave my class 'til the school year ends. I've been working on every skill those kids need for testing and I don't want some new teacher coming in at the last minute and screwing them up."

Eventually they worked out a compromise. Stuart moved into a two-bedroom, two-bath, fully furnished condo unit at the resort with its own private, landscaped garden, while Rachel stayed in their house and completed her contract. When possible, on weekends and holidays, she commuted south. She couldn't help comparing the two cities. On a Friday Rachel would leave Reno all bundled up in a heavy jacket, gloves, and boots in the bone-chilling weather only to be greeted by sunshine, warm air, and a colorful blaze of petunias, paper poppies, and snapdragons at the Palm Springs Airport.

To Rachel's surprise, the aesthetics of the desert inched their way into her heart. She grew to love the sparseness and lack of congestion. At dusk she would stand in awe, soaking in the silhouette of palm trees towering above the roof tops. At night she marveled at the stars that filled the blackened sky like an embroidery pattern. And during the day, with constant sunshine, Rachel found herself dressing more and more casually . . . in walking shorts, tee-shirts, and sandals.

After months of commuting back and forth, Rachel calmed down. One Saturday night as they were driving back to the resort from Rigoletto's, an expensive Italian restaurant, she shot Stuart one of her more mischievous smiles. "I hope no one at school notices that I only call in sick on Fridays and Mondays."

Their house sold in mid-July. As she dealt with the moving company and arranged for their furniture and most personal possessions to once again be placed in storage, a strand of anger welled up inside her. There was no telling where their new adventure might wind up. With a carload of packing boxes and clothes, plus some miscellaneous school stuff, Rachel drove south to join Stuart at Twin Palms Resort. He was beginning to make changes, transforming the rundown hippie haven into an upscale resort. As predicted, Rachel's anger dissipated as she reveled in all the perks—daily housekeeping, the pools, *free* massages, and a fine chef in the dining room.

Stuart got a kick out of his wife and her new lifestyle, taking every opportunity to tease her. "Well, haven't you become the Pampered Princess of Palm Springs! Enjoying the good life, are ya?"

ROSA AND SANTIAGO

Chapter 12

New Life

Desert Oasis, California

NACHO BARELY recalled the Lopez family back in Quezaltepeque. Nevertheless, he felt obliged to help, just as others helped him when he first arrived in California. While driving his beat-up minivan west on the I-10 to pick-up Rosa and Santiago, he reminisced about his own harrowing trek from El Salvador. Even though he had been robbed and beaten too many times to remember, he knew he had been one of the luckier ones. Now older—with a family of his own—he shivered thinking how dangerous it had been riding on top of the boxcars as the train zig-zagged through Mexico. When Nacho snuck across the border, all he had in his pocket was a comb, a telephone number on a scrap of paper, and four dollars.

I was barely nineteen . . . but everything was so much easier then.

For eleven months Nacho had struggled to survive. He washed dishes in a small Mexican restaurant in a beach town near San Diego and bunked on the floor of a low rent apartment with three other illegal men. Things changed dramatically when Yolanda literally walked into his life. A high school senior with a bubbling personality, beseeching eyes the color of charcoal, and long eyelashes started to worked part-time in the restaurant. In the evening she waited on tables, hoping to save enough money to pay for a few junior college classes when she graduated. They developed a mutual attraction. Fortunately, she took him under her wing and showed him the ropes.

In those days, marrying an American legalized his stay, giving him the right to obtain a *green card*. They were married by a priest less than a year after her graduation. With his new designation, he obtained an apprentice job with a local roofing company. When the company received a large contract in Palm Springs, Nacho and Yolanda decided to move. The cost of living was so much less than San Diego. They felt lucky to find a decent, affordable apartment in Desert Oasis, not far from Palm Springs.

As Nacho sped down the freeway, his thoughts returned to Rosa and Santiago. *Without money or speaking the language, it won't be easy. There's so much to learn.*

Nacho arrived at the *stash* house in his work clothes. "Sorry I'm so late. I hope you didn't think I had forgotten you," he said in Spanish. "Traffic's terrible this time of day."

"*Es* okay," Rosa said, relieved beyond words that he finally showed up.

"Are you hungry?"

Not wishing to cause Nacho any undue hardship, Rosa lowered her eyes and replied, "I'm okay." She understood they were completely dependent on his goodwill for everything and didn't want to be an undue burden. However, all she and Santiago had eaten since they left Tijuana were the two small bags of Doritos chili limón tortilla chips and the two small cans of guava juice.

Nacho hung an arm around Santiago's narrow shoulders. "How about you, young man? Hungry?"

Santiago nodded, indicating food was on his mind.

"I thought so. A growing boy. Well, we've got at least a two-hour ride ahead of us . . . depending on traffic. So, we'll stop for dinner first."

Still angry over the loss of his soccer ball and his stomach crying for food, Santiago felt miserable. He eyed everyone at Taco Bell with hostility and suspicion. Caucasians and Hispanics alike. It didn't matter.

After Nacho brought the trays of food to their table, he watched Santiago scarf down three tacos, beans, rice, chips, and a Pepsi. "Want something else to eat?"

Santiago, unable to express himself, harbored a network of invisible insecurities. He lowered his head, afraid to ask for anything else.

Nacho tried hard to make him feel at ease. "Santiago, how old are you?"

"Thirteen. My birthday was last month."

"Ah, a teenager. I have three little girls at home. They'll be so impressed. They can't wait to meet you."

As Nacho drove his minivan back to Desert Oasis, the commute traffic slowed. As they approached the desert floor, the quality of the air changed, suddenly feeling hot and muggy.

"We're almost there."

When Rosa and Santiago viewed Desert Oasis for the first time, their eyes darted back and forth, trying to absorb it all. Several neatly fenced off trailer parks—with their colorful flags and banners—lined the main boulevard. Half-dead palm trees from a failed water system paralleled the sparse sidewalks.

What was not obvious at the time were the demographics of the small town: consisting of released felons from a nearby prison, a handful of survivalists living in decaying houses with boarded-up windows, sex offenders not allowed to live in *family* neighborhoods, African Americans that had been pushed out of their neighborhood in north Palm Springs, Hispanics and Caucasians looking for inexpensive rent and a sprinkling of orthodox Jews that formed their own reclusive enclave.

Nacho pulled up to a shabby two-story apartment complex with a faded *Apartment for Rent* sign out front. Nevertheless, when Santiago saw the small swimming pool set in the center of the unkempt courtyard, his eyes lit up, thinking it paradise. Nacho and his wife Yolanda, and their three daughters—two, four, and six—lived in a two-bedroom unit on the second floor facing the parking lot.

Neither Nacho nor his wife Yolanda had expectations of luxury. Despite the overcrowding, they were more than willing to provide Rosa and Santiago with a temporary refuge. He still remembered how grateful he had been when someone he worked with at the restaurant—someone he barely knew—gave him a place to sack out.

Nacho and Yolanda's little girls were immediately infatuated with Santiago, showering him with attention. "Do you want to see my toys?" the oldest girl asked, trying to be nice.

Overwhelmed by their abundance, Santiago didn't let on that the only possession he ever owned was his soccer ball and now it was gone. All his life he and Javier improvised toys from scraps of wood and discarded boxes. Pointing to the two bunk beds in the girls' tiny bedroom, the six-year-old asked, "Papi, can Santiago sleep in here with us?"

Yolanda laughed. "Ariana, let Tía Rosa sleep with you. Let's make it an all-girls' room. She can have the lower bunk. Now that you are a big girl, you can sleep on top. How's that?"

"What about Santiago?"

"Well, he gets the living room all to himself. We'll make it a boy's room and he can sleep on the couch." Day and night a yellow sheet covered the couch and a soft, fuzzy stuffed monkey rested next to the pillow. A gift from the girls.

"That's Curious George," the oldest one explained, although Santiago didn't understand the word *curious.*

When things calmed down and Rosa got into a routine, she sat down at the kitchen table and penned three letters in her primitive scrawl—one to her father back in El Salvador, one to her son Javier, whom she worried about constantly, and one to Josefina and Diego.

> *Papá,*
> *We are in California staying with Nacho and*
> *his family. Their address:*
> > *24-548 Calle Riviera*
> > *Apartment #107*
> > *Desert Oasis, California*
> *Are you okay? I miss you. In Tijuana, Javier*
> *met a girl and refused to come to California.*
> *I miss him so much. But her father promised*
> *to get him a good job at the Ford factory.*
> *Every night I pray he will be okay. We just*
> *celebrated our first American holiday,*
> *Thanksgiving. I'm learning to drive a car.*
> *We have so much to be thankful for.*

In Tijuana two weeks later, Josefina checked her rusted mailbox after work. To her surprise, she found two letters from Rosa written in an untamed script. She ripped open the envelope addressed to her and Diego. Inside was a note, thanking them for everything. Josefina set the envelope addressed to Javier on the tile counter in her kitchen. Before moving in with Angel, Javier told Josefina where he would be living. On her day off, Josefina planned to personally deliver the letter to him.

Lately Javier had been thinking more and more about his mother and wondering what her life was like in California. When Josefina handed him the letter, he too couldn't wait to open it. He stood there and read and reread it. His mother had printed out Nacho and Yolanda's address and telephone number. She wanted to know if he was getting enough to eat and how he was managing on his own. She ended her letter telling him how much she missed and loved him.

High on his new-found freedom, Javier skimmed over his

mother's concern. Except for his job at the car wash, his days were laced with booze, a little weed, and sex. He was living his dream. Unfortunately, it was nothing he could share with his mother. He did, however, carefully tuck her letter into his duffel bag, so he wouldn't lose it. He planned to write her back when he found the time . . .

In Desert Oasis, Nacho's wife Yolanda continued working as a housekeeper and somehow managed to feed two extra people. Trying to stay within her budget, she kept the meals simple. Soup with bits of chicken or pork. Beans, rice, tortillas and lots of locally grown oranges and grapefruit. But after Sunday Mass, Yolanda invariably made a special dinner. She roasted several chickens simmered in garlic and onions. From time-to-time the ladies she worked for paid her extra to serve or clean-up at their fancy parties and handed her their leftovers. Her plan was to sock away extra money each month hoping that one day they could afford to buy a house.

In exchange for room and board, Rosa offered to babysit the girls while Yolanda worked. Neighbors discovered her babysitting and offered to pay her to watch their children as well. If Yolanda cleaned an extra-large house, she would sometimes ask Rosa to help her. And on those days, Santiago stayed home from school to take her place babysitting.

The apartment manager demanded the first month's rent and a security deposit for a bleak studio apartment. It took Rosa a little more than a year to scrape together enough money for her own apartment. Neither the size nor the condition of the studio apartment mattered. Nor did it matter that the dishwasher and two burners on the greasy old stove were shot. Nor the fact that black mold ringed the bathtub and an occasional cockroach scrambled out from a kitchen cabinet. Pleased that she had gained her independence, Rosa managed to overlook the apartment's faults.

When the wealthy women—whose houses Yolanda cleaned— bought newer and better household goods, they handed her a potpourri of odds and ends. Most were flawed in some way but still usable. Yolanda always figured if she didn't need them, she could always pass them along to someone else in the apartment complex. She gave Rosa what she could: a pot without a lid, some chipped dishes, a few odd glasses, a lamp with a torn shade, some shabby linens, and an old garden table with three chairs, one with a few missing straps.

Most of the tenants in the large apartment complex were Afro-American or Hispanic—some legal, some not. Many of the women worked as housekeepers in Palm Springs and neighboring communities. In the morning when they dropped their babies off in Rosa's austere apartment, they saw how little she and Santiago had. The more generous women gave Rosa additional items passed down by their affluent clients. Rosa and Santiago had been sleeping on the floor for months before Rosa lucked out. One illegal family—fed up with living in fear—planned to return to Mexico. They sold her two used box springs and mattresses, a small dresser, and a 19-inch black and white television set that still worked.

Chapter 13

Javier on his Own

Tijuana, Mexico

JAVIER FELT LIKE AN INTRUDER staying with Diego and Josefina after his mother and brother left for California. He had accumulated a little money working at the car wash and when he found out that Angel's brother had just gotten married, he offered to pay Angel—one of his new buddies—to share his bedroom. After sleeping on the floor for so long, a real bed with a mattress and soft pillow smacked of paradise. Angel's parents were good souls—especially kind—knowing that he was living on his own. They welcomed him as if he were their son. But they left him alone as they did Angel, with no accountability. At night after work, he and Angel hit the bars, listened to music, smoked a little grass, and drank. Sometimes Maria—the voluptuous teenager with whom he was spending more and more time—went along, sometimes not. No longer attending church, Javier relished Sunday mornings and the chance to sleep in.

Months flew by. With no restrictions, he was having the time of his life. One Sunday morning in late February—after another raucous night drinking straight shots of cheap Tequila—Javier crawled out of bed in his shorts. "Jesus, Angel, last night was the best, but I feel like shit."

"Me too. My ears are buzzing."

"God's punishing us," Javier joked. "Getting revenge."

"Really? When did you get so religious?" As Angel slipped into his jeans, he remarked, "someone once told me that gnawing on raw cactus can prevent a hangover."

"Oh, great. Why didn't you tell me that earlier?"

"I didn't think about it 'til now. Maybe it can still help. Look, I'm halfway dressed. There's cactus out front. Maybe it'll work."

Just as Angel opened the door, a *cuiza,* little green gecko, scampered in. "These little buggers are everywhere."

"Go! Get the cactus. Shit, I'm willing to try anything. I'm supposed to meet Maria after eleven o'clock Mass." Javier's head was still reeling as he showered and put on a clean tee-shirt.

With his hair slicked back with pomade, Javier stood in front of the church and watched as Maria emerged. Happy to be together, they wandered the streets aimlessly holding hands. Eventually they caught up with an enthusiastic crowd funneling into the bullfight ring.

"I hate the bullfights," Maria stated. "It's sad to kill an animal just for fun."

"Oh, come on. It takes real guts." Javier always longed to do something heroic. He still fantasized about killing the men who murdered his father.

"You're so mean."

Quickly changing the subject, Javier said, "By the way, last night I heard some hot *tejano,* Tex-Mex music. The singer sounded exactly like Selena. Even sang her song, *Baila Esta Cumbria.* Next time she performs, I'll take you."

Maria let it go.

"Why so quiet?" Javier asked, oblivious to the things that

weighed heavy on her mind. "Are you mad at me 'cuz I didn't take you last night?"

"No," she said evasively. "Just thirsty. Let's get something to drink." She was marking time, petrified to discuss the troubles that dominated her thoughts.

In the park outside the bullring, they stopped at a fruit cart decorated with faded plastic flower. The vendor was selling canned juices, soda pop, and fresh mango. Javier spoke first. "I told you we came to Mexico by bus. It was so boring. Sometimes my mother would buy us slices of mango at a bus stop. Umm. So sugary sweet. Want some?"

"Sure," Maria said, with a tepid smile.

Dodging the swarm of people, they rested on a short cinder-block wall. Mango juice dripped down their arms as they watched the crowd.

"I don't see many gringos here today. That's unusual."

"I guess so," she responded, in a listless voice that let him know she didn't really care one way or the other. "Javier, I've got something important to say. But I'm not sure how you're going to take it." Before he had a chance to brace himself, it gushed out of her like water spilling from a spigot. "I'M PREGNANT!"

"Oh, God, no! How do you know?" he asked, hoping she was wrong.

"I missed two cycles."

Just hearing about girls and their cycles made Javier uncomfortable. For him, it was a mystical subject, and he didn't want to talk about it. His first thought was of himself and his future. "Maria, That's terrible. In another month, I'll be nineteen. I'm not ready to be a father. Get rid of *it*."

"*It?* It's not an *it!* What's wrong with you?"

"Forget what I just said, okay? I'm just a little shocked."

"Well, how *did* you mean it? You're not excited." Tears welled up in her eyes. "You don't care about me. Only yourself."

"No, that's not true and you know it."

"Well, guess what? You're going to be a father, whether you

like it or not. I'm not getting an abortion, if that's what you mean. I could die in some filthy back room. Gloria, my sister's friend, almost bled to death. Is that what you want me to do? Bleed to death." As she spoke, she grew more agitated. "I'm going to have this baby. A baby is a precious gift from God. Who doesn't love a baby?"

"Maria, be reasonable. Who's gonna take care of the baby? You're only sixteen. You're still in school."

"So. Me and my mother, we'll take care of the baby. You can come live with us. Javier. We can be a family. But one way or another, I'm keeping this baby."

Sex was one thing, but Javier never thought of becoming a father. New to absolute freedom, he relished his roust-about nights hanging out with Angel and the guys. Weeks, then months swept by as Javier considered his options. He continued to see Maria throughout her pregnancy. In the beginning, she was constantly tired and nauseous, and in her last month she had to have complete bedrest.

Maria never let up. She kept pushing him to move in. In her final month of pregnancy, Javier—consumed with guilt—finally agreed to live with Maria and her parents. All he brought with him were his clothes stuffed into a duffel bag and the letter his mother had sent from California. He had thought about answering her letter, but never made the time to sit down and write back. In the back of his mind, he knew his mother would neither approve of his new lifestyle nor him becoming a father.

Maria's parents were old and crotchety. They had raised five children, all married and living on their own, except Maria, the youngest. When the Ford factory closed, they had been forced to move into a small apartment on the outskirts of Zona Norte, the *red-light* district. Now they would be burdened with two more mouths to feed. Javier sensed her parents' underlying hostility and barely masked anger towards him.

Despite the hostile environment, Javier was overcome with awe at the birth of Annamaria. He sat for hours and gazed at his sleeping daughter, marveling at her tiny fingers and perfect little toes. On the day of Annamaria's christening, he felt such pride that he sat down at the kitchen table and penned a brief note to his mother, letting her know that she was a grandmother. He enclosed a small black and white photograph taken at the hospital shortly after Annamaria's birth.

Maria spent days and nights nursing and trying to calm their colicky daughter. What was once a torrid love affair between Javier and Maria gradually dissipated like smoke on a windy day. For her, the baby's demands—along with efforts to appease her irritable parents—came before Javier. Patience in their small, overcrowded apartment were in short supply. Tempers flared at the slightest provocation.

Feeling invisible, Javier brooded. He needed to get out of the house, to hang with his buddies, to hit the bars. All he wanted to do was feed the emptiness that floated inside him. He was bored with his job at the car wash, but relieved to get away from his constantly crying daughter and all the squabbling. He badgered Maria's father about the promise of a lucrative job that never materialized. "I didn't go to California with my mother because you promised you'd get me a good job."

"What am I supposed to do? When Ford closed the plant, I lost my job. Look where we're living. Do you think I like it? We had to move. I'm doing the best I can . . . for me, for my family, and, yes, Javier, for you too. Good jobs are hard to come by. If you're so unhappy, go live somewhere else."

At the car wash, Javier lashed out, bullying co-workers and customers alike. One Monday morning a well-dressed, but haughty American woman complained that he didn't do a good enough job polishing the hubcaps on her Mercedes. Javier exploded and yelled back at the angry woman.

His boss—who happened to be outside at the time—overheard his invective tirade. "Javier, in the office. Now. We need to talk."

Javier threw his wet rags down on a rusty barrel and followed his boss.

"Sit down," his boss barked, his face red with anger. "Up 'til now I've been lenient, hoping you'd change your piss poor attitude. But you haven't changed one iota. Get yourself another job. You'll get paid for the days you worked, but you're done here. Finished."

Javier, confused and angry, huffed out of the car wash. He couldn't face the reality of returning to the apartment and admitting to Maria and her parents that he was fired. Wrapped up in his curdled world, he convinced himself that no one appreciated him. Maria and their baby were getting to be troublesome appendages. He was done being a father. He wanted out.

With nothing but the clothes on his back, the few pesos he earned that morning in tips, and his severance pay, Javier made an impetuous decision. The quixotic thought that had been held at bay, exploded. What he wanted most was to return to El Salvador and avenge his father's murder.

Chapter 14

Riding La Bestia

ANGRY WITH THE WORLD, Javier stood under the noonday sun at the Mexican Highway 2 with his thumb out. By the time a long-haul driver pulled over, Javier was sweating profusely.

Hey, kid, where ya headed?" the burly trucker asked in the husky voice of a smoker.

Javier thought it a complicated question. He didn't know whether to say *El Salvador or Mexicali.* Finally, he mumbled, "Mexicali."

"Well then, today's your lucky day. I'm driving there to pick up a load of tires. Climb in. I like talking to people. Takes the boredom out of my job." Even though the windows were rolled down, the cab smelled of stale tobacco and body odor. "Where'd ya want to be dropped?"

"I'm not sure. I'm planning to hitch a ride . . . on a train heading south."

"I'm curious, kid. Why south?"

"To see my grandfather; he's sick." Javier wasn't about to

reveal his real purpose, to track down and kill the men that murdered his father.

"Where's your grandfather live?"

"El Salvador."

"Jesus Christ, that's one heck of a train ride just to see your grandfather. Did you call to tell him you're coming?"

"Naw, it's a surprise."

"Suppose you get down there and he died?"

Without a real answer, Javier shrugged his shoulders.

The truck driver shook his head, thinking he was just another dumb kid. After a short silence, he said, "There's a couple of bottles of water in the blue cooler, right down there by your feet. Get me one, will ya? And grab one for yourself."

As the cool water slid down Javier's parched throat, he felt nothing but gratitude towards this stranger.

The trucker took a couple of swigs, then set his bottle aside. Not one to pull any punches, he asked, "Do you know what you're getting into? The train, *La Bestia,* the beast, is dangerous. They don't call it *la muerte,* the death train for nothing. I'm not telling you what to do, mind you, but I've picked up a lot of innocent kids. Only difference, they were heading north. Those poor kids thought it would be a cinch to ride on top of those freight trains. I bought 'em a meal or two. Heard their hard luck stories. By the time I picked 'em up, they were in pretty bad shape."

Javier wasn't sure he wanted to hear what the trucker had to say.

"When the trains stop, either the corrupt police, *la migra,* or gangs chase them off the boxcars with knives, guns . . . sometimes even machetes. They strip 'em right down to their shorts and rob the poor bastards, taking everything. Even the phone numbers of parents or contacts in the U.S. Then they'd call the contacts and extort money from them. Trust me, they're mean sonsofbitches."

Javier swallowed hard, while remaining silent.

The trucker, who had the weathered face of a man in his sixties, had a coughing jag, then spit phlegm into a dirty rag that was resting on the torn seat. He gulped a little more water, then tried to clear his throat. "Sorry about that. Sometimes when I get to talking a lot, I start to cough. Too much smoking. Say, kid, you don't smoke, do you?"

"Uh, no, can't afford it." *There's no point telling the stranger about the weed.*

"Well, that's a lucky break. It's addictive as hell. Don't ever start. Before you hop on one of them goddamn trains, you need to hear some of the stories I heard. Those kids can't stay on top of the trains forever. And if they lose their concentration or fall asleep, they can topple off and land beneath the wheels . . . maybe lose an arm or a leg. Even worse, die. Eventually they gotta get off and scavenge for food and water. And catch a few winks. *La migra,* immigration is always on their ass, tracking 'em down like animals. Even worse for the girls, you know what I mean."

Javier wished to hell the man would shut up.

"With no money, those poor kids have to beg or steal food to survive. They told me they hide in cemeteries, sleep in mausoleums, near the tracks to catch a few winks. Then wait for another train to come along. Some of the boys I've picked up broke down and cried when they told me about their friends. The ones that didn't make it."

Just then a beer truck tried to pass him and narrowly missed crashing into an oncoming car. "Goddamn it, we could've been killed! Everyone's in such a damn hurry."

It was getting more difficult for Javier to imagine himself hopping on and off the moving freight trains. He wanted to close his mind to the whole thing.

"It can take weeks, sometimes months to get where you're going. And those trains only go through Mexico. Then what? How ya gonna get through Guatemala?"

"I've got money; I'll take a bus."

The trucker scoffed. "Look, kid, you're not hearing me. How long do you think your money's gonna last? Everyone's out to rob you. And I mean everyone."

It was obvious that Javier had not thought his plans through in any detail.

Eventually the trucker stopped talking to concentrate on the tight, curvy mountain roads.

"Do you suppose we could listen to some music?"

"Sorry, a couple of months ago someone snatched my radio when I parked at a PEMEX station. And I haven't got 'round to replacing it. I find it more interesting to pick up hitch-hikers and talk."

After spending two-and-a-half hours with the truck driver, Javier was dropped off in a rural area, not far from the train station in Mexicali.

The trucker handed him a business card. "Kid, if you change your mind and get back to Tijuana, you might check out our warehouse. Every-once-in-a-while they get an opening. A strong young man like you would be perfect for loading and unloading tires."

After listening to all the pitfalls, Javier's resolve had dropped a notch or two. He thanked the driver and absent-mindedly shoved the business card in his front pocket.

It was mid-day and the heat felt oppressive. A rag-tag group of teenage boys and a few men—mostly unhappy and anxious to return home—took cover in the shade of several sycamore trees, not too far from the shimmering railroad tracks. Some were bare-chested with their white tee-shirts slung over their heads, in lieu of a cap. A big metal cross on a thick chain hung around the neck of one young man. Most carried a canteen or backpack. A few had long-sleeve shirts tied around their waist. Javier brought nothing. This disparate group of stragglers had one thing in common. They planned to run alongside a slow-moving train, grab hold of a ladder and pull themselves up to the spine of one of the boxcars before the train picked up speed. With little money, a free but dangerous ride was the best they could do.

A thin man, older than most, spotted Javier standing on the fringes and staring. Out of curiosity, the stranger approached him. "Hey, boy, what's up?"

Javier, now a father, despised being called boy, but didn't want to cause trouble. He had no choice but to answer the direct question. "Heading back to El Salvador. You?"

"Oaxaca. Going back home. Got as far as Phoenix, but to hell with it. Doing shit work. Getting ripped off all the time. Afraid of the crazy sheriff and the Border Patrol. It's not for me. Where'd you go? Arizona? California?"

"Neither," Javier admitted sheepishly, not wanting to be taken for a sissy. With a little swagger in his voice, he said, "I was heading to California but met a beautiful girl in Tijuana and stayed. We had a kid together."

"Nice. So, where's this beautiful girl now?" the stranger asked, raising one eyebrow expectantly. "I don't mind looking at pretty women every now and then. With such a beautiful girlfriend and a baby, why in the hell are you going back to El Salvador?"

Javier was beginning to ask himself the same question. "Long story," is all he said. He had more than a trace of anxiety, as he pivoted to another subject. "Did you ride the trains before?"

"Yeah, didn't you?"

Javier hesitated. "No, I came by bus." He deliberately omitted the fact that he had traveled with his mother and brother. This was the first time in his life that he was totally alone.

"Oh, by the way, I'm Carlos."

"Javier."

"Well, Javier, let me give you some advice," Carlos said, swiping the sweat from his brow with the back of his hand. "If you've never done this before, riding *La Bestia* isn't easy. The thirst alone can drive you mad. Someone gave me a tip. Get a pebble. Keep it in your pocket. When you're dying for water, suck on the pebble. It keeps the saliva in. Here," he said, bending down and picking up a small pebble, "take this. You can thank me later."

For one reason or another, all those heading south had found life in the north so intolerable that they were willing to risk the dangers of *La Bestia* to return home. Javier was right in assuming everyone knew the ropes except him.

Carlos continued. "Unless gangs force you off the train, stay on as long as you can. If you need to jump off to sleep, be careful. Find a place off the ground. The desert's full of snakes. The goddamn diamondback has heat-seeking sensors. I heard about a few guys who got bitten by snakes and died.

Javier, inundated with free advice, sat at the edge of the group. He had hours to weigh his options. *Should I go back to Maria and the baby or head south?*

Finally, one of the guys shouted, "I can feel the rumble of the train. It's coming." This was the clarion call for action.

Several seconds later, Javier heard the clash of metal-on-metal—the squeals, groans, and clanks—as the long train slowly rounded the bend. As if on cue, everyone dashed towards the rusted red cars. Carlos screamed at Javier, "Run. Grab hold of a ladder and pull yourself up."

Along with the others, Javier's adrenaline was pumping fast. He scrambled towards the train. As he got closer—not ten feet from the churning metal wheels—he stopped abruptly. In the pushing and shoving and chaos that ensued, with everyone determined to grab hold of a ladder, someone accidentally knocked Javier to the ground. He questioned himself. *Should I stay or go?*

CONVERGENCE

Chapter 15

Benson Middle School

Desert Oasis, California

BENSON MIDDLE SCHOOL—still in the process of being completed—planned to open that Fall. While still in Reno, Rachel had prepared a binder—a sales pitch of sorts—to highlight her teaching skills. She knew she would be looking for another job. A few weeks after moving to the desert, she called the school district about teaching at the newly constructed middle school near the resort. The personnel department directed her to the principal who was interviewing all summer.

Ms. Webb, the principal of the new middle school flipped through Rachel's binder—that detailed her résumé, award-winning Science Fair projects, and photographs of her classroom endeavors—without saying a word or asking a question. The single thing that got her hired—the silver bullet—was her California teaching credential, issued almost thirty years earlier.

And Ms. Webb caught it.

She closed the binder, looked up, and smiled. "You know the state no longer gives this type of credential. Things have changed drastically. Now, middle school teachers must specialize in a subject, just like high school teachers. Your credential intrigues me. I can place you anywhere and still be compliant."

That's it, Rachel thought. *My credential sold her. I've got the job.*

Benson Middle School was the first new school built in the blighted town of Desert Oasis in over thirty years. In September, school officially started. There were two days of meetings and prep time, to pick up textbooks and organize the classrooms. At fifty-one, Rachel was the oldest and most experienced teacher on the staff. She knew that this first year wasn't going to be a walk in the park. The school was not as luxurious as the resort. And no one would be doting on her like the employees at the resort doted on Stuart.

Even before the students arrived, she returned to the resort exasperated. "Well, how did it go today?" Stuart asked, as they sat in his office.

"It's a brand-new school. I can't understand why the district picked two *newbies* from other districts to get the school up and running. It doesn't make sense. The principal's never been a principal before. And the vice-principal has no administrative experience. It's going to be the blind leading the blind. If the district was smart, they would've picked experienced administrators that knew the ropes."

"The kids haven't even arrived. Stop bitching. Why don't you wait and see how it works out?"

But Rachel was relentless when trying to make her point. "Come on. Don't you think it would have been better to pick experienced administrators? If you were the superintendent, what would you have done?"

"I'm not the superintendent. For God's sakes, Rachel, let it go. Stop analyzing everything."

The district had hired two greenhorns: Sara Webb, a first-time principal and David Belli, a young man with rakish good looks, who had never been a vice-principal before this assignment. The principal hired a coterie of inexperienced friends with emergency or provisional credentials and no teaching experience. Several were still struggling to pass the CBEST test, a basic reading, writing, and math test geared to the sixth grade level. California had put the test in place several years earlier, in one of their spasmodic efforts to make sure teachers were competent before stepping into a classroom.

With no systems in place, the school resembled a shapeless jellyfish, undulating first one way and then the other in ten-foot waves. Adding to the disorder, a chain link fence wrapped itself around an unfinished building—wedged between the administration building and a pod of classrooms. To get to the office, everyone had to walk on planks with heavy overhead scaffolding.

Rachel's new assignment was unique: to keep her students all day and teach them every subject except P.E. and their elective. The rest of the staff, mostly first year teachers, *team taught*, meaning one teacher taught Language Arts and Social Studies and the other taught Math and Science. And they simply traded students. Rachel, the odd man out, wound up with an extra free period. She assumed Ms. Webb dumped the transient students who registered late into her class. She braced herself for the challenge. Nevertheless, she knew she would enjoy teaching all the subjects rather than just two. That way she didn't have to finish each lesson in forty-five-minutes. In her mind, Reading sometimes ran into Social Studies. Science overlapped research, which was essentially Reading and Language Arts. From experience, she understood that one subject frequently merged into another, and this arrangement gave her more flexibility.

In classroom 105, not far from the administration building, Rachel prepared to meet her class. She felt an air of excitement, like performers on opening night. She wrote her name on the chalkboard and in big letters printed WELCOME. When the first bell rang, she stood at the open classroom door and smiled, being sure to greet each new student with a simple "Good Morning." Their indifferent faces avoided eye contact. They passed by her without responding, as if she were a cardboard cutout. *I'll have to work on that,* she thought. *Teach them to look me in the eye and say good morning.* There was no seating chart yet, so the students just grabbed a seat next to someone they knew and chatted.

"Class, could you tone it down a bit, so I can take roll?" she pleaded, trying to hit the right note. She didn't want to appear too strident, but then, not a pushover either.

The din lowered slightly as she called out names. "Jenny Albertson."

"Here."

"Arturo Amado."

"Here."

By the time she got down to Jaime Valencia there was a problem. When Rachel called his name there was silence. Has anyone seen Jaime this morning?"

"No. He'll probably come late," someone shouted from one side of the room. "I think he's in the principal's office."

"Already?" Rachel sighed.

Marco added, "It wasn't Jaime's fault. Someone ripped off his glasses. He didn't do nothing," and a few boys in the class began to snicker.

When the bell rang, the students pushed and shoved, rushing out the door to locate their friends. Rachel pulled a scrawny looking kid aside. From roll call, she remembered his name was Santiago. "Can I speak to you for a sec?"

"Okay," Santiago said meekly.

Thinner than most of the boys in the class, he appeared a bit disheveled. His tennis shoes were worn, with a small hole in the toe on his right foot. He wore grungy silver basketball shorts that hung below his knees and a black tee-shirt. In gray lettering, emblazoned across the front, it read *Shit Happens.*

"Santiago," Rachel said as gently as she knew how, "I have to tell you something personal, okay? Please don't take it the wrong way. But you've got to wear your tee-shirt inside out today or call your mom to bring you another one."

"Why?" he asked, looking down at his faded tee-shirt.

"I'm sorry, Santiago. School rules. *Shit Happens* is not considered appropriate dress. It's not going to fly around here." Years earlier, when Rachel first started to teach middle school, she dared not use the words *shit* or *fuck*. She began her career as a prim and proper teacher. When students flung those words out so casually, she would be offended, and send them to the office. But after years of teaching, she realized those words and others were bantered about more frequently than *homework* or *extra credit.*

"Well," he said looking down at the floor, "she can't bring me no new shirt."

Rachel had an urge to correct Santiago's English, but there were just too many other things to do. "Okay. Then go in the bathroom like I said. Just turn your shirt inside out. You can't wear it the way it is."

Santiago did as he was told.

Chapter 16

Life at the Resort

EVER SINCE RACHEL BEGAN her teaching career, scavenging for school supplies became a way of life. She discovered that California had a major budget crisis on their hands and the district provided minimal supplies. She believed in experiential, hands-on learning. Everything she ran across became a possibility for a teaching opportunity: newspapers, poker chips, beans, straws, string. Whatever. Several weeks after school started, she cornered Stuart in his office at the resort. Half serious, half not, she asked, "Do you think it's stealing if I take a few of your office supplies for my classroom?"

"Well, what'd ya think . . . you're Robin Hood?"

Rachel was incorrigible, like a little kid in a candy shop. And Stuart was always a soft touch. She rationalized, *if it helps the kids, it's a worthy cause. For Stuart, it's just a pittance and for his boss, the flamboyant one being chauffeured around in a Rolls-Royce, it means nothing. But for my class, these supplies are the icing on a very skimpy cake.*

Stuart pulled a brown box from a top shelf. "Here, take this stationery and these envelopes. We've changed our logo and won't be using them."

"Great!" Rachel exclaimed, as if she had discovered the Lost Ark. "The kids can use these to learn to format letters. Can I take some Scotch tape and a decent stapler? The ones at school are crap. They don't even work."

"Do you mind leaving me something to work with?"

Rachel wondered how many Ticonderoga pencils she could snag from a cardboard box without Stuart getting upset. They had much better erasers than the cheap pencils the school provided. She settled on four banded packets.

As Stuart cleared his desk to leave, Rachel stood at the electric sharpener in the supply room, grinding the tip of the pencils to a fine point. She liked handing out sharpened pencils, especially to the students that did not have any school supplies. For whatever reason, she equated a sharp pencil with a sharp mind.

"You're pathetic," Stuart joked, half in jest. Before she could respond, he added, "Ready for dinner? Let's get out of here. I'm starving."

Rachel wasn't sure he was genuinely hungry or just anxious to pull her away from his supply closet. "Sure, let's eat," she replied reluctantly. She had gathered a goldmine of supplies and so far, he hadn't complained bitterly.

"Just leave the stuff on my desk. We'll pick it up later."

As the resort manager, he liked to check the dining room and see how things were running. On their way to the resort's restaurant, Rachel hustled to keep up with Stuart's long strides. Suddenly a roadrunner scampered out from behind some boulders and hopped across their path. "Did you see that?" Rachel asked. "It looks exactly like the roadrunner in the old cartoons we used to watch."

"They like us. They're all over here."

As they climbed the four stairs to the flagstone terrace, Rachel glanced at the river rock bungalows. Turning to Stuart she commented, "No one makes stone buildings anymore. It reminds me of *The Three Little Pigs and the Big Bad Wolf.*"

"Only *you* would think of that. What goes on in that brain of yours?"

"Oh, you'd be surprised."

Although the three, low slung motel-style buildings were old, guests preferred their proximity to the resort's main attraction, a naturally heated grotto sheltered by rare, indigenous palm trees. The healing mineral water welled-up from an opening of the San Andreas fault that ran through the resort.

"It's always so quiet this late in the afternoon," Stuart remarked. "We've got a full house, but nobody's around. Everyone's back in their rooms."

"Well, what'd you expect?" Rachel shot back. "You pitch sex every opportunity you get."

She knew the place earned its reputation. Romantic getaways and nefarious affairs. Cut off from the *real* world by a guarded gate, the pampered guests were coddled royally. Sex was the follow-up to a day of self-indulgence. Food was never on the top of their priority list.

Stuart and Rachel preferred to eat dinner early, beating the guests into the dining room by at least an hour. Marta, the hostess, had been preoccupied lighting the forty or more tealights when they arrived. She hustled over to the reservation podium. "Good evening. Nice to see you, Mr. Roth."

Hey, what about me, Rachel thought, *I'm here too. An acknowledgment would be nice.*

Knowing their habit for not lingering over dinner, the hostess led Stuart and Rachel to the most sought-after table, next to the bay windows with an unobstructed view of the expansive desert floor and Mt. San Jacinto.

With her elbow resting on the table, head held up with her hand, Rachel thought wistfully, *I just want to eat and get back to the condo.* She placed her napkin on her lap and let out a convincing

sigh. Despite the hostess and all the servers doting on her husband, she knew that by default, she too was the beneficiary of their
obsequious service. Rachel reread the effusive statement inside
the resort's new, leather-bound dinner menu with amusement.
She thought, *Billy, the New Age-y chef was way over-the-top.*

The menu read:

> *It is our privilege to greatly influence your*
> *well-being by providing the expressions of our*
> *heart to delight and nourish you. The clean*
> *air, the hot water, and the bright sun is our*
> *inspiration to share in this gift of good health.*

The waiter interrupted Rachel's reverie.

She ordered her favorite dinner: Caesar salad, rack-of-lamb,
and a glass of Callaway Sauvignon Blanc.

After he left, Stuart asked, "So . . . how did it go today?" as he
nibbled on a piece of crusty sourdough bread slathered with butter.

"The kids were a little off the wall, but all-in-all, I can't com-
plain. How'd your day go?"

"Peculiar. Wait 'til you hear this," Stuart lowered his voice so
only Rachel could hear. "Banning called from Reno. He told me to
get some cash out of the safe to give Arlene."

"Who's Arlene?"

"I don't know. Probably one of his girlfriends."

Rachel jabbed her fork into a rather large crouton, shoved it
in her mouth and chewed it slowly, waiting for him to say more.
When he didn't, she pumped him for information. "Well,
what's so unusual about giving money to one of his girlfriends?
He always has girlfriends, and they always need money."

"No, this was different. This was a lot of money. I couldn't
cover it with the cash in the safe. The one we use for our daily operations. So, Banning gave me the combo to the inner safe. Where
he keeps the really big bucks."

"So how much did you give her?"

"Ten grand."

Rachel's eyes grew big. "You just walked over and handed her the cash?"

"Well, I put it in an envelope."

"That was big of you. What's it for?"

"You know I can't ask. Besides, it's probably better not to know."

Banning and his unconventional life-style intrigued Rachel. She thought about her compatriots, the young teachers she worked with. Their lives were conventional. A paycheck. A tract house. Car payments. Raising kids. They all thought *inside* the box. Not that there was anything wrong with that. On the other hand, Banning and his resort—his women, his partying, his chauffeur, his jet, his larger-than-life persona—would be unimaginable to them. Even if his life was made into a soap opera, they probably couldn't relate. And then Rachel reflected on her own extraordinary life-style compared to the kids in her class. She was living this grandiose life in a luxury resort and her students were in survival mode, not knowing what would happen from one day to the next.

Chapter 17

The Classroom

I T HAD BEEN ALMOST TWO YEARS since Santiago crossed into California. With language barriers, he never cared much for school. The only thing he enjoyed was playing soccer with the other boys. He continued to wrestle with the demons that floated freely in his head. For a young boy, he carried the burden of seeing the most grotesque atrocities first-hand. And a day didn't go by that he didn't long for his brother, Javier.

Rachel couldn't help but notice Santiago wearing the same tee-shirt and torn tennis shoes. One day when the bell rang after homeroom, she stopped him. "Santiago, remember what I said? You've got to turn your shirt inside out." After a few more reprimands, Santiago caught on. When he came to school, he wore the same black tee-shirt inside out.

As part of her daily routine, Rachel checked her school mailbox in the morning and at lunch. A month into the school year, the principal, had left a note: Please see me after school. Rachel, always a bit impatient, waited outside the principal's office. She couldn't help overhearing a woman shouting through the closed door. A few minutes later, an obese woman—wearing a tank top with no bra—stormed out of the principal's office in a huff.

Ms. Webb, who was shuffling some folders, invited Rachel in.

As Rachel breezed through the door, she commented, "She sure didn't look like a happy camper."

"There's always some pushy parent wanting to customize their kid's day. It's impossible. I'm just trying to follow the rules. Her daughter refuses to take P.E. I tried telling her it wasn't my call. It's a state requirement. It's mandatory."

It didn't take Rachel long to realize that some of the parents were rougher around the edges than their children.

"Oh, speaking of requirements," Ms. Webb said, "yesterday at the principals' meeting, I learned our school needs to provide English-as-a Second-Language. Since your credential allows you to teach anything, I'm handing you the job."

"You're kidding, right? I'm nowhere near fluent in Spanish. I took it in high school and always got a lousy grade. I've got no ear for it. I can barely put a simple sentence together."

"Well, someone has to teach it. And no one else has the right credential. Look, Rachel, it's only for one period. Just do the best you can, okay."

That was it? Just do the best you can. Rachel felt as if someone had thrown her into the lion's den and told her to work it out. "I'm not sure I can do it." Thinking fast, she added "But if I'm stuck with the job, I'll need an aide. Can I borrow Ofelia? She speaks Spanish."

"Ofelia? She's the attendance clerk. You know she's non-credentialed."

"Isn't attendance pretty much over by noon? Can you just spare her for forty-five minutes? That's all I'm asking."

Ms. Webb snapped the elastic band of her watch a few times. "Well, I'm not supposed to. It's unorthodox. But I guess it'll be okay, if you keep it to yourself. And remember, you must be with the aide at all times."

Rachel, figuring she was on a roll, pushed her advantage. "Since I've got no idea what to do, will you try to keep the class size down?"

"I'll try."

"Oh, and one more thing," Rachel added, "Put Santiago in that class. His English is terrible. He needs all the help he can get." As she stood to go, she had an after-thought. "By the way, what about a textbook or workbook?"

"Come to think of it, the district didn't say anything about materials. But I'll check it out."

Rachel was enraged that Ms. Webb pawned this English-as-a-Second Language class off on her, especially with no teaching materials. Since there would be no department head looking over her shoulder, she took it upon herself to redefine her new, unwelcome assignment.

The next morning while the principal stood outside watching the students get off the buses, Rachel walked into the office wanting to explain the situation to Ofelia, the attendance secretary. "Guess what? You got yourself a new assignment . . . For forty-five minutes a day, you'll be helping me teach English-as-a-Second Language."

Ofelia threw her hands in the air, as if she were pushing a car. "Wait! Aren't you forgetting something? I'm an attendance clerk, not a teacher."

"I know. But Ms. Webb said it's okay."

"Really?"

"Really. Don't worry. I've got it all figured out. Since you're fluent in Spanish, and I'm not, you'll take half the class. Teach them basic English. I'll take the other half and work on their math skills. The next day we'll reverse kids. That way, you'll always teach Spanish to English, and I'll always teach math, okay?"

"Whatever works," Ofelia said with a mischievous smile.

"We'll start next Monday, sixth period."

Two weeks later, Rachel stood in front of her homeroom students. "Since we're a new school, we have an opportunity to pick a school mascot and a logo. Each class will vote and send their picks to the office."

"What's a mascot?" Tameka, a girl with multi-colored little balls at the end of her cornrows, asked.

"Hmm, how can I explain it?" Rachel said, rubbing the back of her neck. "A mascot's something that will identify the school. Football or baseball teams have mascots. Like the Detroit Lions or Miami Dolphins."

A few caught on immediately, but most of the class looked blank. Tameka grew excited. "I got it! We could be the Jaguars."

"Good. Anyone else have an idea. I'll write the ideas down on the blackboard and we'll take a vote."

"What about a scorpion?" Jorge asked. "That would be cool."

Someone in the back asked, "What's a logo? I don't understand?"

"Good question. It's a symbol. Something that we could put on our book covers or yearbook. Tee-shirts and baseball caps. Like the symbols on Adidas or Nikes. Have you ever noticed the symbols on cars? You recognize the car from the symbol.

Before Rachel had a chance to write the word *logo* on the board, Arturo shouted out, "What about a swastika? It's rad."

Rachel tried to contain her revulsion. "Arturo, I don't think that would work. That was the insignia of the NAZI's in Germany during World War II. Do any of you know about the NAZIs? They murdered millions of people," and she couldn't help adding, "six million Jews were killed for no reason at all. I don't think that's a symbol we want to be associated with. It represents cruelty and bullying, not strength and power."

After a brief discussion. Latasha, a smart girl who always put two-and-two together, asked, "Are you Jewish?"

"I am."

The class was stunned. Rachel figured they had never met a Jewish person before. Several inquisitive students asked a few questions.

From Rachel's perspective, teaching was fascinating. She never knew where it would wind up. It was tough striking the right balance. Most of the time she showed restraint. Sometimes she tried not to show her amusement. And sometimes she wanted to strangle the kids. But quite often she just felt sorry for them. Insulated by poverty, she saw her mission . . . to broaden their narrow world. Make them come alive. Be inquisitive. Distinguish fact from fiction. Build vocabulary. There was just so much to teach.

Aha, she thought to herself, *this was a teachable moment even if we aren't supposed to be teaching religion in the classroom.* "I'm assuming most of you are Christians. There are *millions,* no, I take that back, *billions* of people that are. But in America, we have people from countries all over the world. And many of them have different religions."

"I'm Catholic," Isabella blurted out.

"Catholics are Christians," Rachel explained. "All Christians believe in Jesus. But not all people that believe in Jesus are Catholics. There are other religions that believe in Christ. Lutherans, Methodists, Baptists. She wasn't sure what the Episcopalians believed.

"Do you believe in Jesus?" Isabella asked.

Sometimes curiosity could go too far, Rachel thought. *In the matter of religion, she knew it wasn't wise to interject her personal beliefs.* Avoiding a direct answer, she changed direction. "In one way or another we're all different. Yet, in many ways we're all alike." She went over to the chalkboard and printed in bold letters: *Alike* and *Different.* "How are we alike?" she asked the class.

Damian shouted out, "We all got arms and legs."

"True," Rachel said patiently, then scribbled it under the word Alike.

In a scornful way, a boy sitting nearest the window hollered out, "Yeah, and we're all stuck in the same classroom."

As the class tittered, Rachel simply wrote . . . "In same class." There were a few more suggestions and Rachel added a few of her own. Then she asked the class how they were different. "Where were you born?"

The students suddenly picked up on this conversation. It was an easy question.

Most of Rachel's students claimed they were born in the United States or Mexico, but there were a few that came from other places.

Santiago, who usually didn't volunteer, felt comfortable enough to say he was born in El Salvador.

Rachel liked where the conversation was heading. She felt the students were finally engaged. "Can you tell me what city you were born in?" As they shouted out their answers, she wrote on the blackboard: Palm Springs, Thermal. Tijuana. Muleje. "Muleje, where's that?"

"Mexico," a boy shouted as if everyone knew where Muleje was.

In a rare moment of pride, Santiago said he was born in Quezaltepeque.

Rachel rolled her eyes. "You got me on that one. Spell it?"

Afraid he would make a mistake, Santiago lowered his head and shrugged.

Trying to protect his feelings of inadequacy, Rachel admitted, "I don't know how to spell it either. "Why don't you look it up in the big Atlas. It's the big book with the brown cover on top of the bookshelves. If you find it, write it down for me."

The loud buzzer interrupted her lesson. Rachel told Santiago to remain for just a few minutes. Chairs scraped the floor and her students caught up with one another. They shuffled out the door talking and laughing, never giving another thought to what Rachel considered an important lesson.

"Here's where I grew up," Santiago said, handing Rachel a piece of binder paper. In uneven letters he had printed:

Q-U-E-Z-A-L-T-E-P-E-Q-U-E

"Now can I go?"

"No, hang on a minute."

Rachel was aware of Santiago's irregular attendance. And when he was there, he never made eye contact. He slumped down in his chair, but never annoyed his classmates or caused problems. Something about Santiago piqued Rachel's curiosity. She sat down at one of the student's desks alongside him. Trying hard to be gentle, she asked "Santiago, is everything okay at home? You seem to be missing a lot of school. Are you sick?"

Tears welled up in his eyes, but he refused to answer. He simply shrugged, then stared at his lap wishing she'd leave him alone.

"Look, Santiago, you're not in any trouble or anything like that. I'm just concerned, that's all. When you're absent so much, it's hard to teach you."

"Can I go now?" he asked again.

"Yes, of course."

Chapter 18

Looking for the Rolls-Royce

Twin Palms Resort
Desert Oasis, California

S UNDAY WAS Stuart's favorite day. He enjoyed sleeping in, having a leisurely breakfast, and reading the *New York Times*. The rest of the week was invariably rushed . . . a quick shower to get to his office before seven-thirty. Just as he sat down with waffles, warmed syrup, and the newspaper, the phone rang.

"It's probably for you. Do you want me to get it?" Rachel asked.

"No. It's either the resort or Banning. I'll get it." As he headed for the phone, Stuart readjusted the belt on his thick terrycloth bathrobe with the new Twin Palms logo embroidered on the pocket.

With urgency in his voice, Banning said, "Stuart, you gotta do me a favor."

A little perturbed that his Sunday ritual had been disrupted, Stuart replied, "What's up?"

"You gotta find the Rolls for me."

"What?"

"I messed up. When I flew back to Reno a couple of weeks ago, I left the car at the resort. Arlene wanted to drive it, so I loaned her the keys. She called me last night, bawling her eyes out. Said she had been at a party in Palm Springs. And when she went to drive home, the car wouldn't start. She didn't remember exactly, but said it was somewhere off Palm Canyon."

"Is she okay?"

"Fine. She said a friend drove her back to the resort."

"I'll get on it right away." When he hung up, Stuart closed his eyes and pictured a few different scenarios He hoped Arlene wasn't so stoned that she left the car unlocked and the keys inside. *Anything's possible,* he thought, shaking his head in disbelief. He tried calling Arlene, who had usurped one of the new condominium units as her temporary living quarters. When there was no answer, Stuart threw on his casual clothes and hustled over to her unit and banged on the door. No one answered.

He tried to remember what Arlene looked like. Long hair, thin hips, delicate features. But then he couldn't be sure. So many of Banning's girlfriends looked alike. Then it dawned on him. She was the redhead, the one he gave the ten grand to a while back. When Stuart checked the dining room, he spied her in the far corner near the porch windows. She and a distinguished looking gentleman with a mop of wavy gray hair and a Hollywood tan were lingering over mugs of coffee, croissants, and a plate of fresh pineapple and strawberries. Stuart, who never overlooked details, noticed their intimacy, as the man's hands swept over her fingers gently. He could care less about Arlene's sex life. He simply wanted to know what happened to the damn car and the car keys but felt uncomfortable intruding.

The breakfast hostess interrupted his thoughts. "Some man from L.A. called. Claims he's a big film director with Sony. He said it was his wife's birthday and wanted to make a dinner reservation for tonight. When I said no, he had to be a registered guest, he claimed you said it was okay. I told him I'd get back to him."

"Does he have a room reservation?"

"No, that's the problem. He said he tried to make a room reservation, but we're booked. They're staying somewhere else. But the guy went ballistic. Kept insisting that you said it was okay to come in just for dinner."

"No way! I would never say that. The resort, including the dining room, is *only* for registered guests. No one else. Call the man back and explain that no one from the outside comes in. That's what the celebrities love about this place. The privacy."

While they were talking, Stuart periodically glanced over at Arlene's table. He was at his best when in complete control and kept to his intended schedule. His original plan—now spoiled—was to go hiking in the Indian Canyons with Rachel before it got too warm. *Now I'm stuck dealing with one of Banning's irresponsible bimbos.* His patience wore thin, and he eventually barged in. "Arlene," he said in a clipped voice, "please stop by my office after breakfast. And bring the keys to the Rolls."

Stuart sat at his desk checking his watch every three minutes. Tapping his foot, he waited and waited, wondering if she took him seriously. An hour-and-a-half later Arlene came by in white shorts and a halter top, but without her new paramour. She started to explain what happened to the Rolls in Palm Springs.

Pure bullshit, he thought, cutting her short. *A complete waste of a good Sunday.* "Arlene, do you have the keys to the car?"

Returning to the condo, he convinced Rachel to drive with him. "When I find the Rolls, you'll need to drive the Jeep back."

As they headed down the main drive and crossed over the I-10 Freeway, Stuart told Rachel about the director begging for a dinner reservation. "Since he wasn't a registered guest, I told the hostess to tell him he can't come in just for dinner."

Rachel understood Stuart's mentality all too well. "You know what your problem is?"

"No, what?"

"You love being the manager. For you it's all about the kingdom, the power, and the glory."

"Oh, now you're quoting the Bible. Fascinating," Stuart remarked, as he turned right onto Tahquitz. The Rolls was nowhere in sight. They drove for another fifteen minutes, slowing down on adjacent streets. Still no Rolls. Finally, he caught sight of it. Looking abandoned, it was the lone car in the parking lot adjacent to Zelda's, a hip Palm Springs nightclub.

As he pulled up next to the Rolls, he instructed Rachel to wait. "I'm going to see if the damn car starts."

The car was unlocked, and he climbed in. He turned on the ignition and pumped the gas pedal, but nothing happened. He assumed the car probably ran out of gas or hadn't been serviced in a while, if ever.

Using his Blackberry—his amazing new cell phone—he called AAA. "I've got a stalled Rolls," he explained to the dispatcher. "No, I don't know what's the matter. It could be the battery or something big. I really don't know. That's why I'm calling you. I want the car towed to the dealership." Sounding exasperated, he continued. "No. No sir . . . it needs to be serviced regardless. If they're closed, they can service it in the morning."

Always fastidious, Stuart treated his Jeep Cherokee with reverence, never missing an oil or lube check-up. The owner's manual, proof of insurance, and registration were meticulously tucked away in the glove compartment. Ever since he first rode in the Rolls-Royce, he was awed by its luxurious feeling. He didn't understand how anyone could treat such a magnificent car so shabbily.

He grimaced as he retrieved several empty McDonald's French fry containers off the floor along with the entertainment section of a *Desert Sun* newspaper that started to turn yellow around the edges. A sequined top was thrown across the back seat. He knew he needed to search the car for cash or drugs before the tow truck arrived. He had been through this once before.

Stuart still had vivid memories of a frightening incident back in Reno. It involved Banning, his late-night parties, girls, and drugs.

It was three in the morning when Banning called him at home. He spoke in a muffled voice. "Stuart, you got to do me a big favor, man. I'm in the emergency room at St. Mary's Hospital. I've got a real problem on my hands. I had to call 911. Vince—you met Vince—one of the time-share salesmen from L.A. Well anyway, we were partying and he OD'ed." Banning's words sounded jumbled and slightly incoherent. "They're working on him now. They want me to fill out a report. But I don't want the cops involved. Man, you've gotta search the apartment. Clean it out. Clear out the drugs."

Half-groggy, Stuart rubbed his eyes. He tried to focus, knowing this was way out of his league. "The penthouse?"

"No. No. Not the penthouse. The 8th floor apartment. But I'm gonna tell them we were in the penthouse. Just in case . . ." and his voice tapered off.

"Got it." Always a little naive about drugs, Stuart asked, "Where'll I find the drugs?"

Banning grew agitated. "I don't know. Could be anywhere. On the coffee table. The bedrooms. The bathroom. Just look around. But don't talk to anyone."

Stuart, one of Banning's straight men, never smoked a joint and wouldn't know cocaine from sugar. But he didn't have much time to figure it out. As he dressed, he tried piecing it together. The triage nurse was probably insisting Banning fill out an incident report and he was going to fake it. Tell them they were in his penthouse. Stuart gained new respect for his boss. Not only was he wealthy but clever enough to own two places in the tower—his penthouse and a separate two-bedroom condo on the 8th floor, a hideaway where he preferred to party.

As Stuart watched the Rolls being lifted onto the bed of the tow truck, Rachel was grousing about Banning's girlfriends and their irresponsible behavior. But Stuart scoffed it off. "It goes with the territory. Banning and I make a good team."

"Babysitting his girlfriends isn't exactly in your job description."

"You know, I'm not working for corporate America. I'm working for an eccentric, independent, and very wealthy developer. "

"Well," Rachel said, starting to laugh, "I guess your job description should be broader: Vice-president . . . in charge of miracles."

And Stuart laughed with her. "You're right."

Chapter 19

Easy Money

Desert Oasis, California

EVER SINCE ARRIVING in the U.S., Rosa's ambitions grew. She dreamt of moving from their cluttered studio apartment into one with two-bedrooms . . . a bedroom for Santiago and one for herself. But babysitting and occasional housecleaning with Yolanda didn't cut it. To improve their lot, she figured she needed a car of her own. It would make her far less dependent on her neighbors.

One muggy evening while Santiago washed the dinner dishes, Rosa picked up the basket of dirty clothes that sat in the far corner and said casually, "I'll be over in the laundry room." She was relieved to find no one using the few washing machines that worked. While their clothes were washing, she scanned the want ads in the *Penny Pincher*, a free newspaper that was distributed everywhere. As she started to shove her clothes into the dryer, Camilla, a plump, talkative woman who lived two apartments over, slipped through the open door.

Wearing shorts and a tank top, Camilla dropped her yellow laundry basket on the concrete floor. "I'll be right over. I'll start my clothes first," she said in Spanish. She fumbled in her pocket for quarters to put in the coin-operated machine. She jammed her family's dirty laundry into the only washing machine left, then lowered herself onto the rickety wooden bench next to Rosa. "How's the babysitting going?" she asked.

"Okay. The babies are easy. How 'bout you?"

"I just got a new tattoo," Camilla remarked, pointing to the red rose on her upper arm. "Like it?"

"It's beautiful. Does it hurt?"

"A little."

"I was just looking through the paper for more work," Rosa said. "You know, it's hard to find a job when I don't speak good English. But I need more money. At the end of the month, it's rough."

"Oh, I know what you mean. But I didn't know you were looking. Yesterday my cousin told me about a night job. And you don't need good English. I'm still nursing Carlito, otherwise I'd take it for myself. Do you know how to drive?"

"Yes. Nacho taught me. Sometimes he loans me his minivan so I can shop."

Camilla got excited, thinking it might work. "Your boy, he is old enough to stay home alone, yes?"

"Sí,"

"The job requires you to drive people from one town to another. Maybe it takes five or six hours. But it pays good money."

Rosa found out who to contact and the first thing the next morning she called the man-in-charge.

"It's a night job," Armando explained. "The farmers are stingy. Always trying to squeeze by with a smaller crew. But sometimes, at the last minute, they need more field hands, or their fruit won't get planted or harvested in time. That's when they call me. I arrange for extra help to come up from Mexico. Your job would be to pick them up and drive 'em to the fields."

Not only did Rosa accept the transportation job, but worked out an arrangement with Nacho, her cousin's son. "Every time I borrow your minivan, I'll pay you five dollars and fill up the gas tank. Just think," she said negotiating the deal, "you'll earn money while you sleep."

Nacho, who still sent money back to his family in El Salvador, weighed his options. Ultimately, he loaned her the minivan.

And that was a game changer.

In addition to babysitting and housekeeping, Rosa earned extra money shuttling workers from National City, a California town close to the Mexican border, to the fields where they were needed. Rosa felt independent and thought she was on to something. She began to squirrel away a little extra cash in a shoe box on the top shelf in the closet, dreaming of a car, a better job, and ultimately a two-bedroom apartment for herself and Santiago.

"*Mi hijo,* one day soon you will have a room of your own," she said proudly.

With no experience from which to draw, Santiago accepted all their hardships as a normal part of life. He understood that his mother worked days and sometimes late into the night. A good kid, he tried to be helpful, although that didn't stop him from grousing about doing dishes. "It's a girly thing," he said, remembering his father's chauvinistic attitude.

Whenever his mother got an extra housekeeping job, Santiago took her place babysitting the neighbors' children. He liked doing it; that way he could watch television all day. He only went to school because he had to. Since the textbooks were all in English, and he barely understood the language, he never gave any thought to doing homework.

Santiago was scrubbing the large bean pot one evening after dinner when the phone rang. "I'll get it," he shouted.

Rosa had just settled down to watch her favorite series, *Full House,* on their small black and white television set. "Never mind. I've got it," she replied.

Armando, her new boss, never wasted time on chit-chat.

"*Hola.* Another job for you tonight. Around nine, but no later than ten, pick up three people at the usual address in National City. Then deliver them to Carlsbad. You know, to the strawberry fields, where you dropped off the others."

"I understand. I'll be there."

"Santiago, don't worry. I'll be home late again tonight, but in time to take care of the little ones in the morning. You're okay staying by yourself, *sí*?"

"I'm okay, *Mamá.* What time will you be home?"

"Late. Don't worry. You'll be asleep."

Rosa slipped her tennis shoes back on, grabbed her purse, and carried her navy blue sweat jacket with the hood. "Go to bed early and don't get into any trouble." She left the apartment and headed up the flight of stairs to Nacho's apartment.

After their usual greeting, he handed her the keys to the minivan. "Don't forget to fill the tank."

The moon floated behind dark clouds, leaving a rim of silver. Rosa enjoyed this time alone. As she headed west on the I-10, she felt invincible. She had come a long way from the frightened and uncertain immigrant. Half of the money she earned tonight would be socked away for the car she planned to buy. Buoyed with her new sense of adventure, she fiddled with the buttons on the radio. When she heard Gloria Estefan singing *No Me Vaya Enamora, I Will Not Fall in Love Again,* she sang along. On the shy side, she would never sing aloud in front of others, but alone in the car, it felt good.

It's so much better to drive at night, she thought. *The freeway is less crowded.* But like all undocumented workers, Rosa remained cautious. She never drove above the speed limit. She knew being stopped could be disastrous. Suddenly a strong funnel of wind blew through the San Gorgonio Pass, breaking her train of thought. The gust reminded her of the windmills that stood like silent sentinels on both sides of the freeway.

Several hours later Rosa arrived in National City, a part of San Diego county, fourteen miles from the Mexican border. Centuries earlier it was known as *El Rancho del Ray* or the King's Ranch, but now it was just another unremarkable, small, rundown southern California town. Rosa drove through a maze of streets in an unsavory part of town. She parked the minivan on the same side of the street as the low-rise apartment building. Every time she stopped there to make a pick-up, she shuddered at the black metal bars on the windows. *It's as if the renters are in prison.*

Two men, wearing hoodies, and a short woman with long hair, slipped out of the apartment building carrying their belongings in small cloth bundles. The streetlight was broken so Rosa could barely make out the details of their faces. Apprehension hung in the air as they climbed into the minivan. Other than a greeting in Spanish, few words were spoken.

Around the corner, two U.S. Border Patrol agents sat in a customized SUV with the lights out. They had been casing the apartment for three nights, waiting for something to happen. When the agents spotted the three slipping into the minivan, the driver turned to his partner—and with all the heart-pumping excitement of a hunter spotting his prey, he said "Okay, let's go get 'em!"

Rosa had just driven a few yards when she heard the siren. In her rear-view mirror, she spotted a menacing bar of pulsating red and blue lights on the roof of the SUV closing in on her. From a loudspeaker, she heard strident instructions in English: PULL TO THE SIDE OF THE ROAD. PULL TO THE SIDE OF THE ROAD.

Completely unnerved, her hands began to tremble. She had trouble keeping them on the steering wheel. Somehow, she managed to do what she was told. She pulled the car alongside the curb in front of a boarded-up furniture store defaced with graffiti.

The loud, intimidating voice commanded: STEP OUTSIDE THE VEHICLE ... WITH YOUR HANDS IN THE AIR.

Blood rushed to her head. As she slid out of the front seat, her legs began to wobble so hard she was afraid they wouldn't hold her up. The bright beam of a flashlight shone in her face, temporarily blinding her. All she saw was the silhouette of a man heading towards her. She thought she might die on the spot.

A broad-shouldered agent, wearing an olive-green Border Patrol uniform, confronted her. Even though Agent Flores was Hispanic—and spoke Spanish fluently—he deliberately addressed her in English, a common ploy used to taunt and intimidate illegal immigrants. "Ma'am, I need to see your driver's license."

Rosa froze.

"Ma'am, your driver's license. Do you have a driver's license?" Met with a bowed head, down-turned eyes and silence, he asked, "Or other identification? A green card?"

When Rosa could produce nothing, she knew she was headed for trouble. Countless thoughts tumbled through her head. Suddenly she remembered something Nacho had taught her. In America, always address a policeman as sir. Show respect. "Sir, what wrong I do?"

Ignoring her, Agent Flores leaned into the minivan and ordered her passengers to step out with their hands up.

A second agent stood alongside the SUV with one hand wrapped around the handle of his gun. Agent Martinez, also Hispanic, was an inexperienced rookie. Fluent in Spanish, he had been told to only speak English when rounding up illegals. He stepped forward and attempted to question the three docile and frightened passengers. "Do you have identification? What about a driver's license?"

Not knowing a word of English, the panicky trio simply bowed their heads and stared at the ground. This was their first time in the United States, and they were completely intimidated by the swirling blue and red lights, the uniformed agents, and their guns. They had come from a squalid labor camp in Tijuana and had been hired last minute to work in the strawberry fields.

"Hands against the vehicle," Agent Flores commanded. One-by-one he shoved them up against the minivan. After the four were hand-cuffed, he glanced at his watch and began to write out the citations:

Wednesday, September 13, 1985
10:47 pm

Once again Agent Flores addressed Rosa in English. "Under U.S. Penal Code 1324, you're being charged with *reckless disregard that aliens have entered the U.S. and attempted transport of illegal aliens.*"

Rosa did not understand a word he was saying.

Agent Martinez got on his two-way radio and requested back-up. Seven minutes later another Border Patrol SUV arrived. The four were separated. With fear and uncertainty, Rosa and the other woman sat in the back of one vehicle. The two men in the other.

The metal handcuffs hurt Rosa's wrists, cutting off circulation to her hands. *Santiago won't know where I am?* she thought. *Suppose he thinks I've left him. What's going to happen to Nacho's minivan?* She was terrified they were going to dump her across the border or worse, send her back to El Salvador.

"Sir, where you take me? Sir, please. My son, he be home alone. Please . . . let me go. He be so afraid."

Satisfied with their catch for the night, the Border Patrol agents ignored her pleads, pretending they didn't understand a word she said.

Rosa landed in the National City Jail. In a poorly lighted room, she was signed for, fingerprinted, and photographed. That information was fed into a database. Not out of kindness—simply because it was the law—Rosa was allowed one free phone call. Calling an attorney was out of the question. It never entered her mind. Her only thought was to call Santiago. He was such a sound sleeper that she prayed that he'd hear the telephone ring. After what felt like an infinite number of rings, Santiago finally picked up the phone.

"Oh, *mi hijo*, it's so good to hear your voice."

"Mamá, why are you calling so late? Where are you?"

Rosa broke down. She could barely spit out the words, "In jail."

"In jail? You okay?"

"Yes. I'm okay," she repeated. She tried to pull herself together, but laden with emotion, her chest heaved up and down as she gasped for air.

As illegals, Santiago understood the ramifications. He feared his mother could be sent back to El Salvador and he would be left alone. Suddenly, he felt sick to his stomach. Tears ran down his cheeks, still warm from sleep.

"Santiago, listen carefully. You're a big boy now. Take care of yourself. Babysit the little ones 'til I get there. The mothers . . . they'll pay you. If you need food, walk to the market. She continued with her instructions.

He could hear someone telling his mother to end the call. With no one to support him, Santiago panicked. *"Mamá . . ."*

"I've got to go. Remember, do what I said. *Mi hijo,* I love you."

"Mamá, when you coming home?"

"Soon. It's all a big mistake."

Chapter 20

INS and a Detainer

National City Jail
National City, California

AFTER BEING PICKED UP by the Border Patrol, Rosa was arraigned and held over for four additional days in the National City jail. The dank holding cell smelled of urine, vomit, mold, and mildew. She shared it with a parade of crackheads, thieves, drunks, and ladies-of-the-night. Rosa's companions varied from day-to-day, sometimes from hour-to-hour. A few made bail and were out within hours. Even the woman Rosa was going to drive to the strawberry fields disappeared on the second day.

Rosa was fearful or comforted, depending on who shared the holding cell with her. One young woman of color, with Raggedy Ann red hair, had been picked up for possession of crack cocaine. She preferred sitting on the concrete floor with her arms wrapped around her knees. When sadness overwhelmed her, she broke into song. In a pure, angelic voice, she sang *Amazing Grace* as if she were in a church choir on a bright Sunday morning.

An emaciated woman with glassy blue eyes, thin crepe paper arms, and legs that looked like saplings, parked herself on one of the hard benches and kept mumbling to herself, "I didn't do nothin'. I swear to God, I didn't do nothin'." Some who shared the holding cell with Rosa wept quietly, while others screamed angrily at the jailers who periodically shouted back, "Hey, shut the fuck up back there!"

Rosa had no idea that her case was different. She didn't know it at the time, but she was *tagged,* meaning there was a *hold* put on her until a U.S. Immigration and Naturalization Service (INS) officer interviewed her. From time-to-time, depending on the situation, INS officials allowed some undocumented immigrants to be set free on a bond while waiting for a hearing, provided they were not charged with a serious crime.

Not so for Rosa.

Because her crime was deemed more serious—*knowingly transporting illegal aliens*, the U.S. Immigration and Naturalization Service (INS) planned to transfer her directly from National City to a detention facility where her case would be heard. The immigration officer handling Rosa's case knew that the women's section of the Otay Detention Facility in San Diego was filled beyond capacity since it was nearest the border. He found a space for her in another detention facility.

Fear and insecurity engulfed Rosa. Other women arrived later and left before her. She didn't understand why she was stuck in the National City jail. No one bothered to explain to her that INS, Immigration and Naturalization Service—part of the Department of Justice—had arranged for her to be transported to a detention center in the Mojave Desert. She was scheduled to leave early on a Monday morning. But there was a major bureaucratic snafu. The driver also had to pick up other women—all illegal immigrants—from other southern California jails. All of them were headed to the same place.

The van finally arrived to pick up Rosa just before lunch. A thick metal screen separated the women from the driver and his assistant. Neither he nor his assistant worked for the government. They were minimum wage workers in their mid-twenties, working for a *private* company that contracted with INS to transport detainees from one destination to another. In this case, to Apple Valley Detention Center. Not bound by any rules and regulations, the driver and his assistant handled their cargo without fear of being reprimanded, snickering as they referred to their passengers as *onion heads.*

For two-and-a-half hours the van jostled along the freeway, then smaller roads. Rosa felt completely alone and helpless. The handcuffs pinched her skin and cut off her circulation. More than ever, she longed for the solace of her rosary. Despite its absence, she recited the Guardian Angel prayer silently:

> *Angel of God, my Guardian dear,*
> *to whom his love commits me here.*
> *Ever this day be by my side,*
> *to light and guard, to rule and guide.*

Then she pleaded silently: *I don't know where I'm going. Please let Santiago find me.*

Graciela, a young woman from Guatemala, who sat in the back seat, was far more outspoken. "Hey, when do we eat? I'm hungry," she shouted periodically at the driver. "And I need water. I got a bad migraine."

With impunity, either the driver or his assistant shouted, "Shut up back there," to anyone who tried to talk to them.

No one offered the women lunch, not even water, as they traveled north in the midday sun. Requests for bathroom stops were repeatedly ignored. Through the horizontal bars on the side windows, Rosa observed the gradual changes of scenery—from the satellite towns surrounding San Diego to the sparse vegetation and monotonous desert landscape. They finally reached their destination fourteen miles east of Apple Valley, a town that didn't have much going for it, not even apples. In such a remote area, the detention center might well have been cast off the map.

"Jesus, no one will ever find me here," one of the women complained.

Oddly enough, the only thing that Rosa recognized was the American flag waving atop a flagpole as they passed the Visitors Center. A moment later her heart almost stopped when she caught sight of the colorless, concrete detention center buildings, the menacing guard tower, and the high, chain-link fence topped with coiled barbed wire and razors. Slowing up, the van drove into the fenced in courtyard of a low-rise building. The tall security gate slammed shut behind them.

The handcuffed women were marched to the in-take office and signed for, like registered mail. Rosa was given an alien number—an A followed by eight digits. In the tangled web of the legal system, she would hereafter be known as *A-10340795*. At that moment, she lost her individuality. She was instructed to stand on the black tape and face front. Several photos—front and profile—were snapped with her holding a board with her name and alien numbers in big letters.

When the tight handcuffs were finally removed, she rubbed her wrists. Two female guards, who commanded the title of *officers*, took charge. The most vocal, Officer Gomez, had unforgiving black eyes, broad shoulders, and a husky, man-like voice. She let the detainees know she was in charge, ignoring their pleas for food and water. However, she did usher them to the lavatories. She allowed three at a time to use the individual stalls that lacked doors for privacy. Afterwards she herded the frightened, disoriented women into a small, windowless meeting room with three rows of gray folding chairs.

Officer Gomez bellowed, "Into the first or second row. The deputy warden will be here shortly."

The subdued women, with varying degrees of fright, did as they were told. Lost in thoughts of families and home, they sat on the folding chairs and waited. Standing in front of the room,

Officer Conroy struck a take-charge pose with folded arms and an ominous glare. Officer Gomez, holding a clipboard, stationed herself nearest the door.

Twenty minutes later, the deputy warden arrived. From the plastic name tag pinned on his uniform, Rosa assumed he was Hispanic. Standing behind the podium, Deputy Warden Zamora began his routine lecture.

"Ladies, good afternoon." It was a condescending remark, but he was too insensitive to realize it.

"Good afternoon, my ass," a Latina parroted.

"Schuss," the detainee sitting next to her warned.

Ignoring them both, the deputy warden continued. "I'm going to review our rules. It's our policy here at the Apple Valley Detention Center to treat detainees with dignity and respect. We maintain a safe, humane, secure, and sanitary facility. In return, we expect the staff to receive your full cooperation while your case is being processed."

The deputy warden showed no emotion as he opened his black binder. With no inflection in his voice, he droned on and on as he read the rules:

> *You are expected to follow and obey our rules, policies, and procedures.*
> *You will obey all orders given by staff members.*
> *You will respect staff and other detainees.*
> *You will respect facility property and the property of others.*
> *You will keep your clothing and living area clean.*
> *You will obey all safety, security, and sanitation rules.*
> *You will walk, not run throughout the facility.*
> *And, finally, we will respect you.*

A Latina in her early forties mumbled under her breath. "That's bullshit! Trust me. I've been here before."

A few of the women tittered nervously, but Rosa kept quiet, too frightened to respond.

The deputy warden held the women at bay for fifteen additional minutes haranguing them with more expectations and rules . . . everything from the three daily roll call counts, wake-up time, and time for lights out. Finally winding down, he said, "When you hear your name called, line up at the door behind Officer Gomez."

Officer Gomez raised her arm and nodded, all the while looking bored, as if she had done this too many times.

Chapter 21

Locked Doors and Lost Hope

Apple Valley Detention Center
Mojave Desert, California

AS OFFICER GOMEZ led the line of detainees through a labyrinth of corridors, Officer Conroy lagged behind, to make sure no one slipped away from the group. Rosa had officially entered the bleak world of locked doors and lost hope.

Graciela didn't hold back. She turned to the older woman behind her and made a snarky comment. "What's this, some goddamn parade?"

"Shush!" the frightened woman with droopy eyelids responded in Spanish. "I don't want no trouble."

The gaggle of women ended up waiting for further instructions in a large space that resembled a high school locker room with low ceilings, harsh florescent lighting, and wooden benches bolted to the concrete floor. Officer Gomez snarled, *"Espaldas mojadas,* wetbacks, listen up. I'm gonna give each of you a cardboard box. Once you get your carton, remove your clothes."

"All our clothes? Everything?" one of the humiliated women asked in disbelief.

"Yep. Bare-ass naked. Everything except for a plain wedding ring or a watch . . . provided it cost less than $50."

"My boyfriend gave me this watch," Graciela responded. "How am I supposed to know how much it costs?"

"*No seas pendeja!* Don't be an asshole. Guess!" Officer Gomez replied harshly. "Put all your belonging in your box. Everything. Money. Purses. Earrings. Shoes. Clothes. Do I make myself clear?"

"Well, I don't want nobody ripping off my stuff," Graciela remarked.

In an all-out effort to close her down, the authoritarian guard shot back, "Listen, and listen carefully. From now on you'll address me as *Officer Gomez.* And you are not to speak unless you're spoken too. Understood?"

"Yes, Ma'am!" Graciela snarled.

"Sweetie, you got a lot to learn. Try it again." And she demonstrated, "Yes, Officer Gomez."

"Yes, Officer Gomez, Ma'am."

"At the rate you're going, you'll be in an isolation cell in no time."

Ignoring her threat, Graciela asked, "What about my Percocet? I get bad headaches and I need them goddamn pills."

"You heard me. Do I have to say it one more time? EVERYTHING goes into the box except glasses, hearing aids, wedding bands and cheap watches. Give me the pills. Those go to the dispensary. You'll need to talk to them about your medication. Once everything gets put in your box, hold it and stand in line over there." Officer Gomez pointed to the detainee behind a wooden counter. "She'll list each-and-every item. Then she'll ask you to sign for it. Once your name and *alien* number are put on the box, it'll be sealed and stored until you're released."

All the orders confused Rosa, but she dared not speak up. She tried to follow whatever the other women did. They all lowered their heads, averting each other's eyes, as they removed outer clothing and then, feeling degraded and embarrassed, removed their undergarments. Completely naked, Rosa stood in the painstakingly slow-moving line with her cardboard box while each detainee ahead of her forked over all their possessions.

Once they had completed that task, the motley group of women were shepherded into the adjacent group shower room. A dank, moldy odor, laced with chlorine, permeated the area. Individual shower heads jutted out from the walls, but there would be no separation or privacy between them. Officer Gomez handed each of them a pair of rubber flip-flops, a thin bar of anti-bacterial soap, and a special shampoo that rid the hair of lice.

"Find a shower," she ordered. "When I turn on the water, wash up. But be quick about it. We ain't got all day. Be sure and scrub your head with that green shampoo. Damned if we want to bring lice in here."

Rosa withdrew into herself. After the shower with barely warm water, she was given a thin towel to dry her thick hair and body. She dried herself the best she could.

"All right ladies. Stand over there . . . one behind the other. Wait your turn for *clean* clothes and bedding You'll be wearing an orange jumpsuit from now on, courtesy of Apple Valley Detention Center."

With their hair dripping, the naked women stood in another line. Distribution of regulation clothes was a hit-or-miss procedure. A Hispanic detainee who had been incarcerated for well over a year, stood behind the counter. She issued Rosa her allotment of basics:

> *2 jumpsuits, 2 pairs of socks, 1 pair of Crocs, 3*
> *pairs of panties, 2 tee-shirts, 1 pillow, 1 pillowcase,*
> *2 sheets, 2 light-weight blankets, 1 towel, a comb,*
> *one tube of toothpaste, a toothbrush and shampoo.*
> *And a handbook written in English that explained*
> *a myriad of rules.*

The detainee touched Rosa's hand gently and whispered in Spanish, "*Es* okay. You'll be fine *No estás sola.* You are not alone."

As Rosa placed her new possessions on a bench, she couldn't help overhearing one of the detainees complaining. "Lady, I need a bra. Otherwise, my tits are gonna hang down to my waist."

"Sorry. tee-shirts only."

"Come on. Who would it hurt if I wore a bra?"

"Sorry. Regulations."

There was no shortage of grumbling as the recalcitrant women slipped into their panties and plain white tee-shirts. As for the jumpsuits, the newly registered detainees discovered some fit better than others. After they put on their new Crocs, they somehow managed to juggle their remaining clothes and bedding allotments, as they once again lined-up behind Officer Gomez.

Officer Gomez led the gaggle of hungry and disgruntled women—wearing matching orange jumpsuits—through a maze of corridors as if they were children playing *Follow the Leader.* Officer Conroy, who hadn't said much, continued her vigil at the rear of the line. Eventually Officer Gomez swiped the plastic card on a lanyard into a security pad, buzzing them through a set of double doors. At that point, the women didn't realize that guards would be watching them either in person, behind blackened windows, or on computer screens from multiple security cameras twenty-four hours a day.

"Not everyone is in this dorm," Officer Gomez explained. "Don't worry, there's a lot more dorms. There are plenty of beds for all of you. But right now, if I call your name, step to the side."

When Rosa heard her name, she did exactly what she was told. She and two others were handed off to Officer Hartmann, who was sitting inside the dormitory at a small metal desk nearest the double doors. A heavy-set, buxom woman, Officer Hartmann had a temper not to be challenged. She had worked in prisons and detention centers for well over thirteen years. She knew every trick in the book and had zero tolerance for those that didn't adhere to the rules.

Multiple voices echoed off the walls like someone bouncing a basketball in an empty gymnasium. Then suddenly quiet. All eyes focused on the new arrivals. Rosa found that attention nerve-wracking. After their quick assessment, most of the *detainees* returned to whatever they were doing. It was just a moment of curiosity. No big deal. They had grown accustomed to women arbitrarily arriving and departing. Friendships were transitory. Contrary to all known behavioral studies, the detention center had an unrealistic expectation that a group of women—thrown together with multiple ethnicities, religions, nationalities, temperaments, and ages—would somehow manage to get along day and night.

The cavernous dorm room, with the eighteen-foot-high ceiling, held rows of bunk beds, four across and five deep. The bunk beds were squeezed together—head to toe—so tight that one detainee's feet would be close to someone else's head. No bunks touched the walls. Before leading Rosa to her bunk bed, Officer Hartmann carefully printed Rosa's name, alien number and bunk assignment on an official form attached to her clipboard.

"You'll be on the top bunk," she explained. Rosa's personal space now consisted of a narrow bed—second from the end, in the third tier. As they approached her bunk, Officer Hartmann pointed her foot towards the heavy-duty, gray rubber drawers below the bunk bed. In English she explained, "Put your extra belongings in drawer marked 3-5-A. If you want, you can sleep with both blankets. But the rule is . . . during the day, you must leave one blanket folded neatly at the foot of your bunk. If you nap, only use the folded blanket. That way your bunk don't get messed up. Wake-up's at six. Your bunk's gotta be made before roll-call at seven."

Rosa looked blank. Even if she understood English, there were too many instructions. It didn't help that she had no food or water all day, had a splitting headache, and her arms ached from carrying her extra clothes and bedding.

A wiry woman of color, with kinky black hair, had the lower bunk. In Rwanda, her entire family—and most of the people in her village—had been slaughtered by the Tutsis. It was miraculous that she had escaped and somehow made her way into the U.S. begging for asylum. As soon as Officer Hartmann left, the woman sprinted from her bed. She pointed to her chest and smiled. "Me Saba." Without a common language, she somehow managed to convey compassion. She helped Rosa put her things away and make her bunk.

All her life, Rosa had slept in a pitch-black room with an open window. It was almost impossible to sleep in the detention center. A protective cage covered the florescent lights in the ceiling. Even though the garish lights were dimmed at nine o'clock, they were never completely turned off. There were constant disturbances: arguments, weeping women, some calling out names in their sleep, or loud snoring. In addition, the guards making the rounds shone flashlights in their faces.

Some detainees were able to talk with their loved ones by telephone or in prearranged one-hour visits with friends or relatives. Not so, Rosa. Bleached of spirit, she lived in a vacuum. Isolated. Completely shut off. And worse, she had absolutely zero control over her life. There was no time—not even her husband's murder—when she felt so down-hearted and depressed. While those on the *outside* tended to their families and laughed with their friends, Rosa lived in silent desperation, alone, powerless, and out-of-sight.

The only thing sustaining her was prayer.

For the first six weeks she never stopped crying and obsessing about her new situation. To add to her misery, she caught a bad cold and developed a chronic cough. Constantly running in the back of her mind, she worried what would become of her two sons—Javier in Tijuana and Santiago, alone, without anyone to guide him. Often her thoughts returned to El Salvador. When she couldn't sleep, she replayed the events that led to her husband's murder. She wondered where she would be if he hadn't fought against the government.

The detention center supplied the first bottle of shampoo and tube of toothpaste. After that, the detainees were forced to buy these and any other hygiene products from the commissary. Out of necessity, Rosa signed up to work. She earned a dollar a day mopping floors, cleaning toilets, or working in the laundry. Although the need to buy these products motivated her, keeping busy also helped alleviate the utter monotony.

When not working, she sat passively in a white plastic chair in the so-called *rec* room, staring blankly at the single television screen while the more aggressive, ill-tempered women fought like alley cats over their choices of programs. Only two things brightened her sagging spirits: the hour-a-day that she could breathe fresh air in the fenced-in exercise yard and attending Sunday Mass. Father Sanchez, a stooped priest with a gentle heart, brought in a wooden cross and placed it on a cloth-covered banquet table in a nondescript meeting room. His were the only kind words she heard, and they gave her temporary solace.

Chapter 22

Rosa's Hearing

Apple Valley Detention Center
Mojave Desert, California

WHEN A LOATHSOME security guard came for Rosa, she had her third bout of a cold and a lingering cough. Her nose was runny, her ears rang, and she thought she might have a low-grade fever. Hand-cuffed, she could barely wipe her nose with her arm. Regardless of how she was feeling, court hearings were set in stone. There was no consideration for sickness, only for the detention center's schedule.

An unsympathetic guard led Rosa through a labyrinth of hallways that ended in a courtyard. She blinked several times as her eyes adjusted to the sunlight and splashes of color. She inhaled the rush of fresh air. No matter where she was—inside or outside—she realized she had been living in a colorless world. Except for the orange jumpsuits, everything was gray. The metal furnishings. The walls. The doors. Even the exercise yard . . . which consisted of asphalt, gravel, and a ten-foot-high fence topped with concertina wire. The landscaped courtyard was like a therapeutic tonic. Rosa drank-in the palette of vibrant colors: red bottlebrush, purple agapanthus, green leaves, fluffy white clouds, robin-egg blue sky. It reminded her of the intense colors of the birds and the flowers back in Quazaltepeque. *And at that moment, despite the bloodshed, she wished she had never left El Salvador.*

Inside the courthouse, she was placed in the locked, window-less holding area along with other women detainees, each awaiting their turn to be heard in the immigration courtrooms. Although she had no knowledge of it, one floor above was the INS (Immi-gration and Nationalization Service) offices, filled with a stagger-ing backload of paperwork and not enough staff to process it.

Eventually a stern-faced bailiff, with a thick, double chin, and a belly that rolled over the belt of his uniform, called her name. "Rosa Lopez. *Es Rosa Lopez aquí?*"

She trembled as the bailiff led her into the unfamiliar court-room. The American flag that stood to the left of the judge was the only décor, except for an official photo of Ronald Reagan. In her innocence, she had no idea that Judge L. Martin would be rushing through multiple cases that day.

Undocumented workers—frequently called *wetbacks*—weren't welcomed by a majority of the California voters and the lingering mind-set permeated the immigration courts. INS was picking up illegal immigrants faster than the courts could handle them.

The judge cleared his throat. In an intimidating voice he asked, "Are you Rosa Lopez?"

"*Sí.*" Rosa sat in the witness stand with her back straight up and fingers laced together in front of her to keep them from shaking.

The judge scanned her file. Then for the court reporter, he repeated her name and *alien* number.

Less than ten minutes into her hearing—which was con-ducted in English—a slightly bent Caucasian man with a crown of gray hair stuck several papers in front of her. "Sign here." Then he repeated it in Spanish, "*Firma aquí.*" He smiled benevolently as he handed Rosa a pen and pointed to several lines marked with paper arrows.

Unaccustomed to seeing a man wearing a dark suit and tie, she assumed he was somebody important. Not wishing to cause trouble, Rosa dutifully printed her first and last name, not fully understanding the ramifications of pleading guilty to the two charges against her: *Reckless Disregard that Aliens Have Entered the United States . . . and Attempted Transport of Illegal Aliens.*

Judge Martin considered the charges serious and ruled that Rosa be held over for deportation. With utter disregard, Rosa's hearing—like those of other illegal immigrants—was rushed. No one did any research. The entire process was akin to an over-crowded night court, without a reality check or proper defense. And for many, the judge's ruling had life or death consequences.

Hour-after-hour, day-after-day, Rosa existed in a never-never land. It was only natural that the incarcerated women gravitated towards those who spoke the same language. Those from Mexico, Central and South America—whether young, old, fat, thin, beautiful, or beat and bedraggled—stuck together. From time to time, Rosa and the others sat on the bunk beds in their pod or in the so-called *rec room* swapping stories about their pathetic encounters in detention. The dependent women laughed and cried on each other's shoulders. They reminisced about their families, children, parents, and longings for their native lands. They spoke of their worries and dreams and confessed their sins.

A few of the women had completed their chores one afternoon before supper and gathered in the rec room to chat. Maricella, barely out of her teens, with thick black hair pulled into a ponytail and the delicate features of a Madonna, unexpectedly burst into tears. "I'm sorry. I'm sorry," she cried out hesitantly, trying not to burden the other women with her troubles.

"It's okay," Rosa said, patting her arm. "Why are you crying?"

Maricella started to explain but raw emotions got in the way. Between sobs, she explained, "I got picked up for drugs when I was four months pregnant. I had my baby here . . . in detention. But they took him away and placed him in foster care. Now they're gonna send me back to Nicaragua. It's not fair," she complained. "I'll never see my baby. He'll never know his mother."

Stunned, no one knew what to say.

Quickly Lupe broke the silence, adding her own tale of woe. "You know, not long after I got here, my eye got infected. For weeks, I begged to see a doctor. They didn't like me making a fuss, so they threw me in solitary confinement. When they took me to the infirmary, no one spoke Spanish. Some lady—maybe a nurse maybe a doctor, maybe a nobody—looked at my eye and handed me some drops. They didn't help. Nothin' happened. My eye just got worse. Finally, when they let me go back, the lady she give to me different drops. But nothin' worked." Always vain about her looks, Lupe was broken-hearted that she could no longer see out of her left eye. Since there were no mirrors, she didn't realize that her eye was glazed over like that of a dead fish.

Valentina usually didn't say much. But after hearing all this, she shared her story. In Guatemala, she had been raped repeatedly by an uncle. He threatened to kill her younger brother if she didn't submit. "I couldn't take it no more," she sobbed. "So, one day I ran away. I risked everything. Now look at me. Locked up. A caged animal. I don't even know if my brother is alive or dead."

Each told their own humiliating or sad story about gangs, rapes, and threats, until an officer rounded them up to do a head count. Then she escorted them to the cafeteria for another meager supper.

Chapter 23

You've Got to be Taught to Hate

Benson Middle School
Desert Oasis, California

SEVERAL MEETINGS had been called to parse out just the right wording for a mission statement. Rachel scoffed at its futility. *No one ever bothered to read it and even if they did, so what. Nothing ever changed.* A bottom-line person, she thought her job had three essential components: to make sure her students were proficient in basic math and reading, to build their self-confidence, and create a sense of curiosity, the urge to keep learning. Something her students sorely lacked.

Ms. Webb, the principal, called for yet another after school meeting. Rachel set her lesson plans aside and hustled over to the barely finished library, wondering what craziness was coming down the turnpike. Stacks of books, not yet catalogued and shelved, sat on the librarian's counter. The staff grew restless as they waited for the principal. Rachel's mind wandered off to other things.

Ms. Webb finally breezed into the library twenty minutes late. "Sorry," she apologized, "but I had a situation in the office." For a moment she stopped, as if still processing the last incident. "Okay," she sighed, "let's get started." Quickly glancing at her clipboard, she said, "The purpose of today's meeting is to discuss AIDS and the risk of exchanging body fluids."

What did this have to do with teaching? Rachel wondered. *Meetings, always meetings. The only consistent thing the principal did was call meetings and show up late.*

A first-year P.E. teacher who just graduated from Cal State, San Bernardino, raised his hand. "What're we supposed to do if someone falls and is bleeding out in the school yard?"

After a seven-minute discussion on the transmittable disease, it was decided they needed to keep latex gloves available out in the yard. A young, attractive blonde teacher, a summer recruit from Kansas asked, "Suppose someone gets a bloody nose?"

Same thing, Rachel thought. For someone who would rather work than sit through meetings, it was tedious to sit there while teachers asked inane questions just to hear their own voices. She knew everyone feared AIDS. But she tried to calculate the odds that some middle school kid that happened to get bloody on the playground would test positive.

A cynical math and science teacher sat across from her, snapping her gum. Rachel laughed inwardly when she heard her comment. "I'd just tell the kid to get up and go to the office."

Ms. Webb let the comment go. Looking down at her notes, she said, "We need to talk about school supplies. The district gave me a list and I made a copy for each of you. Would someone pass these around?"

When everyone received a copy, Ms. Webb continued. "Each student needs a full-size binder and separators." She lifted her black binder high in the air and flipped through the dividers. "Can everyone see? Have them label a section for each class. It will help to keep them organized. Also, they'll need at least three #2 pencils, an eraser, a pack of binder paper, a small bottle of Elmer's glue, crayons, and scissors."

Who was she kidding? Some of these kids don't get enough to eat. They're lucky if they have shoes that fit. Their parents aren't worried about binders with separators. This is another half-cocked idea from the district or some high-priced consultant, who never stepped into a classroom full of dirt-poor kids. And if this was the key to learning, why didn't the district supply the student with all of it?

"Oh, another reminder from the district office," Ms. Webb added, "make sure your students pledge the flag each morning. We need to slip in a little patriotism. Does everyone have an American flag in their room? If not, see me after the meeting."

Before school began the following Monday, Rachel stood at the blackboard and wrote a few easy math problems, a sponge assignment to keep the class quiet while she took roll.

Roxane Robinson, a bi-racial girl in her class, wandered in, clearly upset. "Can I talk to you?"

"Sure," Rachel said, as she laid the chalk down on the metal shelf below the blackboard. "What's up?"

Roxane broke into tears. "The boys keep teasing me. Calling me an Oreo cookie."

Rachel's mind stalled, not sure how to handle this situation. She moved to the door and locked it. "Let me get you some tissues to wipe away those tears." After patting Roxane's shoulder—a no-no according to strict school rules about touching the students—Rachel told her how beautiful she was. Her skin was the color of creamy coffee, a full mop of kinky blonde hair, and gorgeous green cat's eyes. "You're absolutely stunning. Beautiful. Someday, that is . . . if you want to, you could be a top model." Rachel chastised herself. *Why did I say that? It's not always about looks. She can be anything she wants to be. A top scientist, an artist, whatever.* "You're a perfect human being. Kind and sweet. Smart. One day these little bullies—*she wanted to say little shitheads but restrained herself*—will grow up and appreciate you."

They were not finished with their conversation when the 8:10 bell rang. Rachel could hear some of the rude students pounding, then kicking the door. "Let us in." Then she heard someone who she thought was screaming, "Hey, *Jew,* open up." At first, she thought she imagined it. She assumed they were yelling, "Hey *you,* open up." When she heard it for the third time, she knew it was not her imagination.

She wrapped up her conversation with Roxane and opened the door. "Who was yelling *Hey, Jew, open up?"* Not daring to tattle, most of the students looked at her with blank eyes or looked away. But two girls in the back of the pack pointed to Arturo. "Okay, everyone, get inside and settle down. Arturo, stay here. We need to talk." After the rest of the students filed inside, Rachel and Arturo remained outside with the door open. "Were you the one saying *Hey, Jew?"*

He shrugged. "So?"

"You don't talk to people like that," she said, losing her cool. "I'm your teacher. You need to show some respect. Everyone has a name. Use it. We never refer to people by their religion."

Arturo didn't look smug or belligerent. He simply said, "What's the big deal? My dad says stuff like that all the time."

He truly didn't see the problem. It's what he heard at home.

Hopping mad, Rachel left her class unattended—another big no-no—and dragged him to the vice-principal's office. She didn't know why or where it came from but the song from the musical *South Pacific* popped into her head: *You've Got to be Taught to Hate.* To her surprise, Rachel discovered, the meek, good-looking, Italian vice-principal's mother was Jewish. So, it turned out he knew enough about the Holocaust and Jewish history to land into Arturo. Satisfied that someone else was handling it, Rachel hustled back, praying that no one got hurt while she left her students in an unsupervised classroom.

"Good morning, everyone," Rachel said, trying to calm herself down. "Sorry I was delayed. Please rise and face the flag. We're going to recite the Pledge of Allegiance together."

The chairs scratched the floor as the class reluctantly rose.

"Put your right hand over your heart and begin, *I pledge allegiance . . .*"

Chapter 24

Twin Palms

OVER TIME Stuart smoothed over the funkier qualities of the resort. A man-made lake was built on the lower level and stocked with koi fish. The original swimming pool painted an old-fashion blue—a trend in the 30's—was resurfaced and modernized. A misting system was installed to cool the sunbathers when the outside temperature grew uncomfortably hot. Tons of fine, gritty desert rock had been hauled in to cover the cracked asphalt in the parking lots and the road leading down to the newer condos. Rather than rundown, it gave the resort a more rustic feeling. French doors replaced sliding glass doors in the condo units. And two tennis courts were built, although few people played on them.

The front guard house—at one time a nondescript building that resembled a coffin standing on its head—was transformed into a small entry building using the same river rock as the original units and an authentic Mexican tile roof. Stuart hired security guards for 24/7 exclusivity and provided them with uniforms.

Strict rules were set in place. Absolutely no one was allowed on the property unless they were eighteen or older and a registered guest. Putting age restrictions in place was not legal, but Stuart was not averse to making up his own rules. All went smoothly until a woman judge made a reservation for two people. When she and her young teenage daughter drove up to the guard gate all hell broke loose. But Stuart held his ground. And they were not admitted. A stickler for detail, he created a manual with specific job descriptions for all employees. He wanted to add an employee benefit package, so well-trained employees would stick and stay. However, the CPA in Reno—always tight-fisted with money—overruled him.

"But it would help us get more qualified employees," Stuart argued. "And they'll stick around longer. We'd have trained people and that's better for the resort."

"Absolutely not. It's an unnecessary expense."

Stuart dropped the idea in disgust, hoping to fight the battle another day.

A creature of habit, Stuart routinely left his condo unit early. He ambled up the gritty path to his office, another quaint river rock building barely large enough for him, a secretary, and the infamous supply room. Before he did anything else, he skimmed the nightly reports, looking for any irregularities. After prioritizing his day, he locked his office door and set out for the dining room to make sure the kitchen staff showed up for work and the breakfast buffet was ready.

One morning on his way up, he passed the sixteen original rock units. With no one in sight, he mused, *this wasn't the kind of place where guests jogged first thing in the morning.* As he ambled by the mineral pool, his searching eyes spotted a black bikini top—barely more than two postage stamps—wedged into the crevice between two rocks. He chuckled to himself. It was no secret. Plenty of nefarious goings on happened under the cover of darkness.

There was something about the small, intimate resort that enhanced the libido. Because the desert had few lights, the blackened sky filled with a panoply of stars. The hot mineral water spirited away any aches and pains. Guests' moods were transformed by the isolation and the exclusivity. Some New Agers claimed there was a vortex of energy. But whatever it was, it was the perfect out-of-the-way place for a romantic liaison, illicit or otherwise.

Stuart's first call came through right after breakfast. The reservation clerk called claiming a woman named Judith insisted on speaking to the manager.

"She claims she's a regular and sends us a ton of clients. But the dates she wants are all booked up."

Setting aside his paperwork, Stuart sighed, "Okay, put her through."

"This is Judith Brant with the Arnold M. Gold Agency," she announced with an imperious New York accent, assuming everyone knew that Arnold Gold was a well- known talent agency. "I need a room for a client. You'd recognize his name, but I'm not allowed to mention it. He's a big-time actor. Anyway, he just finished three months of filming in Turkey, and he's completely burned out. He desperately needs a break."

"Look, I'd really like to help," Stuart replied, "but there's nothing available. We're booked solid for the next three weeks."

"Come on. It's just for a week. Seriously, my client is on the brink of a nervous breakdown. Help me out. I come out there all the time. I'm a regular. And I can send a lot of business your way. Surely you can squeeze out another room for a good client."

"I'm sorry. I wish I could, but we're full. There's simply no space. Everyone has sent in their deposits."

Banning, Stuart's boss, had his reasons for making it hard to get a reservation. A consummate salesman, he had developed a sure-fire technique and it worked like a charm. Offer something for sale—then take it away—making the person want it all-the-more. Build the demand. And with that exclusivity, it followed that the price of a room went up and up.

Stuart smiled inwardly as he hung up the phone. The more he turned potential guests away, the more they clamored to get in. Twin Palms Resort now claimed a certain panache. In a short time, the hippie haven had been transformed into a sought after get-away. In addition, the resort was his boss's personal playground. With no mortgage, no partners, and no need to make a profit, Banning could do with it whatever he pleased.

It was unusual that Banning called Stuart before noon. "Listen, I got the name and number of a top public relations guy. Alain Beaulieu. Sounds French. I think he could be useful. We need to beef up our press exposure. Squeeze out some good publicity. Beaulieu heads a hot-shot firm in San Francisco. I'm told he was instrumental in getting the governor elected. I think he's got the right connections and knows what to do."

Stuart latched on to the idea immediately.

"Get hold of him. Fly him down. Give him whatever he wants. Let him get a feel for the place. Then I'll fly down. Hear what he's got to say. And we'll take it from there."

Stuart called A.B. Marketing and played telephone tag for several days before he got hold of Alain Beaulieu. He explained what they were looking for. "But the only way you can do this is to come down. Be our guest. After you get the feel of Twin Palms, we'd love to pick your brain. I hear you're the man."

Alain, not short on self-esteem, thrived on accolades. Banning had no way of knowing that Alain played the same *hard-to-get* game he did. "I'm swamped right now. Too many irons in the fire. How about Christmas? That's when things slow down a bit."

With one small suitcase and a copy of the best-seller *Capone*, Alain Beaulieu flew into Los Angeles, rented a black Mercedes, and drove to the resort. Stuart met him in his office and laid out his plan. "Alain, we want you to get a feel for the resort. Everything's *comped*. Get a few massages. Sign for your meals. It's all on us. Talk to people. Have a good time."

Stuart put Alain up in a suite in the old-fashioned rock units. Although the suite was nothing more than a bedroom and living room filled with cheap 20's style reproductions, it was the most sought-after suite at the resort. Guests clamored for its "old world" charm.

Enthralled with the resort, Alain wasn't in any rush to get back to foggy San Francisco. Five days passed before Alain—a handsome divorcee in his mid-forties—reconnected with Stuart over lunch in the dining room.

"Well," Stuart said, putting down his Coke, "What's your take?"

Swiping a lock of straight blond hair from his forehead, Alain said, "What's not to like? The water worked wonders on my trick knee. And I've met some outrageous women."

Stuart dismissed the chit-chat about Alain's personal life and zeroed in on business. "I'm curious. Have you given any thought to a marketing plan?"

Alain, one of the slickest public relations guys in the business, painted a rosy picture. However, he was careful not to get into specifics until the company settled on his fee. "This place is unique. And it's sure as hell relaxing. I've no doubt that I can help you spread the word. Your brochure could use a bit of tweaking. I haven't seen a press kit. Do you have one?"

"No, truthfully we never thought of that."

"Well, I'm good at creating press kits. Then I'll do some press releases. Get you written-up in all the important newspapers and travel magazines."

Stuart took to his ideas immediately.

Alain milked the *freebie* into the new year. He reveled in the dry air and blue skies. With his French accent, broad shoulders, flat stomach, and skimpy European cut Speedo, he charmed everyone he met, especially the ladies. Every morning he awakened just in time for the low-key breakfast buffet. Then spent most of his time marinating in the hot mineral water, swapping stories around the swimming pool, or getting a variety of exotic massages.

"Well, Banning's anxious to meet you," Stuart said. "He's flying down Thursday morning. He wants to hear what you've got to say. By the way, would you like to join my wife and me for dinner tomorrow night?" Stuart wanted to sound him out before Banning arrived.

The next morning, Stuart talked to Rachel. "Don't hang out at school too long. I forgot to tell you we've got dinner plans."

"Tonight?"

"Yeah. You're about to dine with the great Alain Beaulieu, the Crown Prince of Public Relations. I think you'll like him. When it comes to sales, I'm beginning to think he's every bit as slick as Banning."

Rachel asked, "What time's dinner?"

"Six, our usual dinner time."

Despite the early hour, Rachel couldn't resist adding her two cents worth. "You know when we *entertain*," and she emphasized the word *entertain*, "it's more continental to dine later. Not many people eat dinner on the stroke of six like we do. They look forward to a nice, leisurely dining experience."

Stuart simply remarked, "Oh, really. We've been entertaining for years, and so far, everyone's managed to come to dinner at six."

"Just saying," Rachel said, not willing to concede the point.

Chapter 25

Dinner with Alain

AT DINNER Stuart introduced Rachel to Alain, the public relations guru. Rachel relished the idea of entertaining in the resort's dining room. She didn't have to shop, cook, or clean-up. Plus, she had an insatiable curiosity and reveled in meeting new people. Stuart was amused that Alain, a natural born kibitzer, who had only been at the resort a short time, knew more people in the dining room than he did.

After they were seated, Stuart asked, "What's your preference in wine?"

Alain had no shame in suggesting an expensive bottle of French burgundy. While they sipped their wine, Rachel pounded Alain with a myriad of questions.

A showman first-class, he loved an audience and was happy to oblige. "I was sixteen when my family moved from Cassis to New Orleans."

"We've been to France several times but I'm not exactly sure where Cassis is."

"It's a quaint fishing village in southern France. An incredibly picturesque place. Primo," Alain said, making a circle with his thumb and index fingers. "When I came here, I barely spoke English. I was really shy. It took years before I felt fluent."

Rachel, who was always a little too forward, commented, "You shy? Somehow I can't visualize that."

"Yeah, afraid people would laugh at me. Your idioms are killers. At first I took them literally."

Enchanted by his French accent, Rachel flattered him. "Oh, well. Now your English is perfect."

"I still mispronounce some words."

"English is tough. I teach school and work on language every day. Some of my students are new to this country. They're terrified to speak in English. Truthfully English doesn't always make sense. Just when you think you've got it down pat, there's an exception to the rule."

"Tell me about it," Alain confided. "My family had a special tutor. She came to the house and gave all of us English lessons."

"I'm curious," Rachel admitted, "if you don't mind me asking, what brought your family to New Orleans?"

"My father was a spy," Alain said with a straight face. When he saw their stunned look, he cracked a smile. "Just kidding."

"You really had me going," Rachel said. "Seriously . . ."

Alain chuckled. "It wasn't quite that dramatic. My father belonged to a fishing co-op in Cassis. They sent him here to learn about fish packing and distribution. Can you believe it? Fish packing."

"Well, it's an honest living. Does your family still live in New Orleans?"

"No, no, no. After two years, they moved back to France. I got lucky. I got a soccer scholarship to Stanford and moved west. After college I worked for a big P.R. agency in Frisco. But after ten years, I started my own business."

Rachel cringed when she heard the word *Frisco*. That was a no-no for native San Franciscans. A euphemism made famous by sailors during the second world war. But she decided to let it go since he was their guest. She pushed on, squeezing him for more information.

"What's this, twenty questions?" Stuart finally remarked, giving her one of his looks. "I don't think Alain wants to be interrogated." Anxious to get down to business, Stuart took control and changed the subject. "So . . . Alain, any thoughts about a new brochure?"

"Well . . . there's nothing wrong with the old brochure," he remarked diplomatically, not wanting to step on anyone's toes. "But I think it could use a bit more sophistication."

"I've got an idea," Rachel said, feeling loose after all the wine. "Want to hear it?"

Stuart gave Rachel another glaring look, as if to say shut up. But she pretended she didn't notice.

"Sure. Let's hear it," Alain replied as Stuart ran his fingers through his thick wavy hair and cringed, not knowing what Rachel would come up with next.

"I'm no marketing expert," Rachel postured, "but today during my lunch break a slogan popped into my head. I was thinking how everything around me—the kids, the school, even the town—is chaotic. The only thing around here that's peaceful is the resort. It sticks out like a sore thumb. You know. . . in a good way. So anyhow, how does this sound? *Twin Palms, an island in a sea of stress.*"

Alain repeated it. "*Twin Palms . . . an island in a sea of stress. Good. Good. Yes. It really pops.*"

Not sure how her idea would be received, Rachel was pleased to see his face light up.

"Hey, you're pretty good at this. If I may," Alain said, "I'd take it one step further. *Twin Palms Resort and Spa . . . an island in a sea of stress.* Sounds like a place to go, a destination. Rachel, ever think of changing jobs?"

"Are you kidding? Every day. But despite all my bitching, I love teaching. If I do it right, I can influence the lives of these kids . . ." Almost as an afterthought, Rachel added, "And I hope for the better."

Stuart and Alain began to speak at once. Stuart caught himself and allowed Alain to speak first.

"Yes, I think I can use your idea. But I've got to write it down; otherwise, I may lose it. Ideas are constantly swirling around in my head."

Stuart raised his index finger and motioned for the server. "Could you bring us a piece of paper and a pen? There's a notebook on the shelf below the reception desk."

Alain scribbled the slogan down, folded it and shoved it into the pocket of his silk Hawaiian shirt. Then he began his spiel. "You know, words have power. They create vivid images in the mind." It was clear Alain was in his element. With his wine glass empty, he sipped some water. "For example, by changing the name to Twin Palms *Resort and Spa*, the resort congers up a more upscale image."

Stuart concurred.

"Here's another little tweak. We could change *mineral water pool* to *grotto pool*. Mineral water sounds medicinal. Too antiseptic. Like going to Baden-Baden for the cure. *Grotto pool* creates an image of soaking in luxurious water. See what I mean?"

Stuart and Rachel were enthralled. Rachel thought *grotto pool* was redundant but didn't want to say anything.

"There's definitely good vibes here. I'm totally relaxed. That's when my creative juices kick in."

Stuart looked pleased. This was his territory. "You're right. You know, we get lots of people from the entertainment world. Actors. Writers. Producers. A famous couple, well-known song writers, just checked out a couple of weeks ago. They were here for a month."

"I can see why. While we're on the subject," Alain continued, "another idea crossed my mind. I'd really like to run it by you."

Stuart had tucked away too much food and wine. He had a long day and was more than ready to call it quits for the night. But as a good host, he played along. "Let's hear it."

"Okay. This will slay you. Tonight, while getting dressed, I noticed the old mirror above the bureau had a small round hole in it . . . the size of a bullet. Before I flew down here, I bought a copy of *Capone* at the airport. You know, it's been on the best seller list for weeks. I'd been meaning to read it, but never got around to it 'til now. It's about Al Capone, the famous gangster. So, I got this crazy idea. Suppose I create a legend, something for people to latch on to. Since the rock house is right out of the 20's, suppose we claimed this was Capone's western hideaway? Then we could call the suite I'm in . . . the Capone Suite."

"Listen, everything you've said tonight sounds fantastic. When Banning flies down tomorrow, make your presentation. He's a great listener."

Chapter 26

Banning Meets Alain

S TUART—who believed punctuality was the eleventh com-
mandment—invariably got edgy waiting for people. Without
realizing it, he had been drumming his fingers impatiently on the polished walnut table. He drank a Coke and Alain, the
public relations genius, sipped Perrier as they schmoozed about
the NFL draft picks while waiting for Banning.

Twenty minutes late, Banning, the very wealthy owner-devel-
oper, waltzed into the small banquet room adjacent to the dining
room and interrupted their conversation. Carrying an ice-cold
beer, he simply said, "Sorry I'm late," but offered no explanation.
He took off his finely woven Panama hat and flung it onto one of
the empty chairs, removed his sunglasses, and casually slipped off
his Birkenstock sandals.

Stuart chuckled inwardly, wondering if Alain was expecting a
more conventional man to appear. He made the introductions quickly.

Sitting at the head of the table, Banning did a quick overview
of his plans for the property, then pumped Alain for new ideas.

Always at his best when making presentations, Alain spent the better part of five minutes complimenting the two men on their vision for the resort. "I've got to hand it to you both. You've really turned this place around. It's a little *Shangri-La,* a sybaritic paradise." Then he went about hooking them. "What you need now is something outlandish. Something that will capture the imagination of every travel writer and magazine. Something with pow. Different." Pitching Banning, Alain's eyes grew intense. "I've already told this to Stuart, but I'll repeat it now. While staying here, I read the story of *Al Capone.* The book's been on the best seller list for weeks. Maybe years. In America it seems that everyone loves a good gangster story. Remember the television series *The Untouchables.* It went on for years. What I'm proposing may sound a little outlandish but hear me out. Suppose we invent a Capone story?"

"What's on your mind?" Banning asked.

"What if we say Al Capone used this place as a hideaway . . . to get away from the feds. It happened over fifty years ago. Who could dispute it?"

Stuart couldn't contain himself. "Alain, your story is not so far-fetched. From the info I've gathered at the historical society, back in the 20's this place actually was an out-of-the-way roadhouse . . . with gambling and prostitutes."

"Perfect," Alain said. "It fits right in. Picture this. Way out here in the desert . . . no one could track him down. Think of the elevation and how the resort slopes down towards Palm Springs."

"In those days," Stuart interjected, "there was nothing around here but sand dunes. Capone would have a perfect view of the unpaved road leading out this way. Any car heading in this direction would kick up a cloud of dust. Capone's henchmen would be able to see them coming from miles away."

Banning, the consummate salesman, bought it . . . hook, line, and sinker. "It's great! People gobble up stories like this. We could even embellish it."

The three men fed off each other.

Alain threw in another idea. "Remember the hole in the mirror in the suite where I'm staying? It looks exactly like a bullet hole. That's what got me thinking about Capone in the first place."

"Perfect. We'll claim it was a bullet hole," Banning piped in. "I'm beginning to like this idea more and more. If you want, I can carve Capone's initials into the desk. I did that all the time back in high school. My teacher caught me and sent me to the principal's office. I nearly got suspended for that little caper."

They all laughed.

"There's actually a rooftop sunbathing terrace above your suite," Stuart said. "We could build a lookout tower. It would make it seem more authentic."

Banning remarked, "I've got one question. Where would Capone hide if he saw the Fed's coming?"

By this time, Stuart—who knew every inch of the property—was almost giddy. "We've got a basement half-covered in sand about seventy-five feet from the rock house and half-way to the dining room. A building must have been there at one time. There's a crazy fortified passage that leads off from there and it suddenly dead ends. There's even an old Mosler safe down there. Huge. Probably too heavy to be hauled up. We could claim that's where Capone stashed his money."

Alain broke into a wide smile. He was pleased that the two men were energized by his pitch. "We could call the rooms where I'm staying the Capone Suite." With his adrenaline pumping, he pushed further. "We could even go so far as to rename the dining room. Call it the casino. It'll give the place character, makes it more colorful. Believe me when I tell you, this will put the resort on the map. In addition to a more enticing brochure, I can create a fantastic press kit complete with the Capone legend. We'll invite the travel writers here, hand them a press kit and let 'em write. I guarantee, they'll eat it up. It's dynamite."

Banning, who rarely thought to give a compliment, smiled widely. "You know, Alain, you live up to your reputation. You're damn good at what you do. You've got my vote. Let's do it!"

Chapter 27

Looking for Santiago

Benson Middle School

AS RACHEL TOOK ATTENDANCE during homeroom, she noticed that Santiago had been continuously absent. *For God's sake, she complained, how am I supposed to teach him? Everything, especially math, builds sequentially. At the end of the year, when the administration evaluates the progress my class makes—or doesn't make—they'll blame me that he hasn't learned anything.*

During her lunch break Rachel headed to the office to discuss Santiago's spotty attendance with Ofelia, the attendance clerk. A good-natured Hispanic woman, Ofelia helped Rachel out every afternoon with her English-as-a-Second-Language class.

"What's the story on Santiago? Did he drop out."

"Not that I know of. But you never can tell. I've called his house, but no one answers. That's all I can do. Should I notify the truant officer?"

It's probably a good idea. He's either cutting school or he's lying in a pool of blood. Or his family moved somewhere else."

Ofelia phoned Ms. Paulsen, the overworked truant officer, whose job it was to cover the whole district. She explained Santiago's absences and urged her to get on it as soon as she could.

Every day before their English-as-a-Second-Language class began, Rachel asked Ofelia if she heard anything more about Santiago. She heard the same answer every day. "Ms. Paulsen hasn't returned my phone call."

Rachel, who had grown impatient, expected her to respond right away. "Ofelia, call her again. Raise bloody hell."

When Ofelia finally got hold of the truant officer, Ms. Paulsen apologized profusely. "I sprained my ankle playing tennis a couple of weeks ago and couldn't get around. Things got backed-up. I'll get on it as soon as I can."

Another two weeks passed before Ms. Paulsen physically checked on Santiago. As she neared the apartment, she heard a television blaring and surmised someone was home. After ringing the doorbell—which she wasn't sure was working—and banging on the door, she spotted Santiago peeking through the closed blinds.

Santiago hesitated, not sure whether to open the door. After incessant knocking, he eventually cracked it open, as far as the chain would allow.

From her perspective, Ms. Paulsen saw a darkened living room and the glow of the black-and-white television. She saw the silhouette of a few toddlers sitting on the floor. As gently as she could, she introduced herself. "May I speak to your mom?"

"She no home."

"When will she be back?"

"I don't know."

Ms. Paulsen had to look at her clipboard because his name escaped her. "Well then, Santiago, may I speak to your father?"

"NO!" he said, and slammed the door shut.

Ms. Paulsen understood that he was afraid he would get into trouble. From past experiences with other truant kids, she knew how futile it was to stand there and plead with him. It was not uncommon for students to babysit younger brothers and sisters while their parents went to work. First thing the next morning, she called Ofelia, the attendance clerk. "I'll send you a copy of my report. But I had no success. Look, I'm so far behind, I'm going to hand his case over to Children's Protective Services. Maybe they have more clout."

At Children's Protective Services, a fresh-out-of-college social worker, Ms. Morgan, was assigned to Santiago's case. She got around to Santiago two weeks later because she had more urgent situations to deal with—plus she had taken a few extra days off before Thanksgiving to be with her family. When she drove over to the apartment, she encountered the same negative response.

Santiago still wasn't in school, and Rachel expected some resolution. She caught up with Ofelia in the office. "What's the word on Santiago? He's still missing-in-action."

"Santiago won't open the door for the truant officer or Ms. Morgan. Neither of them could get in to talk to his parents."

Rachel was irate. "This has dragged on long enough. Santiago knows me. Maybe he'll respond better to me. Get his address and put it in my mailbox. I've got a dentist appointment today after school, but I'll drive over there tomorrow."

Rachel took matters into her own hands. And she had been right. Santiago responded to her. As he led her into the dark studio apartment that smelled stale from lack of air, she glanced around at the hodge-podge of furniture. *So, this is how it is for the immigrants,* she thought. *They start with nothing.* A small black and white television sat on a plastic garden table. Two single beds were pushed up against separate walls. Above one was an inexpensive gold-framed rendering of Jesus. A lamp with a torn shade and a chipped statue of the Virgin Mary sat on a table. In the space at the end of the kitchen sat an old garden table with three chairs.

Two babies strapped in infant seats were on the floor sleeping, their diaper bags alongside them. Three toddlers sat with their legs crisscrossed—mesmerized by a silly cartoon. Empty baby bottles sat on the kitchen counter.

"Santiago, may I sit down?" Rachel asked, convinced that what the apartment needed most was a good airing out. Without a couch, Rachel and Santiago sat side-by-side on one of the rumpled beds. "I'm here 'cause I care about you. Is everything all right?"

Santiago's hands flew up to his face to cover an avalanche of tears. Then, without warning, he began to sob so hard his body shook.

"It's okay. It's okay." Rachel whispered, putting the flat of her hand on his back. "You're going to be all right. I'm here to help you."

Time passed. Nothing further was said until Santiago regained his composure.

"Let me get a tissue to wipe your tears." Rachel headed to the bathroom. She looked around but couldn't find any. In a hurry, she grabbed a roll of toilet paper that was sitting on the floor. Returning, she offered him a wad of paper. She brushed aside a tuft of long, unkempt hair that fell over Santiago's face. "You're not in trouble. I'm here 'cause I care about you. What's going on?"

It took a while, but in his broken English Santiago tried to explain. "My mother, she gone. One night she leaved for work, but never come back. She call only one time and say she in jail. She tell to me to watch the kids. She be home soon."

One of the tots ambled over and put his chubby little fingers on Santiago's knee. "You okay?" he asked.

In a gentle voice, Rachel said, "Yes, he's fine. Now go watch your program."

The little one weaved his way back to his place in front of the television. Rachel held Santiago's hand and waited for him to continue.

"Then no more calls. I not know where she is. Maybe dead."

"No, Santiago, don't jump to conclusions." Not sure he understood, she clarified her thoughts. "Let's get the facts first. I want you to think hard. Do you know where she was going?"

He told her as much as he knew. "I clean dishes when she go.

She gots job somewhere near San Diego. She did that a lot. I forgets the name of the place she go. She drive people to work."

"That's helpful. By any chance, did you call the police?"

"I be too afraid."

"What about your dad? Is your dad home?" she asked, still innocent of the circumstances.

Santiago started to sob again. Her question brought back horrifying images for him. He relived the terrifying scene with his father lying in the dirt.

Rachel had no idea what triggered more tears but had the decency not to press. Once again, she placed her hand on his back for reassurance and waited.

"In El Salvador, he be murdered."

Chills ran down Rachel's spine. Murder, that was something she didn't bargain for.

"Oh, Santiago, I'm so sorry. I didn't know." She began to put the pieces together, to see the bigger picture. He had been on his own since his mother disappeared. Rachel couldn't believe his mother would simply abandon him. "Santiago, if you trust me well enough, I can check into her disappearance." She reworded herself, attempting to use simpler, more familiar words. "I can look for your mom."

"Maybe you find her?" he said, with an innocence that pierced Rachel's heart.

"I'll try very hard. I promise. Do you have enough to eat?"

"Sometimes Nacho brings to me food. But Nacho, he be mad. His minivan gone. Mamá, when she leaved, take his van. Sometimes when mothers bring to me their kids, they bring to me food. I gots money for babysitting. Sometimes at night I go to the 7-Eleven. Buy burritos and chips."

Rachel cringed but didn't say aloud what she was thinking. *The resort throws away a ton of food every day. The contrast between his apartment and the resort was unfathomable: from abject poverty to pampered guests 24/7.*

Santiago continued. "I okay 'cept the apartment boss. He want money for to pay the rent. He handed to me papers. But if I gives to him the money, then I won't gots nothin' to eat."

Chapter 28

Searching for Rosa

A FTER FINDING SANTIAGO living alone, Rachel could think of nothing else as she drove back to the resort. She glanced at her watch. Almost five o'clock. She needed to talk to Stuart, tell him what she found out. She parked her car near the condo and scrambled up the gritty path to his office. Rachel barged in only to find Stuart on the telephone.

He waved her off, indicating he'd be with her in a moment. While he talked on the phone, Rachel headed for the storage room behind his desk to take inventory of what was there and what she needed.

When he hung up, Stuart apologized. "Sorry I couldn't talk. Banning had me on the phone for ten minutes. He's got another crazy idea. Someone told him that we should start an organic vegetable garden." Rubbing his forehead, he groused, "I need another project like I need a hole in my head. We'd have to hire another gardener just to take care of it. God, I can just pick up the phone and have organic produce delivered any day of the week. Sorry for ranting. It's been a helluva day. Anyway, what's up with you?"

"Where do I start?" Rachel responded, the pitch of her voice rising with her frustration level. "Remember that kid I told you about? That Hispanic boy . . . Santiago. The one that hardly ever comes to school. Well, I checked on him after school today."

"What do you mean, you checked on him?"

"I drove over to his apartment and found out he's living by himself. With no adults. Stuart, when I questioned him about it, he told me his father was murdered."

"Here . . . in Desert Oasis?"

"No," she said, shaking her head and giving him an exasperated look, as if to say *get a clue*. "In El Salvador. He was murdered by soldiers."

"Rachel, don't get involved. It could be dangerous. You've got no idea what you're getting yourself into."

She ignored his comments. "I'm guessing that's the reason Santiago and his mother came to California. Now she's in jail . . . somewhere."

"Why? Why's she in jail? What did she do?"

"Maybe she robbed a bank. How do I know?" she snapped. "But my gut feeling is she probably got picked up for being illegal. Stuart, the kid's living alone. I'm not sure I've got the story straight, but supposedly his mother drove some people to work one night and got arrested. She called him once . . . to tell him she landed in jail. Santiago doesn't know what jail. So, I promised him I'd try to track her down."

"I don't believe you," he said, slamming his hand down on his desk. "Why do you get yourself into these messes?"

"Just lucky, I guess."

Stuart hesitated; not sure Rachel wanted to hear his advice. "Well . . . if you don't mind me sticking my nose in, if I were you, I'd call the Riverside County Sheriff's Department." Then he added, "And if she's not in a county jail, I'd call INS."

"What's INS?"

"I don't know, but they're the guys that round-up illegal immigrants."

"Well, how do you know about INS . . . or whatever it's called?"

"I just know. Take my word for it. I hired a couple of illegals for the hotel in Reno. I didn't know they were illegal until INS came and scooped them up."

For the first time, Rachel realized that she had a daunting task ahead of her. By the time she headed back to their condo, she felt drained. The first thing she did was flip on the air-conditioner. She slipped off her sandals, opened a can of diet Coke—something she only did when she was frustrated—and pulled Santiago's mother's name from her purse. She put the paper on the end table, called information to get the number, and placed a call to the County Sheriff's Department.

"I'm looking for a woman that's gone missing," Rachel explained.

"How long has she been missing? A day, a month, a year, what?"

"That's what I'm trying to find out. Maybe two to three months. Maybe longer."

"Can you give me her name?"

"Rosa Lopez," Rachel said, and then tried to explain the odd circumstances. "The last her son heard . . . she'd been arrested. But since then, he hasn't heard a word. Look, I'm his teacher and I'm just trying to help him out. I'm trying to piece it all together."

"Does he know where she was arrested?"

"No. That's the point. That's what I'm trying to find out. She's disappeared. He hasn't heard from her since that one call. Can you help me?"

"Ma'am," the sluggish voice responded, "I can't help you today. For all intents and purposes the office is about to close. But if you give me your telephone number, I'll have someone search our records. And they'll get back to you."

Not adverse to being pushy, Rachel asked for his name and when she could expect an answer. Trying to put some urgency into the request, she explained that Rosa Lopez's thirteen-year-old son was living alone, and he needed to find her.

The deputy didn't like being put on the spot. "Ma'am, we're pretty busy 'round here. Someone will call . . . just as soon as they can get to it,"

Rachel grew angry when no one returned her call. The following Friday she took matters into her own hands. On her lunch break, she headed over to the trailer that doubled as a temporary teachers' lunchroom/lounge and called the County Sheriff's Office again. After repeating the whole situation, she was transferred to missing persons, and finally to Officer Hennessey, in the records department.

"Look, ma'am, I'm sorry nobody got back to you. But I can see that someone did check the county jails. Nears I can tell, Rosa Lopez is nowheres in our system. You can give INS a try. They've got a big processing center down in El Centro. Would you like that number?"

Rachel jumped all over it. "Yes, please. That would be great." At the same time, she chastised herself for not heeding Stuart's suggestion in the first place. "By the way," she said, trying to keep her voice calm, "if I might ask, what do those initials stand for?"

"Immigration and Naturalization Services, ma'am."
She thanked him and immediately called the INS Processing Center. Rachel repeated the situation. "I'm looking for a woman named Rosa Lopez. Her young son's living alone, and I don't know what to do with him. I can't emphasize how important this call is. I need to find her."

"Where was she living? And what country did she come from, Ma'am?"

Rachel was sick of being called ma'am, but let it go. "Desert Oasis, California. And she's from El Salvador."

"Please hold the line. This might take a few minutes, but I'll check her name against our data base."

It felt like five minutes had passed. Rachel grew hostile, wondering if the person on the other end of the line had left her hanging. Absent-mindedly she doodled squares and question marks on an expired lunch calendar. Beginning to feel enclosed, she glanced around the small room. A group of teachers—some correcting papers—were eating their lunches and talking quietly amongst themselves.

Jonathan, the prissy art teacher stood by the phone. He pointed to his watch, letting Rachel know that he'd been waiting a long time to use the phone.

Rachel covered the mouth of the phone. "I can't help it. I'm on hold," she said looking frustrated.

The clerk finally came back on the line. He told Rachel that he had located a Rosa Lopez from Desert Oasis in their computer. "Ma'am, if it's the right one, she's in the Apple Valley Detention Center."

Bingo! I found her I found her!

Her mind raced with new scenarios. *I don't want to tell Santiago until I find a place for him to live. Then, I can call his mother and let her know exactly where he's living 'til she comes back.* Then she corrected herself and added *if she comes back.* Rachel still hadn't eaten her lunch when the bell rang, indicating the end of the lunch period.

As she was about to leave, Jonathan, who had been listening to the constant saga of Santiago, made a snide remark. "You know other people need to use the phone. Why are you so hung up on this kid, anyway?"

Not wishing to get into an argument, Rachel ignored his comment and walked away.

Chapter 29

Children's Protective Services

BEFORE SCHOOL STARTED, Rachel smiled as she ambled over to the office. She couldn't wait to discuss Santiago's situation with Ofelia, the attendance clerk. "Hey, you'll never guess what happened? Before Ofelia had a chance to respond, Rachel blurted it out. "I finally found out what happened to Santiago's mother. She's in a detention center."

"Really. That's awful. Poor thing. I heard they're like prisons."

"You're probably right. But one way or another, I need to talk to her. He can't go on like this. I don't know how long it's been since anyone paid rent on his apartment. But if the landlord kicks him out, the poor kid's gonna be homeless, living on the street. Someone needs to take him in, at least temporarily."

"Call Children's Protective Services?"

"They're useless!" When Rachel heard herself shouting at the one person on her side, she lowered her voice. "I'm sorry. I'm sorry, Ofelia. It's just that so far Children's Protective Services has done nothing to help him."

"Rachel, I know you're frustrated. I can hear it in your voice. But it's worth a try. Ask for Ms. Morgan. She's worked with a few of our students."

"I've called her before. Remember? She got nowhere with Santiago. He refused to talk to her."

"Seriously, do you have a better suggestion?"

"Okay, okay. I'll call at lunch time."

With her bag lunch in hand, Rachel once again headed for the trailer, the temporary teacher's lounge/lunchroom, to make her call. She had no choice but to sit at the long banquet table shoved against the wall, where the phone was connected. Privacy was hard to come by. Before she ate her sandwich, she called Children's Protective Services and asked for Ms. Morgan.

After Rachel explained Santiago's predicament, Ms. Morgan immediately suggested foster care.

Rachel groused, "Uh-uh. I've heard pros and cons. But if that's the only choice, and Santiago's placed with a family, you've got to promise me it will be a loving family, not one of those just looking for the money or wanting a workhorse. He's shy and ultra-sensitive. And truthfully, so far his life hasn't been a bed of roses."

Ms. Morgan periodically punctuated Rachel's tirade. "I get it. Yes, I agree. Uh-huh." In the end, the social worker promised to find a place for Santiago.

After hanging up, Rachel moved to one of the round banquet tables and tried to calm herself down. As she ate, a few of the teachers sitting there began to make snide comments.

"He's probably here illegally," Kimberly, the young blonde teacher said.

"So what?" Rachel growled, dismissing her comments out-of-hand. *Another one of those dingbat recruits from Kansas. She'll only last a few years in California and then head back home. The district loves to bring them out 'cause they go back home before they're vested in the retirement system.*

"I'm just saying."

"Don't say."

The P.E. teacher—who flunked the math segment on the CBEST test three times and was working on a provisional credential—remarked, "If he doesn't come to school, there'd be one less kid in your class. Did you ever think about that?"

Rachel refused to respond but thought, *why would you worry about it? All you do in P.E. is have the kids run around the track or cut them loose to play tetherball.*

Some teachers were even more harsh. They thought he should be sent back to Mexico or wherever he came from. The speech therapist, a gentle grandmotherly type, who came to their school one day a week, simply stated, "Maybe you're too involved."

How would you know? Rachel thought. *You only see your charges for fifteen minutes, one day a week.* Growing hostile, she shoved a couple of almonds in her mouth and reviewed her options. She decided to ignore all the negative comments *If only I had a Blackberry, I could stay in my classroom and call without everybody adding their two cents worth.*

Rachel couldn't help obsessing about Santiago. She worried that he didn't have enough to eat. After school, she drove over to the shopping center and bought two bags of groceries: milk, cereal, orange juice, packaged lunch meats, peanut butter, strawberry jelly, and a loaf of bread and hauled them over to Santiago's apartment.

On Friday Ms. Morgan left a message with Ofelia, the attendance clerk. "Tell Rachel to call me. I've got some good news."

At lunch Rachel read the call-back slip that had been placed in her mailbox. She waited her turn to use the phone. A teacher was checking on her daughter, who was home sick. Finally, it was Rachel's turn. "What's up?" she asked Ms. Morgan, from Children's Protective Services.

"I think I've found just the right spot for Santiago. Not a foster home. Ever hear of Bar 8 Ranch for Boys?"

"No, should I?"

"Well, no. Not really. I just found out about it myself. Five years ago, an ex-baseball player and his wife started it. It's up in Sky Valley. They lost their only son to drugs and they're trying to turn his death into something positive. Apparently, they've made it their life's mission to look after troubled boys."

Feeling slightly disappointed, Rachel interrupted her. "But he's not troubled."

"I know. But listen. Yesterday I called Andy and told him about Santiago's unusual circumstances. He said that's no problem. They often care for boys that somehow fall through the cracks. I shouldn't be telling you this, but last week one of their boys ran away. He tried to rob the Dunkin' Donut shop. And he got caught. He's now in a facility for youthful offenders. And Bar 8 Ranch won't take him back. That's how come there's the empty bed."

Chapter 30

Classroom Observation

RACHEL LOVED THE ENVIRONMENT she had created. An overhead projector would have made it perfect. At the beginning of the year, she had filled out a requisition form in hopes of getting one but was still waiting for its arrival. At the rate things were going, she suspected that it would be a long time before her request got filled, if ever. Since there was a nomadic component to her life, Rachel *had taught in more districts than most teachers. In each school district, the principal had the duty to frequently evaluate new* teachers. So, in theory, Rachel was considered a *new, probationary* teacher even though she had taught for many years. For the evaluations, the standard procedure was for the principal to slip unannounced into a classroom, find an empty seat, and take notes on their observations of the classroom, the teacher, and the students.

Rachel took a deep breath when she noticed the principal had slipped through the door after the lunch bell rang. Ms. Webb found an empty chair, sat down quietly and immediately began to jot down her observations. *Did she have to pick my English-as-a-Second Language class for an evaluation? Oh, well. It is, what it is.* Rachel tried to convince herself things could be worse. *At least I'm teaching something.* Knowing there was going to be hell to pay, she had no choice but to plow through her math lesson.

"Do I have your attention?" Rachel asked her group of students. She waited until all eyes focused on her. "Today we're going to review two-digit multiplication." *Dammit, this would be so much easier, if I had an overhead projector.* On the blackboard, she demonstrated how important it was to set the problem up in a specific way. She gave her group a problem and walked around the table to see how they were doing. "I don't get it," one girl shouted out.

Lord, give me patience, Rachel thought, as she went over to help her. Ofelia, the attendance monitor from the office, was working with the other half of the students using home-made Spanish to English flash cards. She held up a Spanish word and her charges repeated it in English. All the students in Ophelia's area of the room were paying attention, except Carlotta. She was prancing around the room screaming *puta. PUTA!*

Rachel wasn't sure what it meant but knew in her gut it wasn't a nice word. For the most part, the class ignored Carlotta. But since the principal was observing her classroom management skills as well as everything else, Rachel stopped what she was doing, walked over to Carlotta, and insisted she sit down. She put her hand on Carlotta's shoulder and tried to talk to her softly. Agitated, Carlotta pulled away and started to pace the room again. Rachel left her alone and returned to her math group.

Early the next morning, when Rachel checked her mailbox, there was a note from the principal. It read:

Please see me after school to discuss your observation.

"Sorry I'm late," Rachel explained as she rushed in. "But I had bus duty."

"No problem," Mrs. Webb said, slipping some papers into a red file folder. "Please close the door and have a seat. I've got your evaluation here. Look it over, then we can talk about it. I'm not sure this is the way it was done in Reno, but this is the way it's done in California. It's divided into three parts: a positive section, one for self-improvement, and one to set a goal."

"Yeah, it's pretty much the same." Immediately Rachel chastised herself for her sloppy language. *Watch the YEAHS. Show respect,* she thought, *even though you're older and have more classroom experience.*

As expected, her evaluation started out with a positive comment, but quickly morphed into something else. "I know that you're trying hard to work with these kids, but I have several concerns. Number one, I noticed you were teaching math in your English-as-a-Second Language class. According to the district's regulations, that's a no-no. Strictly speaking, you need to be working on English with these kids."

"Yes, but . . . remember when you asked me to do this, I told you I wasn't fluent in Spanish. In my last district, I only taught math. That's what I'm good at. And every one of these kids can use a little extra help since they're such a small group."

"Rachel," Ms. Webb said firmly, "put yourself in my shoes. As a principal in charge of assignments, you've got one of those rare, might I say old-fashion credentials. It allows you to teach every subject from kindergarten through eighth grade. You're the only one that I could call on to teach English-as-a-Second-Language."

"I don't mean to be difficult, but I've got a problem with that. I stink at foreign languages. When I went to college, English-as-a-Second Language wasn't even around. I don't even have a teacher's manual or outline to follow. My credential allows me to teach reading and math, social studies, and science. Nothing about a foreign language. May I speak frankly?"

"Be my guest."

"The district is aware that many of the kids at our school are non-English speakers. Why didn't they hire a Spanish speaking teacher or two? Or supply me with a teacher's guide or workbooks, flashcards, SOMETHING?" When Rachel grew emotional, her voice grew louder. She realized she needed to calm down, modulate it to make her point more effectively. "In the other district where I taught, they had a legitimate program. Every morning, they pulled *all* non-English speaking kids out of their classes, not just a select few. They provided a systematic and comprehensive program with headsets and tapes, videos, workbooks, the whole shebang. I don't even have an overhead projector."

The principal toyed with the top of a ballpoint pen. "Well," and she paused to collect her thoughts, "this is the way it works here. And, frankly, we're all doing the best we can."

"I agree. We're all doing the best we can, with what we've got to work with. In ESL, I've got nothing. Ofelia's working on their English and I'm teaching them basic math. Actually, they're lucky. They're getting both."

Pivoting to another subject, Ms. Webb said, "By the way, what's with that girl running around the classroom disrupting everyone? She was out-of-control."

"Oh . . . that's Carlotta. She's impossible. You ought to thank me that I haven't sent her to the office. What would you do with her? She's got severe emotional problems. Now that we're talking about it, she probably should be evaluated by the school psychologist. What's his name? I keep forgetting . . ."

"Steve Kennedy. If you want an I.E.P, you'll have to fill out a behavioral survey and a few forms first."

With all the school's acronyms, Rachel thought for a moment. Then she got it; I.E.P., *Individual Educational Plan.*

"With all our special needs kids, the psychologist is swamped. One day a week is insufficient. You'll have to be patient. It'll be a while before he can test her."

Rachel sighed. *By the time they get around to testing her, she'll be ready to move on to high school.* She knew enough to hold back the myriad of thoughts racing through her head. That was exactly why most teachers didn't take the time to fill out the complex forms. Then commit to a bunch of extra meetings. Even if the school psychologist did an evaluation, there was only so much room in Special Education. *Besides,* she thought, *what Special Education programs were available to Carlotta, a non-English speaking student with the reading ability of a second grader and emotional and behavioral problems to boot. It was easier to just let her be.*

Just then Ms. Webb's secretary burst in, explaining that another obnoxious parent was outside her office, demanding to see her. Rachel strolled back to her classroom thinking nothing ever gets resolved. Everyone gets dumped on. Her job wasn't easy, but neither was the principal's nor the psychologist's.

Chapter 31

Good Day, Bad Day

O N FRIDAY EVENING, Stuart returned to the condo earlier than usual. In a bad mood, he groaned inwardly, knowing that Rachel expected him to go to temple that night for a Hanukkah party. All day the temperature had bounced around in the mid-seventies and the air was still warm enough to sit outside. Stuart had gone to work in khaki shorts and a powder blue polo shirt with the resort's logo. He savored this time of day. He slipped off his socks and shoes and paraded around barefoot. *Dammit,* he thought, stretching his arms above his head, *there's still a little daylight left and I'm going to take advantage of it.*

Rachel sat at the dining room table correcting her students' writing assignments.

"It's been a rough day and I'm dog tired," Stuart warned. Always needing a quick pick-me-up, he opened the refrigerator and surveyed its contents. He managed to scoot through the French doors into the garden with a tray of green olives, hummus and chips. He placed them on a low-slung table under the trellis.

"I'll be out in a minute," Rachel said dismissively. "I'm almost done."

"When you come out, bring the open bottle of wine. I couldn't carry everything."

Rachel had barely plunked herself down on her chaise lounge when she blurted out, "I've got good news. Remember Santiago, that kid I've been telling you about? The one that's been living alone."

"Yeah. How could I forget? You're obsessed with him. Lately, that's all you talk about."

"Well, I think I found a place for him to live."

Visibly irritated, Stuart snapped. "What's with you? Why are you so involved with this kid anyway?"

"I don't know. It just sort of happened. What was I supposed to do? Leave him alone in that grungy apartment? Why so grouchy?"

"Bad day. You know Quinn, the gardener, the one with the long scar on his neck? He must have come in with another hangover. He and the maintenance guy got into a beef. They almost came to blows over the timer on the sprinklers. I swear, that man's a pain in the ass. Then . . . just as I was getting ready to leave, some bitchy broad tracked me down, insisting that we *comp* her stay 'cause she found a couple of dead cockroaches under her bed. For chrissakes, this is the desert. There are bugs. We spray every week. And the damn cockroaches were dead."

"Eww! I can't stand those things. I freak out whenever I see them. And I saw a couple of those little reddish ones crawling on the kitchen counter in Santiago's apartment. The poor kid lives with them."

"Can't you just forget Santiago for two minutes? Rachel, he's not your responsibility. You know there are agencies that deal with kids like him."

"Yeah, but he doesn't trust them; he trusts me."

Stuart dipped another pita chip into the hummus. "So, now what?"

"I don't know. Children's Protective Services found a temporary home for him. And I'm kind of the liaison between Santiago and them. Ever hear of Bar 8 Ranch for Boys?"

"No."

"It's not far from here. But they keep a low profile."

Stuart had little patience for the Santiago saga. All he wanted was a little peace and quiet. "Not to change the subject, but can we skip the temple's party tonight? I'm not in the mood to socialize."

"Oh, come on. It's the first night of Hanukkah. How bad can a vodka and *latke* party be?"

"I'm exhausted. I just filled up on chips. Besides, I could live without the *latkes*," Stuart said, pointing to the start of a paunch.

"Yeah. I noticed that. We're both getting fat. Too much rich food. But here's an interesting factoid. I kept your mother's menorah. When I packed up the house to come down here, I didn't have the heart to put it in storage. You know, it's a family heirloom. I think it's in one of those unopened boxes stored in the closet in the extra bedroom. If I can find it, let's have our own Hanukkah here. We can light the candles and say the blessing."

"You kept it? That's great. You know that menorah has quite a history. Someone gave it to my grandmother when they were forced to live in Golden Gate Park after the 1906 earthquake in San Francisco."

"When we first got married, your grandmother told me the story. It's a miracle it survived this long. But then . . . Hanukkah's about a miracle. You know, I've got a miracle of my own. Want to hear it?"

"Sure. I'm crazy about miracles," he said, mocking her.

"Actually, I've got two miracles."

"Oh, that's twice as good."

"Chalk 'em up. Number one, I located Santiago's mother, and two, I found a place for Santiago to live."

"You did good," Stuart conceded, although he thought Rachel was stretching the miracle thing a bit. Now . . . can we please skip the Hanukkah party?

"Fine." With a smug, mischievous smile, Rachel added, "I knew all along I only had a fifty-fifty chance of getting you to go to the temple Hanukkah party."

Stuart rolled his eyes. "Hey, isn't tomorrow the official start of Christmas vacation?"

"Yep."

"Then let's celebrate that, too."

Saturday morning Rachel planned to sleep in, but her mind kept swirling with thoughts about Santiago. Just before ten, she phoned Andy Owens, owner-director of the boys' ranch. "I believe Ms. Morgan from Children's Protective Services has already spoken to you about Santiago Lopez. I was wondering if I could drive him up to tour the ranch sometime this afternoon?"

After finalizing her plan, Rachel tried to call Santiago. His phone was dead so she drove over to his apartment. "Are you babysitting anyone today?"

"No," he said flatly.

Noting his melancholy voice, she asked, "How about McDonald's for lunch?"

Santiago had often seen it advertised on television. He had only eaten there once before, when Nacho took him and his daughters one Sunday after church.

Once inside, they waited in a line four-deep. Rachel told him he could order anything he wanted.

"Really?" he said, as if he hadn't heard her right.

"Yeah. Today's a very special day."

Unsure of his English, he was too insecure to place his order. So, Rachel ordered for him. *Life is good,* she thought. *At least for me. Daily maid service. Soaking in the mineral water, the comp massages, and rich dinners. Even my new job is perfect. A ridiculously easy commute from the resort. A self-contained class, except for the English-as-a-Second-Language class.* She knew her hedonistic lifestyle was light-years away from Santiago's. She suspected that he had never experienced a single frill in his life.

Rachel watched silently as the chocolate shake slid over his Adam's apple. His eyes never left his Big Mac and fries. When nothing remained, Rachel said, "I've got a big surprise for you."

Not sure what she meant, Santiago frowned, saying nothing.

Rachel reached across the table and gently touched his hand. "I found your mom. She's okay."

Suddenly his mournful face exploded with joy. "Where? Where'd you find her? Can I talk to her?"

"Well, it's kind of hard to explain. Nothing bad happened to her, but she's in a detention center." Santiago sat quietly for a moment, but Rachel sensed the wheels spinning in his head.

"Detention center?" He recognized the word *detention* from school. Students who got in trouble went to detention. "Did she do something bad?"

"No, she didn't do anything bad?"

"Then, when can she come home?"

"Not just yet." What could Rachel say? *She's locked up in a prison. No, she thought better of that.* Trying to make him understand, she said, "She's what's called an *immigrant.* That means she started out from a different country. And before she can be with you, she has to go through the court system. But," she added cheerfully, "she's here in California. I'm not making any promises, but maybe we can arrange for you to talk to her."

Santiago jumped in, "Can I see her? Where's she?"

"She's in a place near Apple Valley. That's about eighty miles from here."

"When she be coming home?" Santiago repeated, with all the innocence of a young boy longing for his mother.

"To be honest, I don't know. It's kind of complicated. But before you talk to her, let's get you settled, so she won't worry about you. Santiago, there's nothing wrong with babysitting, but you're too young to be living alone. You've done a fantastic job taking care of yourself. I'm really proud of you. But you need to be outside, playing with kids your own age . . . and in school. I think you'll love the place I found. It's a nearby boys' ranch. The man who started it, used to be a professional baseball player. Andy Owens. Ever hear of him?"

Santiago shook his head.

"Well, anyway, he's pretty famous. He used to pitch for the New York Mets. He loves sports, especially baseball. How 'bout you? Do you like baseball?"

"No I like soccer."

"Andy loves all sports," Rachel said, spinning it to entice him. "From what I understand some of the boys play soccer, too. Is that something that might interest you?"

"Uh-huh. I carry my soccer ball all the way from El Salvador. But someone stealed it in the first day I be in California."

"Oh, Santiago, that's horrible. You must feel so sad. I had no idea you liked soccer. I bet you're pretty good at it."

"My father teached to me." With that memory, Santiago's fingers tightened into fists and his face scrunched up trying to hold back the tears.

Rachel quickly changed the subject. "You'll live in a nice cottage with boys your age. Some, I'm guessing, even go to Benson Middle School, same as you. Would you like me to drive you to the ranch? We can hang-out there today. Kind of look around."

With his emotions bottled up inside, Santiago gave his customary non-committal shrug. So much was happening at once. At last, he said what was on his mind. "If I move, Mamá, she won't know where to find me."

"You're right. We'll have to call her. Make sure she knows where you are. Then she can stop worrying about you . . . and you can stop worrying about her."

Chapter 32

Visit to Bar 8 Ranch

A S RACHEL AND SANTIAGO drove up the mountain, a vicious sandstorm developed out of nowhere. Tumbleweed flew helter-skelter across the road. Rachel's vision grew sketchy. From the sand and dust, she could barely make out the mustard yellow color of her Volkswagen Rabbit convertible. She wondered what damage it was doing to the car's black canvas top. The high desert landscape looked bleak, except for the yucca trees—with their dagger-like spikes, the mesquite, and the ever-present tumbleweed. While they climbed another thousand feet on curvy mountain roads towards Sky Valley, Santiago sat quietly, picking at the skin around his nails. Fortunately, the sandstorm passed as suddenly as it started.

Although Rachel had been focused on her driving, she almost missed the inconspicuous, sun-bleached sign that read Bar 8 Boys' Ranch and showed a faded red arrow. She turned off the road and pulled up to a rusted entry gate. A copse of tall tamarisk trees stood like sentinels on either side, providing a modicum of privacy from those passing. She turned off the motor and slipped out of the car. She swung the creaky gate open, securing it on a wooden post with a thistle rope. Not bothering to close the gate, she concentrated on driving down the crunchy, gravel road that led into a protected valley.

Rachel spotted an inconspicuous wooden sign tacked to a tree. It said office and pointed to a large trailer two hundred feet away. Well, this is it. Are you ready to look around?"

Feeling alone and forsaken, Santiago bit his lower lip and shrugged. "Yes," he said meekly, knowing what was expected of him. Without realizing it, Rachel had become his anchor, his protector, and his security blanket. She had become the center of his small universe.

They climbed two wobbly wooden steps leading to a partially opened sliding glass door. Inside the office trailer, Andy Owens pushed his chair back and rose from his desk. He was a tall muscular man with black hair slicked back, and enormous hands that could easily wrap around a baseball. He shook hands with Rachel and attempted to shake Santiago's hand.

Santiago, whose hands were sweaty from nerves, recoiled. He thought Andy a giant, with the lightest blue eyes he had ever seen.

"Welcome. Please . . . have a seat." Andy's eyes sparkled through his clear glass aviator frames. "Glad to meet you both. Suppose ya'll call me Andy."

Rachel appreciated his informality.

After some generalized chitchat about his baseball career, he looked directly at Santiago. "Hey kiddo, want to see what's around here? I know you'll love it. Afterwards we can come back to the office, and I'll answer your questions. How's that?"

Not realizing it was Santiago's chance to connect with Andy, Rachel interrupted. "Truthfully, until a few days ago, I didn't even know this place existed. I think we'd both love to look around."

Naturally shy—and without the English words to express his uneasiness—Santiago had no choice, but to remain silent.

Finally, Andy stood, indicating they were about to walk the

property. He grabbed his royal blue and orange Met's cap off the wooden coat rack near the door. "Let's go, Biloxi," he said, clapping his hands. When the lethargic basset hound rose from her wicker bed behind his desk, Andy noticed Santiago step back. "Biloxi won't hurt you. She's perfectly harmless."

"Funny name," Rachel commented.

"I named her after my hometown. In case you couldn't tell by my accent, I'm from good ol' Mississippi."

Once outdoors, Andy pulled his handkerchief from his pocket and casually wiped his glasses. When he put them back on, the lenses were a bronze color. The change did not go unnoticed by Santiago, who was intrigued by Andy's eyes. He remembered them being blue. Now he couldn't even see Andy's eyes through the colored lenses.

Biloxi tagged alongside as they headed down the lane towards Cottage B—the building that housed thirteen to fifteen-year-olds. In the cottage, four separate bedrooms, plus the house father's room, surrounded a central living area. As they entered one of the bedrooms, Andy said, "This is it. If you like it here, Santiago, you'll be sharing this room with Jimmy. You'd have your own dresser and desk. Take a look at that bulletin board. *Pretty snazzy, isn't it?*"

Confused by the word *snazzy*, Santiago said nothing. But he did notice Andy's glasses were clear again.

"Jimmy's a pretty nice fella. Loves horses. I'm willin' to bet that right now he's down at the barn or over at the corral talkin' to the horses." Then, as an afterthought Andy asked, "Have you ever ridden a horse?"

"No," Santiago said, shaking his head back and forth.

Just as they were about to walk outside, they ran into another boy, with a little more heft than Santiago. "Hey, Michael, how's it going?"

"Good."

"Santiago, this is Michael. Michael, this is Santiago. He may be bunkin' with Jimmy."

Michael smiled at him and said nothing.

As they ambled over to the dining hall, Andy greeted a few more boys by name. The dining hall was light and bright, with refectory tables and long wooden benches. Colorful drawings of Christmas trees were pinned to a handful of bulletin boards, strategically placed between the long, rectangular windows. Several home-made mobiles left over from Thanksgiving hung from the ceiling. The sweet, intoxicating aroma of freshly baked cookies wafted through the dining room.

Santiago, fixated on Andy's glasses, noticing that they were clear again.

When they stepped into the kitchen—the largest one Santiago had ever seen—Andy introduced Rachel and Santiago to his wife Jenny and two of the older boys. The tall one in a white tee-shirt and red apron was kneading dough, and a younger boy was peeling potatoes. Jenny had just removed several batches of chocolate chip cookies from the oven and was sliding them onto metal racks to cool.

"Nice to meet you," Jenny said. "Here. Take a cookie. But be careful, they're still hot. It can burn your mouth."

Not sure what to do, Santiago looked at Rachel.

Andy said, "Aw, go ahead. Take one. It's fine." As Santiago began to chew the cookie, Andy tousled his hair. "Isn't that the best cookie you ever tasted?"

Santiago flinched and stepped away, resenting his familiarity. Although the piping hot chocolate chip cookie burned his tongue, it truly was the sweetest thing he had ever tasted. From a window in the kitchen, he spotted a group of boys playing basketball.

As they continued the tour, Rachel kept stride with Andy; Biloxi and Santiago slogged behind. Rachel sensed that Santiago was growing tired and couldn't process too much more. She stopped and waited for him to catch up. When they neared a small building behind a windscreen of tamarisk trees, they heard the rhythmic clanking coming from the washers and dryers.

Andy explained, "This here's the laundry room. Check out

that wall chart. You'll see that every cottage does their wash on different days. Billy, he's a senior in high school, well, he's sorting clothes into different baskets."

Santiago—who never thought about changing clothes—was inattentive. When they reached the corral, Santiago hung back. The size and bulk of the horses frightened him. Sure enough, Jimmy, who was to be his new roommate, had been checking on the animals' water supply. When Santiago was introduced, Jimmy sized him up and nodded.

Santiago lost interest in Jimmy and the horses. Once again, he was staring at the lenses on Andy's glasses. Inside the cottage and the laundry room they were light. Now they were dark again. He had never seen anything like that and convinced himself that Andy had magical powers.

The vegetable garden, not far from the barn, was fenced in with two layers of chicken wire. Right before Halloween, several of the boys made two scarecrows out of old clothes and straw. A bit faded and disheveled with old straw hats, they were staked at opposite ends of the garden, between the lettuce and tomato plants. "We try to grow some of our own vegetables, but the damn jackrabbits . . . Oops! Excuse me for swearin', but those cute little critters somehow get in and eat everything in sight."

Santiago heard the squawking chickens on the other side of the dirt road. When he glanced over, he saw them scratching at some scraps of left-over food. Still haunted by the vision of the chickens pecking at his father's dead body, Santiago thought he might throw up right then and there. He turned his body away from everyone, covered his mouth with his hand, and lowered his head towards the ground. He tried to stem the flow of tears gathering in his eyes.

Sensitive to his every move, Rachel approached him. "Santiago, are you okay?"

Not wanting to talk about it, he just shrugged.

Oblivious to Santiago's problem, Andy continued talking. "In the morning, the boys walk up to the main road. School buses come by at various times. They drop the boys off at different schools. Did you notice the van in the driveway? Someone from here, usually my wife or me—sometimes both of us—pick the boys up if they stay after school for sports or other activities."

On their drive back to his apartment, Santiago was once again picking at the skin around his nails. Rachel sensed something sad clouded his mind. Intuitively she knew he wasn't inclined to talk about it. Trying to distract him, she said, "I grew up in San Francisco. It's a big city. When I was your age, I always wished I could grow vegetables in a big garden."

"My mother, she gots a garden." Then he clammed up again, lost in a kaleidoscope of bad memories.

Rachel changed the subject. "Tell me again, Santiago, where'd you live in El Salvador?"

"Quezaltepeque."

"What does Quezal..." and she stumbled trying to remember the whole word.

"Quezaltepeque," he corrected.

"Sorry, my Spanish is pretty bad. What's it mean?"

"Quezal is bird. Tepeque, hills."

"Ah, I get it. Birds in the hills. Do you miss living there?"

"All the time."

"What'd you miss most?"

"My *familia*. My father, *Mamá* and my brother, Javier."

"I didn't know you had a brother. You never mentioned it before. Where does he live?"

"Tijuana. He gots a girlfriend."

Rachel felt his deep longing but chose not to dwell on it. "Tell me about Quezaltepeque? Do you still remember it?"

"The parrots. Sometimes in the day, they fly to our big tree."

"Oh, I bet that was beautiful. What about friends? Did you have friends there?"

Santiago surprised her again by opening-up a bit. "Francisco, he be my best friend. All the time, after school we play soccer.

When I leave, he give to me his soccer shirt. With Pele's number."

"Wow! Your friend sounds like a pretty nice guy."

"But Mamá, she make me to leave the shirt in Tijuana."

Rachel didn't understand why and thought better than to ask. *There is so much about him I don't know.*

Chapter 33

Call to Detention Center

O N THE REMAINDER of the drive back from visiting the Bar 8 Ranch, Santiago once again turned inward. Rachel garnered what little information he shared. She surmised that his revelation about his friend and the soccer shirt set off a series of memories. But she had no idea what was on his mind. Physically, she thought he resembled a pathetic ragamuffin, desperately in need of clean clothes and a haircut. Without a mother to fuss over him, she was afraid he would just become another lost soul. The one thing she knew for sure was that he desperately needed to connect with his mother. And Rachel needed to contact her as well. But not for the same reasons. She needed to let Rosa know where her son would be living.

The only thing that put a smile on Santiago's face, was when Rachel announced that they would call his mother as soon as they got to his apartment.

His eyes came alive. "Really! I want to talk to my her. Can I talk to her first?"

"Absolutely," she said, hoping this would be a defining moment.

As they entered his disheveled apartment, Rachel pulled the telephone number for Apple Valley Detention Center out of her shoulder bag and laid the paper on the plastic garden table.

"Santiago, would you open the blinds? I can hardly make out the numbers."

That was simply a ruse. Rachel could see well enough but felt claustrophobic in the dark, closed-off apartment that smelled of stale air.

She punched in the number, but the phone didn't connect. She repeated the process several more times and got the same results. Then it occurred to her that the telephone had been disconnected.

"I'm so sorry, Santiago. Your phone isn't working. We can't call today. But I promise you, I'll see to it that you talk to her real soon."

Santiago fought back tears. Rachel felt terrible. She knew she had let him down. To brighten his mood, she took him to McDonald's for an early supper. Afterwards, they stopped at the market, and she bought him more milk, bread, fruit, cookies, and another big jar of peanut butter.

The following morning after she showered and dressed, Rachel tried to reach Rosa again. This time without Santiago. She didn't want to disappoint him again if it went wrong. She placed the call to the Apple Valley Detention Center from her condominium. She expected a little bureaucratic run-around, but nothing like what she got. It took patience to finally get to the right department.

"I need to speak to Rosa Lopez, a *detainee* at your facility. How can I reach her? Yes. It's a personal matter. Very important."

"Ma'am, you can't just call her. It's not that simple. There's a process. She's gotta call *you*. Can you hold the line a sec? Let me check the computer. I'll see if she's got a calling card?" More than a minute passed. "I'm looking at the screen and I see she don't have a calling card. And there's zero money in her account to buy one. If you want to talk to her, you'll need to send her money."

"Come on. That's ridiculous. I just want to let her know her son's okay. He's going to be moving. And she needs to know where. Look, I've got to know how long she's going to be there. I don't know what to do with her apartment. With all her stuff."

"I understand, ma'am, but that's our procedure. We got close to a thousand beds here. *Detainees* from all over the world. And everyone wants to talk on the phone."

Rachel didn't like the connotation of the word *detainee* any more than she liked being called *ma'am*, but both were facts of life. "Okay. Just tell me what I need to do to get her a calling card or whatever?"

"Ma'am, I just told you. If you want to talk to Rosa Lopez, you'll need to deposit money in her general account, so she can purchase a calling card."

"I get it. But who do I make the check out to?"

"Sorry ma'am, no credit cards. No checks. We don't accept personal checks or payroll checks. We only accept checks from Federal, State, City and County Agencies. If you're planning to send money, it must be a money order. And those can only be from the U.S. Postal Service or Western Union. The only other way to give a *detainee* money, is to come directly to our facility on a visitation day. There's a machine in our lobby that allows you to deposit cash directly into her account. But before you do any of that, you need her *alien number*?"

Rachel massaged her forehead. "Can you give me her *alien number*?"

"Yes, Ma'am. Got a pencil and paper?"

"Yep. I'm ready."

"Her alien number is A-10349795."

"Let me repeat that to make sure I got it right. A-10349975."

"No. No." He repeated the series of numbers, and she finally got all the digits in the right order.

"Let me be clear," Rachel said. "Rosa needs money in a personal account before she can call anyone outside the detention center. Do I have that correct?"

"Yes, ma'am. You got that correct."

Frustrated with the bureaucracy, Rachel took a deep breath. "Okay. Okay. Suppose I just send her a letter?"

"Easier," the detached voice responded. He repeated the address twice. "Ma'am, if you send her a letter, make sure you add that *alien* number. There may be more than one Rosa Lopez in here."

It was getting too complicated. Rachel realized that a letter was too impersonal. She needed feed-back. Besides, she promised Santiago he could talk to her. So many thoughts raced through her head. On a deeper level, something else bothered her. *The alien numbers. By giving Rosa alien numbers, the authorities succeeded in stripping her of her identity. No longer a person, she was just a catalogue number in a warehouse. It reminded Rachel of the Nazi concentration camps that she had read about, where they tattooed numbers on each prisoner's arm.*

"If I drive there, will I be able to see her?"

"Yes, but you can't just go any old time. We got set hours and days. No visitors on Tuesdays or Wednesdays except attorneys. On other days you can visit for almost an hour. Visitations run from 8:00 to 11:00 a.m. and again from 1:00 to 4:00 p.m. But you've gotta make an appointment."

"Okay," Rachel said in a clipped tone. "I'll get back to you on that." *She didn't want to make an appointment to see Rosa until she got Santiago settled. So much was still in limbo.*

After she hung up, Rachel decided to join Stuart for lunch. In the resort's dining room, she poured her heart out. She spoke about the detention center, Santiago, the apartment, and the Bar 8 Ranch for Boys. Stuart listened attentively, only interrupting her when he couldn't follow the thread. "Look, I know I've said this before, but why don't you butt out? Let someone else handle it? You're just a teacher, not a social worker."

"Funny you should say that. I used to think I was just a teacher. But that's not true. Something changed my mind. When we were living in Reno, a cute little girl in my class told me it was her birthday. I wished her a happy birthday and let it go at that. The next day I asked her what she did for her birthday, thinking of the three-day celebrations we used to have when our kids were little. Cakes and parties and grandparents. That girl had tears in her eyes and such a sad face. She told me her mother—who I happened to know was single—didn't get home 'til later that night. She had to work the four-to-midnight shift at one of the casinos. That's when I realized I had to make those kids feel special. For the most part, I saw them more than their parents. And everything they needed, wasn't found in a textbook."

"Look, I get it. But he's not your responsibility. We've got three kids of our own. Isn't that enough."

"Yes, and they're doing fine. Thank God, I don't have to micro-manage their lives. Tell me . . . what better use of my time can there be? No one really gives a bleep about this kid except me. If I abandon him now, he'll just be another statistic, another kid lost in a bureaucratic maze. And maybe his mother would never find him again."

"Look, Rachel, you can't save the world."

"That's not the point . . . and you know it. He needs a place to live, and his mother deserves to know where he's at. That's it. But I can't get through to his mother. The detention center has the dumbest system I've ever heard of. I can't call her. And she can't call me unless she has money in her stupid account. It's a Catch-22. She's being treated like Jack the Ripper."

"Don't exaggerate."

"I'm not! She's done nothing wrong. All she ever wanted, was a safe place to live. Why's that a crime? You know as well as I do that everyone loves hiring the illegal immigrants. They get paid *bupkas*, nothing, to do our dirty work. So, why's she being treated like a murderer?"

"Okay. Calm down. Let's take this one step at a time. She's not in jail; she's in a detention center, right?"

"Same thing. It's just a euphemism for prison." Rachel's throat clamped shut and she started to cough. For the moment, she stopped talking to drink some water.

"Are you okay?"

"Yeah, I'm fine. But that poor lady. One minute they treat her like a prisoner and the next minute they make her pay for her calls . . . as if she was staying at the Four Seasons. Santiago's mother must be freaking out with worry. I've got to tell her where her son's going to live."

Chapter 34

Bar 8 Boys' Ranch

Wednesday, December 20

REGARDLESS OF STUART'S admonishment to back off, Rachel got caught up in helping Santiago make the transition to the boys' ranch. "Today's an important day. Santiago," Rachel remarked, hoping to put a positive spin on his move. "I need to tell the apartment manager you're leaving." Frankly, she didn't think there was much in Rosa's apartment worth keeping but thought it better to ask. "Is there anything special you want to take with you?"

For the moment, he stood still, a pensive look on his face. "*Mamá's* rosary. I give to her when she come home."

"That's all? Any books or toys?"

"*Nada*. Oh, maybe I take my Superman comic book."

"That's it?"

Neither of them knew about Rosa's nest egg, the money she hid in a shoebox on the top shelf in the closet. Hard earned money she had been saving to buy a car.

"Don't forget, we've got to tell the people that count on you to babysit. Tell them that you can't do it anymore. I'll go with you, but remember, I don't speak Spanish. So . . . you'll have to do all the talking."

As they climbed the exterior stairs, Santiago tried to explain that he and his mother stayed with Nacho and Yolanda for over a year. He thought they were some sort of relative, but he didn't know exactly how.

When Nacho opened the door, Rachel was relieved to discovered that he spoke English. Despite his heavy accent, she grasped most of what he was saying. She explained that she was Santiago's teacher, and she was taking him to live at the Boys' Ranch temporarily.

Naturally curious about Santiago, Nacho invited the two in. His wife was working, but he knew that she'd want to know all the details. For the moment, he set aside the loss of his minivan and his anger towards Rosa. Even though Santiago had nothing to do with it, his presence jogged Nacho's memory. It reminded him of Rosa and the time he loaned her his minivan. When she didn't return, he waited a few days figuring either she was in an accident or arrested. But it took him weeks and weeks to track down his minivan. When he finally located it and discovered how much the storage fees were, he figured he was better off buying another minivan.

"Have a seat," he said, trying to be hospitable. He grabbed a notepad and pencil by the telephone and jotted down Rachel's telephone number and that of the Bar 8 Boys' Ranch.

"When we're finished in the apartment, I'll leave the door unlocked," Rachel explained. "You know Rosa. Take whatever you think she might need from the apartment. I suspect that if no one picks up the furnishings, the manager will dump 'em. He'll probably want to re-rent the apartment as soon as he can."

"Oh," Nacho said, almost as an afterthought, "Santiago, we got a letter from your brother. He probably thought you and your mom still lived here. It's here in the kitchen somewhere. I'll look in the drawers. We've been meaning to give it to you."

"From Javier?"

"Yeah, from Javier."

Nacho and Rachel stood back and watched, as Santiago took the letter and ripped it open. "Look! A picture of a baby. Javier gots a baby!"

They all focused on the small photograph. "Wow! By the looks of it, she must have just been born. Does she have a name?" Rachel asked.

"Annamaria."

"Don't lose the letter. When you show your mom, she'll be so happy."

After contacting the parents that Santiago would no longer be babysitting, Rachel drove Santiago to the new Walmart. She grabbed a shopping cart and made a beeline for the boys' department. As far as she was concerned, he needed a fresh start: new shirts, a couple of pairs of jeans, a jacket, underwear, pajamas, the works. She eyeballed his size and, except for the tennis shoes, didn't expect him to try on each item. Anything fresh and clean would be an improvement. "How about a baseball hat?"

His response lacked enthusiasm.

"Let's see if this one fits," Rachel said, taking an orange and black San Francisco Giants hat off the shelf. "Let's take it. The Giants are my favorite baseball team." It was obvious she was having more fun than he was. As she rolled the shopping cart towards the cashiers, they passed the sporting goods department. At the end of the aisle was a large display of soccer balls.

"Santiago, why don't you pick out a soccer ball? It will make up for the one that got stolen."

Suddenly his eyes brightened. This was close to his heart. He touched the soccer balls, comparing one to the other. He had never seen so many in one place, in so many colors. Ultimately, he picked a traditional black and white ball and held on to it. There was no way he was going to dump it in the shopping cart.

Rachel tried hard to engage Santiago in conversation as they drove up the mountain to the Bar 8 Ranch. But true to form,

Santiago responded in one or two words or a neutral shrug. His thoughts were heavy. He feared that he would never see his mother again. And he wasn't sure that the Boys' Ranch was for him. All he knew was the apartment building where he lived. As they turned off the winding road and headed east, down the long-rutted drive-way, Rachel also grew apprehensive. This situation—committing a young boy to live in a group home—was much harder emotion-ally than she thought. Up to this point Rachel felt she was doing the right thing, but suddenly she developed major reservations, *I pray this works out for him. The poor kid has no choice but to trust those of us in on the decisions. It's horrible to put someone in an institution, even though it seems like a wonderful place.*

When Andy heard the wheels of the car crunching along the gravel driveway, he scrambled out of the office to greet them. Bi-loxi followed behind. "Welcome! Welcome!" In an obsequious manner, he dominated the conversation. "God sure did give us another wonderful day, didn't he?" Putting his arm on Santiago's shoulder, Andy said, "We're looking forward to having you as part of our ranch family."

Not liking the touch, Santiago stepped away.

Rachel reached into the back seat of her car and began to pull out the plastic shopping bags with Santiago's new clothes.

"Whoa," Andy cautioned. "I think you'd be better off driving down to the cottage with all those bags." He turned to Santiago. "Man, it sure looks like you've got yourself some new duds."

The stoic expression on Santiago's face indicated he had no understanding of the word *duds*. He stood there in silence, not knowing what to say.

Andy tried to break the obvious tension. Turning to Rachel, he said, "You know, the bright mustard color of your car and the black convertible top reminds me of a giant bumble bee."

"I've been told that before."

Rachel and Santiago slowly drove down to Cottage B, while Andy and Biloxi followed. As they were unloading and bringing things into the cottage, a dog began to bark furiously.

"Every cottage has its own dog or cat to care for. Don't you worry, Santiago, Tippy's bark's bigger than his bite. He's just saying hello to Biloxi. They're old friends."

Then, in an aside to Rachel—as if Santiago couldn't hear—he said, "It's good for the boys to learn to care for the animals. Gives 'em responsibility. Also gives 'em someone special to love."

Santiago wasn't convinced. Pets weren't his thing.

Considering eight teenage boys lived there, the cottage was neat and orderly. Tippy, the cottage mutt, had an oval-shaped wicker basket topped with a soft, plaid blanket, set right outside the house father's bedroom.

"Well, Santiago, this is it. Your bedroom." Andy enthused.

Santiago, unconsciously picking at the skin around his nails, eyed the room with caution.

"Looks pretty nice," Rachel remarked. "When I was your age, I always wanted a bulletin board. You know, I never did get one." She began organizing his new clothes on the bed. "I need to remove these tags. Andy, do you have a scissors I can borrow?"

"Sure. I'll get it. It'll just take a sec. Tomorrow the house father will label Santiago's things, so they don't get mixed up with someone else's in the laundry."

"Sorry. I never thought about that."

"No problem. We do it for all the boys." With his master key, Andy trod across the cottage's living room and unlocked the house father's bedroom door. He grabbed a pair of scissors from inside the desk. As Rachel removed the prices and stickers on the clothes, she handed them to Santiago to put in his dresser. *It's déjà vu, like helping my kids when they went off to college. Then she thought, but this is different. There's no going home for Thanksgiving and Christmas. This will be Santiago's permanent home. A bed, a dresser, a desk, and a bulletin board. Nothing more.*

Santiago placed his treasures—the Superman comic, the letter from Javier, and his mother's rosary—in the corner of the top drawer along with his new socks, shorts, and pajamas. Then, not knowing what to do with the new soccer ball he had been holding, he dropped it on his crisply made bed.

With one fell swoop, Andy wrapped his long fingers around the ball with one hand and slid it under his other arm. "Listen, Santiago," he said in that slow southern drawl, "you want to keep this, I know, but around here, I've found too many boys fighting over a ball. Mark my word, it'll be better if we just toss it in with our other sports equipment. There's a sign-up sheet. You can get it out any time you want. But, so can the other boys. We're a community here. We need to share everything."

Santiago blinked his eyes to hold back the tears. His fists tightened. Disappointment and anger consumed him. "But it's mine! She gave it to me," he snapped, too shy to use his teacher's name.

"Oh, Santiago," Rachel interjected, "I'm so sorry. I didn't know the rules. It's my fault. It'll all work out. You'll see. But sweetheart, please call me Rachel. We're good friends now. Will you be okay with that?"

Ignoring what she said, he responded sharply, "She gave it to me!" Then he raised his voice even higher. "Rachel gave it to me!"

"Buddy, you'll be fine. You'll get to know our rules and routine. Understand how it works around here. And when you do, trust me, you'll feel a whole lot better than you're feeling now."

Rachel felt horrible that she had given Santiago the ball only to have it taken away. She knew what it meant to him. On the other hand, she couldn't argue with Andy. She saw his point. She felt guilty, as if she had set Santiago up for a major disappointment, on the one day he needed positive reinforcement. She had wanted the transition to go smoothly.

As if on cue, Andy's wife entered the cottage. "Hi, Santiago. Remember me? I'm the lady in the kitchen. The one that gave you a cookie. Remember that?"

"Uh huh."

"Why don't you walk over to the kitchen with me. I'm shorthanded and really could use some help making some sugar cookies for tonight's dinner."

That was the signal for Rachel to leave. "Oh, that ought to be fun," Rachel said, hoping this distraction would preoccupy him as she slipped away. "Lucky you," she said, trying to pacify him. "I remember how good those cookies were. Santiago, I'm going to say good-bye to you now. But I'll be back soon. I promise. How about a big hug?"

Santiago, frightened and still brooding over the soccer ball, allowed Rachel to hug him but he didn't hug her back, even though she was the only kind and steady person in his small universe.

"Santiago, I'm expecting to see you in class after Christmas vacation, okay?"

Andy walked her to her car. Just before she climbed in, he gave her some last-minute instructions. "Don't send anything or visit Santiago for at least three weeks. He needs time to acclimate to his new surroundings, make friends, you know, learn the ropes."

"But it's almost Christmas. He won't have anything to open."

"We'll take care of it. We take the boys on some special outing and give them each a small sum of money to buy something." Always needing more money, Andy added, "If you want, you can send us a check and we'll add it to our Christmas fund."

Rachel had an empty feeling as she drove away. She opened the window, switched on the car radio, and listened to Michael Bolton singing *Love is a Wonderful Thing*. But her head felt heavy. She longed for peace and quiet. Feeling empty, she snapped off the radio, preferring silence. Deep down she wondered if she made the right choice for Santiago.

She had an uncanny ability to see things from more than one point of view. And that invariably created a problem. Rachel had a horrible time making choices in her own life, much less for someone else. But truth be told, she didn't think there was any alternative. *What do you do with a kid that has been living alone?* On reflection, she wondered how she got so involved in the first place. She hated to admit it, but maybe Stuart was right. Maybe a social worker should have handled Santiago's situation.

Chapter 35

Santiago's First Night

Sky Valley, California

AFTER RACHESL'S EMOTIONAL good-bye, Andy's wife Jenny tried to ease Santiago into the Bar 8 routine. She insisted Santiago walk with her to the dining room kitchen. Many of the boys she dealt with on a day-to-day basis had never experienced a positive home life and lacked rudimentary kitchen skills. He watched as she showed him how to take a large spoonful of cookie dough and arrange it in even rows on the oversized cookie sheets. Then she handed him the spoon to try it on his own.

On edge, Santiago jumped when he heard the shrill sound of the five-thirty buzzer announcing dinner. In the dining room, he and Jenny stood to one side listening to the clamor as the boys filed in and picked up a tray.

A young man, wearing a tee-shirt that said *staff* across the chest, came up and introduced himself to Santiago. "Hey, buddy, I'm Ted. You must be Santiago. I hear you're going to be bunking in my cottage. See you after dinner, okay? We can walk back to the cottage together."

"That's Ted," Jenny explained. "He's in charge of your cottage. A real nice guy. You'll like him."

At the tail end of the cafeteria line, Jenny showed Santiago what to do. He recoiled when he saw the chicken fried steak with thick brownish gravy, mashed potatoes, and carrots she had scooped onto his plate. She led him to the Cottage B table.

After everyone said grace, Andy rose from his chair, raised his hand, and blew a shrill whistle. When the boys settled down, he said, "I've got an announcement. We've got a new member of our Bar 8 family. Santiago Lopez. Santiago, please stand up."

Santiago looked to Jenny for direction, and she nodded. Feeling awkward and shy, he rose slowly.

"How about a big Bar 8 welcome. Let's hear the big hello for Santiago."

In the crowded dining room, the boys shouted, "Hello, Santiago" so loud that it echoed off the walls.

"That was nice. Good job everybody. Since it's Christmas vacation, ya'll have plenty of time to introduce yourselves. Santiago loves to play soccer. I know ya'll be kind and include him in your games. You know, show him the ropes. Okay . . . Santiago, you can sit back down." Then Andy continues with his announcements. "Now then, tomorrow the boys from Cottage D will be helping me set up our Christmas tree. After breakfast tomorrow, anyone who's interested in making decorations should remain in the dining room. Jenny has some things for ya'll to make for the Christmas tree. And everyone, from all cottages are welcome to join in."

Jenny continued to stand behind Santiago, feeling it was up to her to keep a watchful eye on him. She touched his shoulder and introduced him to the boys sitting next to him. "Malcolm, Damian, Earl, this is Santiago. You're all in the same cottage. And

Santiago, that's your roommate Jimmy . . . sitting down at the end in the white tee-shirt, next to Eduardo."

Above the clamor, Jimmy heard his name mentioned and looked over.

"Jimmy, you'll be in-charge of Santiago. Make him feel welcome."

Jimmy scowled and jammed a fork full of mashed potatoes into his mouth.

Andy insisted on routines. After dinner, the boys from Cottage C washed tables and trays. Those in Cottage D helped clean up the serving station, wrapped the food and put it away. The rest of the boys squeezed in a little more play time. Even though they were on vacation, the boys maintained the same rigid schedule. From 8:00 p.m. to 9:00 p.m. was supposed to be a quiet hour, reserved for homework or reading. The boys were expected to be washed up and in their beds by 9:30 p.m. except the older ones, who could read for an additional half hour before lights out.

As Santiago completed day one at Bar 8 Ranch, he began to undress and get ready for bed. His roommate Jimmy stared at him coldly. "Hey, Santiago," he taunted, "your dick's the size of a peanut. And you got no balls. What's with that long hair? You look like a girl."

Fearful of a fight, Santiago simply told him to shut up. He quickly put on his new pajamas, carelessly threw his clothes over the desk chair, and climbed into bed.

But Jimmy continued to needle him. "You know, I ain't never slept in the same room as a spick before."

"Shut up, stupid. Leave me alone."

"Don't call me stupid. Why are you here, anyway?"

Santiago didn't know how to answer. He withheld the information about his father being murdered. He didn't want Jimmy to desecrate that memory. "My mother, she gots picked up by the police. She's in a detention place."

"Oh . . . now I get it," Jimmy mocked. "A couple of wetbacks."

Santiago was afraid to tangle with him. "Shut up. Leave me alone."

"Leave me alone; leave me alone," Jimmy taunted. "You know, you're a little pussy, a wuss!" Once Jimmy's adrenaline started pumping, there was no stopping him. Seeing that he had the upper hand, he sprang from his bed and started to rummage through the top drawer in Santiago's dresser. "Lookie here. Lookie here," he mocked, holding up the Superman comic book. "Look what I found."

"Put it down!"

"Don't tell me, you believe that someday Superman's gonna swoop down and save your sorry little ass. I bet you still believe in Santa Claus." With that, he ripped the comic book in half.

Santiago jumped out of bed and tried to shove Jimmy away from his things. But Jimmy was stronger and stood his ground.

"That's my mother's rosary! Please . . . don't touch it. Give it to me."

"Ohhhh . . . a little Jesus bracelet, how sweet. Hey, pussy, just so you know, that Jesus thing never works out."

Just before Ted, their house father, charged through the boys' bedroom door to break up the ruckus, Jimmy had pulled the rosary apart. Beads were bouncing in all directions on the linoleum floor. "Hey, you guys, knock it off!" He separated them. One in a rage and the other with an avalanche of tears streaming down his cheeks. "Jimmy, calm down and go to my room!"

"Santiago, I'll help you pick up the beads in a second. First, I've got to deal with Jimmy." In an authoritative voice, Ted said, "Jimmy, we're trading beds for the night. You'll sleep in my room, and I'll sleep here."

When Jimmy started to mouth off, Ted raised his voice. "Get to my room. NOW!"

Some boys in the cottage heard the commotion and gathered outside the bedroom to see what was happening. "Everything's fine," Ted barked, "now get back to your rooms. Shifting to a gentler tone, he talked to Santiago who had been sobbing quietly. "I'll help you pick up the beads. Get a pair of your socks. For now, we'll stuff the beads in the socks, okay? We can try to restring them in the morning."

Ted bounced back and forth between rooms, trying to calm both boys. He sat on the side of Santiago's bed. "Tomorrow I'll find you another roommate . . . in a different cottage." He understood many boys who had been placed at the ranch had emotional problems, some worse than others. It was not unusual for fights to break out. When he thought that all the boys had quieted down, he climbed into Jimmy's bed and fell fast asleep.

Still revved, Santiago couldn't sleep. His mind raced, and his heart thumped hard against his chest. *Rachel left me here. That big man swiped my soccer ball. My roommate picked a fight and wrecked my mother's rosary. All I heard all day long was cottage this . . . and cottage that. The food stinks. That big glob of something was awful, nothing like my mom's cooking.*

Frightened, Santiago thought that Jimmy or one of the other boys would pounce on him in the morning. He just wanted to run away. As soon as he heard Ted snoring, he crept out of bed quietly. Without turning on the light, he fumbled for his jeans and the long-sleeved shirt that he had tossed over the desk chair earlier. He nabbed his new tennis shoes that were tucked half-way under the desk. On cat-feet Santiago tip-toed out of the unlocked cottage, not quite closing the door behind him. It took a while for his eyes to adjust to the darkness. He found his way to Andy's office.

Santiago's thoughts were jumbled as he slipped his pants and shirt on over his pajamas. He sat down on the wooden steps leading to Andy's mobile office to lace-up his shoes. As he slogged up the steep gravel driveway to the rural road, his teeth chattered in the frigid winter air. He chastised himself for not bringing his jacket. But the one thing he knew for sure, he was never going back to the boys' ranch. He hated it there.

Where should I go? Without a real plan, he only knew two places. The school or the apartment. The fact that it was Christmas vacation posed a problem. Rachel would not be at the school, and he had no idea where she lived. He had neither money nor identification. His breath grew short. He held out his thumb, wanting, needing, hoping for a ride down to Desert Oasis. In El Salvador hitchhiking was a way of life—an alternate means of transportation—but not so in California. He felt the whoosh of a few cars that rushed by him on the narrow road. In the middle of the night, no one was eager to pick up a stranger, a mere silhouette in their headlights.

A daunting wind caused the moon to weave in and out of a series of pewter clouds. Unable to see details, Santiago stepped into a pothole, lost his balance, and stumbled, ripping the skin open on his right hand as he hit the gravel. He forced himself to get up. In a daze, he picked the pebbles from his palms. With no other choice, he placed one foot in front of the other and began the long trek down the winding mountain road towards Desert Oasis.

His jumbled mind bounced from the present to the past and back again. He could still visualize the soldier holding a teacher's head on a stick. And the dead and dying people left in the streets. At times, Santiago wasn't sure if he was hallucinating or not. Sometimes he imagined his father's body floating alongside him, just as it did when he was on the long bus rides from El Salvador. At times, he even heard his father's voice: *Mi hijo, mi hijo, be brave.*

When his thoughts returned to the present, it was worse. He felt scared and alone. He wondered where his mother was. Would he ever see her again? He remembered his friend Francisco and wondered if he was still alive. He missed his brother Javier. Suddenly, he panicked, remembering the letter with the photo of Javier's baby that he left in the cottage. He heard the symphonic howl of coyotes, imagining a pack of them just beyond an outcropping of boulders.

Santiago could hardly contain his fear. Quickening his pace, he didn't slow down until the howls of the coyotes became a faint cry in the distance. In the dark, his hearing perked up. Anything that broke the stillness of the night—a car approaching, a branch snapping—frightened him. In survival mode, he tried, but couldn't convince himself that the mysterious noises were merely jackrabbits scampering under a bush, not rattlesnakes about to strike.

In his misery, he trekked down the hill for hours, wondering when the road would finally level off. He felt the blisters on the bottom of his feet breaking open but could not see or feel the pooling blood. He longed for water to quench his thirst. Periodically he cried for himself and all that had happened, but there was nobody to wipe away his tears. Eventually a pinkish-red ribbon peeked over the hills on the eastern horizon. Gradually the bleakness of night transitioned into morning light. Emotionally and physically drained, he finally felt the soothing warmth of the rising sun.

On the outskirts of town, Santiago recognized a familiar intersection. He figured he could find his way from there. When he finally arrived at his apartment complex, he found the front door locked. Not deterred, he trampled through a bed of half-dead oleander bushes to the front window. It took some ingenuity, but he finally figured out how to remove the broken screen and pry the window open. Weary beyond measure, he climbed into his apartment unit and plopped down on the bed.

With the sweet sense of accomplishment, Santiago finally felt secure. He was home.

Chapter 36

Finding Santiago

Desert Oasis, California

S OMEDAY TED WANTED to become a psychologist, so he
took his job seriously. As was his habit, he awakened earlier
than the boys in his cottage, needing quiet time to organize
his day. It took a second or two before he remembered why he
woke up in one of the boys' rooms instead of his own. *The fight.*
He glanced over at Santiago's bed. Empty. The clothes that had
been tossed so carelessly over Santiago's desk chair the night before, were also gone. Quickly, he put two and two together. Peeking in on the other bedrooms, he found all the boys fast asleep,
including Jimmy, who was in his bed in a fetal position.

Where in the hell did Santiago go? He checked the communal
bathroom but found it empty. He put on his jeans and tennis
shoes, without any socks, and began searching outside. His gut
told him it was possible that Santiago ran away after being bul-
lied by Jimmy. If so, he would not be the first to disappear under

the cover of darkness. Ted chastised himself, thinking he should have done a better job of handling the fight; perhaps counseling Santiago, rather than just breaking up the fight. He knew he needed help and headed over to Jenny and Andy's private cottage.

When Ted knocked on their door, no one stirred. Worried about Santiago and a bit panicky, he pounded harder. Andy, the founder of the boys' ranch and his boss, still in his pajama bottoms, white tee-shirt, and barefoot, finally opened the door. "What's going on?" he asked in a groggy voice.

"Sorry to bother you so early, but Santiago's gone." Ted summarized the situation and brought him up to date. He had broken up a horrible fight the night before. Jimmy had started it and he wouldn't let up on Santiago.

"Okay. We'll deal with Jimmy later. Now. . . about Santiago, the poor kid may just need time to think. Did you check the barn?" Swiping his fingers through his unruly hair, Andy said, "The kid could be anywhere. If we can't find him, we've gotta notify the authorities. But let's not jump the gun." Turning back to his wife, who by this time had put on a bathrobe, Andy said, "Jenny, go up to Ted's cottage and watch the boys." Then back to Ted, he said, "I'll get dressed and meet you in my office. We'll work out a search plan."

Without alarming the boys, Andy and Ted scoured every inch of the ranch, hoping that Santiago simply needed some time to work out his anger. When their search came up empty, they reconvened in Andy's office. "So far we're batting zero. Ted, you need to get back to your boys. I've got one play left. I'm trying to get into Santiago's mind. Maybe he contacted Rachel. You know, the teacher who brought him here. I'll try her one time before calling the police."

Hearing that Santiago ran away, Rachel became visibly upset. "What happened?"

Andy glossed over the fight with his roommate.

Rachel agreed that they should wait before calling the police. She was afraid that if the authorities found him, they'd place him in foster care. "I'll look for him. If I find him, I'll get back to you."

Stuart, who had been in the kitchen making Rachel coffee, overheard her side of the conversation. After hanging up the phone, she turned to him. "Santiago's missing."

Swept up in the drama, Stuart surprised Rachel and himself. "If you're going out to look for him, I'm going with you." Though he'd never actually set eyes on Santiago, he had been following every segment of Santiago's saga, right from the beginning. "But what if we find him? We can't even bring him here, to the resort. You know the rules. No children under eighteen allowed. That's an ironclad rule. We didn't even do it for the judge's daughter."

Rachel panicked. "Oh, God! This is all my fault. I've no idea why he ran away. Maybe he'll go back to the ranch. If not, the welfare department will probably stick him in foster care. And that may or may not be disastrous."

Stuart said, "Don't get ahead of yourself. First we've got to find him."

Still in the same crazy get-up—pants and shirt over pajamas— Santiago simply plopped down on one the unmade single beds in his former apartment and was sound asleep. When he heard the loud, insistent rapping and Rachel's voice, he wasn't sure if he was dreaming or if it was for real. He stumbled to the front door and opened it.

"Santiago, you have no idea how happy I am to see you! You gave us such a scare."

Santiago immediately spotted the unknown man standing slightly behind Rachel and felt threatened. Rachel quickly introduced Santiago to her husband, reassuring him that no harm would come to him.

Stuart didn't know whether to put out his hand for the boy to shake but decided to let it go with a simple smile and a few kind words.

"May we come in?" Rachel asked.

As they stepped into the studio apartment, Stuart couldn't help noticing the disarray. Running a resort, his first instinct was to send someone over from housekeeping to clean everything up but remained silent. *Now wasn't the time.*

"What happened?" Rachel asked. "Why'd you run away? Want to talk about it?"

"No!" Santiago said decisively.

Rachel couldn't help noticing the dirt on his face and hands. Taking charge, she simply said, "Let's clean you up."

He used an almost flat, sliver of soap to remove the grit from his hands, then splashed cold water on his face.

Always the practical one, Stuart reminded Rachel to call the ranch and let them know you found him.

"I can't. The phone's dead. Their service has been cut off. Santiago, do you think we can use your friend's phone? What's his name again? Taco or something."

"Nacho," Santiago corrected.

Within minutes the three of them climbed the flight of stairs to Nacho's apartment.   Yolanda heard the knocking and opened the door. She was startled to see Santiago standing there. Nacho had told her he was going to a boys' ranch. "Santiago, what are you doing here?"

Before he could respond, Rachel intervened. She introduced herself and Stuart. "I think you were out when I met your husband." Cryptically she explained that Santiago had run away from the boys' ranch. "We just found him back in his old apartment. I was wondering if we could use your phone. The phone in his apartment doesn't work. And I need to let the people at the ranch know he's okay. . . I don't want them calling the police."

"Sure. Go ahead. Use my phone." Then she addressed her girls, "Turn off the television. This lady needs to make a very important phone call . . . and she needs quiet. Go play in your room."

Even though the girls knew Santiago, there were suddenly two strangers in their small apartment. By the tone in their mom's voice, they sensed the urgency. They knew better than to argue. The little one touched Santiago's knee, as she trod into their bedroom.

Yolanda, always kind-hearted, had been riddled with guilt for leaving Santiago alone in his apartment after Rosa disappeared. But at the time, she had been overwhelmed, dealing with her own problems. A raging flu had hit her family one-by-one and then her back went out. She was laid up for months. To make matters worse, she had to pacify Nacho, who was infuriated that Rosa was responsible for his minivan being impounded.

Now concerned, she asked, "Santiago, are you okay?"

Santiago nodded. He had no words to describe his feelings. Tired. Angry. Sad. Scared. Lonely.

While Rachel placed the call to Andy, head of the boys' ranch, Yolanda offered Santiago something to eat. "Sit at the table. You must be hungry. She grabbed an orange from a bowl on the counter. Here, eat this while I pour you some milk."

The stress and anxiety of the last twenty-four hours clung to Santiago like a shroud.

"How about some reheated rice and beans? It'll only take a minute to heat up in the microwave."

While Santiago ate, Stuart surveyed their apartment. An artificial Christmas tree, strung with tiny lights and decorated with home-made and store-bought ornaments, stood in the corner of the living room near the front window. A manger with miniature ceramic figurines rested on a side table. As he watched Santiago eat, Stuart realized he too was hungry.

Patting Santiago's shoulder, Rachel said, "Andy and Ted are so relieved we found you. Andy told me he heard about the fight. He promised to move you to another cottage. He thinks you'll be much happier there."

Santiago's hands tightened into fists and tears welled-up in his eyes. Afraid to look at Rachel, he stared down at the emptied glass. Shaking his head back and forth, he finally voiced his opinion. "NO! I no go back! I run away again!"

Chapter 37

Temporary Home

STILL IN YOLANDA'S APARTMENT, Rachel began to panic. *If Santiago didn't go back to the ranch, where was he going to live?* He had nowhere to go. She knew he couldn't stay with her. Even if Stuart would allow it, the resort had a strict rule: no children under eighteen allowed. Running out of ideas, she fell back on the only other option, a foster home.

Unexpectedly, Yolanda popped up with the perfect solution. Responding to Santiago's obvious fear of returning to the boys' ranch, she offered him a way out. "Santiago, if you like, you could stay here. Live with us." Then correcting herself, she added, "Of course, that is until your mom comes home."

"Yes," he said with conviction. "I wanna be here." For Santiago, her invitation was the next best thing to being with his mother.

"You know the girls love you. They always wanted a brother."

Rachel was pleased that he finally had the gumption to speak for himself. She could hardly believe her ears. She thought Yolanda's offer almost too good to be true. A temporary home among familiar people . . . with his own family, no matter how remote. "Are you sure it's okay?"

"Yes, of course. He can sleep here . . . on the couch, like he used to."

"That's wonderful. Just wonderful. Such good news." Suddenly Rachel remembered how this all started, how she got involved in the first place. "But there's a catch. No more babysitting on school days. He needs to go to school regularly. He's already missed way too much. May I make a suggestion?"

Stuart gave her one of his looks, like why don't you quit while you're ahead. But Yolanda indicated she was willing to listen.

"It's just a thought, really. The Boys' and Girls' Club is terrific. They pick the kids up after school. They play games. Do sports stuff. Even help them with their homework. Some of the kids in my class go there after school and they love it. I don't know what they charge but it's probably pretty reasonable."

Stuart surmised that even if the program turned out to be inexpensive, Yolanda couldn't afford it. After all, she had children of her own to contend with. "I've got an idea that should make everyone happy. Yolanda, suppose Rachel and I give you seventy-five dollars a month. You know, for Santiago's room and board . . . and if it works out, to pay the monthly fee for the Boys' and Girls' Club. You're making a huge commitment. Frankly, nobody knows when Santiago's mother will be released." And in front of Santiago, Stuart did not want to state the obvious, *Santiago's mother may well be deported back to El Salvador.*

Overwhelmed by his generosity, Yolanda took to the idea immediately. She figured the Boys' and Girls' Club would keep Santiago busy and out of trouble after school.

"Great. Then it's all settled. Turning to his wife, Stuart said, "I'm starving. You know how I get if I don't eat." Then he directed a question to Santiago, "You must be really tired. Would you like to go out to breakfast with us or stay here and sleep?"

"Sleep."

"That's what I figured."

Yolanda zipped into the girls' room and pulled the cotton Cinderella bedspread, pillow, and sheet off the empty bunk bed in the girls' room. "Here . . . I'll fix up the couch for you."

With no sleep in twenty-four hours, physically exhausted from the hike back to the apartment, and emotionally drained from all the tumult, Santiago jumped at the chance to sleep. As he shed his outer clothes and shoes, everyone realized he was still wearing his pajamas. He climbed under the cover and fell asleep instantly.

In a soft voice Rachel explained to Yolanda that she had bought him some new clothes before he went to live at the boys' ranch. "I'll drive up to the ranch later today and collect them." Then she hugged Yolanda, thanking her profusely for taking Santiago in.

Stuart pulled his brown leather wallet out of his back pocket, peeled off seventy-five dollars, and handed it to Yolanda.

"You know, I would have taken Santiago in for nothing."

Rachel and Stuart had no sooner driven away, when Stuart asked, "What'd you know about the Boys' and Girls' Club?"

"Not much. Why?"

"Well, you seemed to push something you know nothing about."

"It's got to be better than sitting around watching television all day. He's not doing well in school. He needs to run around, be with kids his own age. He likes soccer. Maybe they have a soccer team. In the next few days. I'll find out about their programs. Oh, by the way, where'd your sudden generosity come from? You've done nothing but hound me not to get involved. It's unlike you to be doling out money."

"I don't know. The kid got to me. He looked so . . ." and Stuart searched for the right words, "so lost and pathetic. His father's dead. His mom is in detention. He's got no one. Besides, it'll probably just be for a month or two. We're not exactly rolling in the dough. But we're not paying rent or buying too much food. So, I figured it's not that big a deal."

"Well, well, well, look who turned into a bleeding heart. Tell the truth, don't you feel good about what you just did?" As awful as the day began, Rachel now felt euphoric. Santiago had a safe place to live and—never mind the money. For once Stuart offered to help rather than hassle her about Santiago. Rachel smiled inwardly. *Everything in incremental steps. Stuart has empathy after all.*

Later that afternoon Rachel drove up the mountain to the boys' ranch to collect Santiago's things. Before meeting her in the office, Andy had boxed up Santiago's possessions. He had tucked the letter from Javier inside. His soccer ball rested precariously on top.

"Thanks Andy. One thing's for sure," Rachel said, "he'll be the happiest kid around to get back his soccer ball. I'm sorry that episode with the ball caused him such pain. If I had known the rules, I never would have bought it for him in the first place."

"Well, you meant well."

"He told me that on his first night in the U.S., someone stole his soccer ball, the one he carried all the way from El Salvador. And then you grabbed the second soccer ball right out from under him." Trying to be tactful, she pivoted. "But I totally understand why you had to do it. I can just imagine how many fights start over a bat or a ball. Speaking of fights, besides the soccer ball incident, what'd you think caused Santiago to run away?"

Andy hesitated before speaking. "You know, I made a horrible mistake. Jimmy, his roommate, the one that got into a fight with him, is far more troubled than I thought. I probably shouldn't be telling you this, but maybe you'll understand. Jimmy never knew his father. No one could be sure who is father was. He was shuffled back and forth between his mom, who was heavy into meth, and his grandma. The grandma was also raising her son's two kids. I'm guessing Jimmy was always a handful. When he was almost eleven, his mom drugged him up late one night and drove him to the big shopping center in Palm Desert. She put a gun in his hand and abandoned him."

"Oh, my God! I never heard such a horrible story," Rachel exclaimed, "and I've heard a lot of awful stories. The poor kid could have shot someone or been killed by the police."

"Fortunately, one of the security guards found him. It must have been cold that night. He was curled up next to the loading dock, fast asleep. He didn't remember how he got there. Security took the gun away and called the police. It took some time 'til they located his mother. She was living in some beat-up trailer in Whitewater. Strung out on meth. The cops didn't know what to do with him. They checked on his grandma. And she didn't want the better part of him. Since Jimmy did nothing wrong, the authorities figured he'd be better off living here."

"What happened to his mother?"

"There were some legal proceedings. Technically, Jimmy's a ward of the court. For almost two years, he's had extensive counseling and training in conflict management. He's had some minor run-ins, you know, normal boy's stuff, but nothing like the vicious outburst last night. I'm not sure what set him off. Maybe it hurt him to see all Santiago's new clothes, knowing someone cared for him. Who knows? Maybe one of the bigger and stronger boys picked on him that day. It's hard to say. But I'm sure sorry that he took it out on Santiago. He seems like a nice, quiet kid."

"I feel bad too. I guess I was assuming the boys' ranch was like summer camp, the kind where my kids went. Now I realize you've got your hands full dealing with a bunch of troubled boys."

With his Southern Baptist upbringing, Andy spoke like a true believer. "You've gotta remember, they're all God's children. Someone has to take them in, give 'em a chance. Try to salvage their lives. And somewhere along the way, teach them a few survival skills."

"Andy, my hat's off to you. Your job's way tougher than a teacher's."

By the time Rachel left the ranch it was almost dinner time. She juggled the cardboard box of clothes with the soccer ball up the flight of stairs to Yolanda's apartment, hoping the ball wouldn't roll off the top. She rang the doorbell with her little finger, hoping it could be heard over the blaring television. When Yolanda greeted her at the door, Rachel immediately commented, "What's cooking on the stove? Smells like garlic. I could smell it from the street."

Yolanda wiped her hands on her apron. The edge of her lips turned up into a smile. "I'm making *pollo encebollado*, chicken and onions. Santiago's favorite."

"Oh, it's the onions. Yummy." She picked up the box and brought it in, including the soccer ball.

With his hair still rumpled from sleep, Santiago had been watching cartoons with Yolanda's young daughters. When Santiago eyed the soccer ball on top of the box, he turned away from the television. But out of shyness or politeness, he did not grab it. He waited patiently for Rachel to hand it to him. "The letter from Javier is in the box with your new clothes. Don't lose it. Someday you can show your mom." *Silently, she wondered if that would ever happen.* Rachel only stayed briefly, feeling like her job was complete, at least for the day. However, before saying good-bye, she had an idea. She asked Santiago if he had ever been to a *Star Wars* movie.

"No."

"Well, would you like to see one?"

"Yes. Yes," he said, his face brightening. He had seen so many *Star Wars* advertisements on television.

"Great. That'll be my Christmas present to you. How about the *Return of the Jedi* next Saturday? Just you, me, and Stuart. We'll pick you up and head to the movies.

As Rachel bowed out, she sighed, *Enough for one day.*

Chapter 38

Visit to Detention Center

RACHEL KNEW SANTIAGO would never be happy until his mother returned. And personally, she would feel guilty if she did not drive him to see her at least once now that they knew where she was. She wanted to let his mother know he was okay. Right before Christmas, she punched in the numbers for the Apple Valley Detention Center, bracing herself for another wave of bureaucracy. To her surprise, the call was quickly transferred to the Visitor's Scheduling Department. No longer intimidated, she demanded specific information on what day and time she could take Santiago to see his mother.

"How about some time this week?" Rachel asked, thinking that since it was still Christmas vacation, neither she nor Santiago would miss any school.

"Sorry ma'am. This week, being Christmas and all, it's all booked up"

Rachel sighed. "Well, then . . . when's the next available time?"

"Thursday, January 11th. I got an 11 o'clock slot open."

"Ugh, that's kinda early. We have a three-hour drive to get there." Realizing they didn't care about any inconveniences she might have, she switched gears. "Okay, I'll take it. There'll be two of us."

"Under what names?"

"Santiago Lopez. He's visiting his mother, Rosa Lopez. And me, Rachel Roth. I'll be driving him."

"Ma'am, there's lots of people here named Lopez. I need to make sure we get the right Lopez. By any chance do you happen to have her alien numbers?

Rachel resented his request but was prepared. "As a matter of fact, I do," she said, looking at her notes. "Her alien numbers are A-10340795." Distrustful of the bureaucracy, she asked him to repeat the numbers.

He asked again for their names and spelled them back to her.

"Have you been here before?"

"No. What'd we do when we get there?"

"You'll see a sign. Visitors' Center. Park there. Inside is a registration desk. Have your identification out. After signing in, you'll see a bunch of lockers. You'll need a quarter to lock up your belongings. You can't bring nothing beyond that point. Not even your purse. Just so you know . . . and nothing for the detainees. From there, you'll be guided through the visitation process. Visitors must be dressed appropriately. No shorts. No sandals. No gang colors. No gang displays of any kind."

As soon as she got off the phone, Rachel punched in Yolanda's number. "It's a done deal."

"I'm excited for him."

"That Thursday he's got to be ready no later than seven in the morning."

"We're both going to miss school, but there's nothing I can do about that."

Yolanda wanted Rosa to see for herself that he was being well taken care of. On Sunday, before his visit with his mother, Santiago showered and washed his hair. Afterwards, she wrapped an old towel around his shoulders and trimmed his hair carefully. In addition, she washed and ironed his khaki pants and his new white shirt.

The day before they were to drive to the detention center, Rachel prepared detailed lesson plans for her substitute teacher. That night—feigning a cold—she called the substitute line to have someone take her class the following morning. Technically, it was much easier for Santiago. On the day of their visitation, he simply didn't show up for school.

Early Thursday morning, Yolanda and Santiago were up before everyone else. She saw to it that he showered and washed his hair again. She prepared an unusually hearty breakfast and constantly fussed over him, reassuring him that it would all work out. When Rachel arrived, she too exclaimed, "Wow! Santiago, you look especially handsome this morning. Your mom's going to be so surprised at how much you've grown."

Santiago lowered his eyes self-consciously. But Rachel could tell that underneath his usual reticence, he was excited.

Yolanda wrapped her arm around his shoulder and gave him a big hug. "You watch, Santiago, you are going to make your mother so happy. Do you have the letter from your brother?"

"Here," he said pulling it out of his pocket.

Rachel and Santiago set off on their three-hour drive. From the corner of her eye, Rachel glanced over and saw Santiago nervously picking at the skin around his nails again.

"What are you thinking about?"

"Nothing."

"Oh, come on. You must be thinking about something?"

"Why they put her in detention? What she do bad?"

Rachel didn't have a ready answer. What could she say? *Because of fear and prejudice. Because some people in Congress don't want Hispanics to live here.* "I don't know why," she confessed. "I know your mom's a good person, and so are you. How about a little music? Turn on the radio. That shiny little knob right there," she said pointing. "Pick any station you want."

Not used to choices—not even small ones that most people take for granted—he fiddled with the knob until he recognized some Spanish music.

"Do you know that song?"

"No," he said, smiling shyly.

Rachel let it pass.

The monotonous drive along Route 62—a backroad—went smoothly enough. They saw a few cars and trucks but mostly a vast, empty space pock-marked with desert vegetation—sagebrush, Joshua trees, and cacti—hearty plants able to survive extreme hot and cold temperatures. Every now and then Rachel sped past a rickety old shack that had been pounded to oblivion by the sun and wind. Always curious, she couldn't help wondering what type of person lived there . . . in the middle of nowhere.

After a brief pit stop in Yucca Valley, they headed west on Route 247. At one point a gang of cyclists on Harleys—in black from helmets to boots—revved their engines as they roared by. As the motorcycles faded over a small hillock, Rachel exclaimed, "Did you see those guys? They all looked like Darth Vader."

Santiago smiled, remembering the *Star Wars* movie. "Cool."

As they neared Lucerne Valley, Rachel realized the radio, not Santiago, had been filling the air with noise. "Would you mind turning the radio off now?" Desperate to make conversation, she said, "We're approaching Old Woman Springs Road. Isn't that a funny name?"

"Yeah, weird."

It wasn't exactly a dialogue, but Santiago was communicating. Ever the teacher, Rachel asked, "Do you know what animals live out here in *no-man's-land*?" Then she corrected her use of words. *English has too many idioms.* "Do you know what animals live here in the desert?"

"Coyotes. I hear them when I run away from the ranch. And snakes."

She was surprised that he answered her. "You're right. Owls, mice, and jackrabbits live here too. The coyotes eat the jackrabbits, and the owls eat the rats and mice . . . and spit out the bones."

"Eeew, gross."

Rachel chuckled inwardly at his new vocabulary. *Cool. Weird. Gross.* So American. She surmised that he picked up these words living with Yolanda's girls, who spoke English since birth.

When Rachel and Santiago finally arrived at the Apple Valley Detention Center, she drove through several check points, one with guard dogs. She resented the high level of security, assuming most of the people incarcerated were not hardened criminals. At the Visitors Center, she slipped her Volkswagen into the first open stall and glanced at her watch.

"Well, here we are. Santiago, have you got the letter from your brother?"

He raised the envelope in the air.

"Good."

They had no sooner taken a few steps when Rachel noticed the irony of the place. In front of the Visitors Center, the American flag—the symbol of freedom—billowed and snapped atop the flagpole. *How many people are locked up here?* she wondered. *What about their freedom?*

Even though the sprawling detention center resembled an impenetrable fortress, she tried to put a positive spin on it for Santiago's sake. "Aren't you happy that you're finally going to see your mom?"

The excitement in his eyes and his wide smile told the story.

They eventually caught up with the others as they neared the Visitors' Center. They took their place at the end of a line that crawled out from the double doors at the entrance. When it was finally their turn, Rachel showed her driver's license to the uniformed guard who checked her name off a clipboard that rested on top of his desk.

The man registering people asked, "Is he your son?"

"No," Rachel explained, looking over at Santiago, whose face was a mask. "He's Rosa Lopez's son. I'm his teacher. We're here to visit his mother. Do you need her alien number?"

A burly guard stood nearby, scrutinizing everyone registering. Without saying it, he was letting everyone know this was a serious place and there was no joking around.

Another male guard, with a slight build and coarse black hair, stood further in, constantly repeating his instructions to all that entered. "Purses and wallets . . . and any other possessions must be stowed in one of the lockers before going through the metal detector. And you'll need a quarter to use the locker. If you don't have change, that machine," he said, pointing, "can change paper money into coins."

At a nearby metal table used for just this purpose, Rachel fumbled through her purse and wallet, scrounging for a quarter. *God, they don't even supply a free locker. They're even making money off the visitors.*

When she thought she had followed all the rules, another guard with intense eyes noticed the envelope Santiago was carrying. "You can't bring nothin' in with you. You gotta put that envelope back in the locker."

"WHAT?!" Rachel exclaimed. "Oh, come on. It's just a letter . . . with a photograph. For God's sakes, it's only paper. It's not going to hurt anyone."

"Sorry, ma'am. Rules are rules."

The two of them traipsed out of the line. "I know you're disappointed, Santiago, but you heard the guy. We've got to lock it up. But you can still tell your mother about the baby, okay?"

Once again, they returned to the end of the line. One-by-one, individuals were guided through the metal detector. When it was their turn, Santiago hesitated. He had never gone through one. He looked up at Rachel with a quizzical expression. She could see that he was frightened by the unfamiliar procedures, the intimidating guards, and the metal detector. "Go on. Just walk through it," she urged. "I promise it won't hurt you."

As soon as they passed, another male guard, with a sonorous voice that bellowed off the walls, directed them down the hall to a large windowless waiting room. The uninviting room had harsh, florescent lighting and gray folding chairs arranged in rows, auditorium style.

"Are you okay?"

"Yeah," he said, although Rachel could almost feel his anxiety. "When can I see my mom?"

"Soon. Very soon."

Rachel and Santiago joined the motley mass of humanity. Anticipation and restlessness filled the hot, stuffy room. Scanning the crowded room, she realized the one thing that all the visitors shared was their desire to see a loved one. She imagined that they too had left their homes hours earlier and driven from various parts of California—maybe even from other states—to this desolate destination, even if it was only for one measly hour.

With no magazines or newspapers to scan, or television screen to focus on, the room itself provided the only diversion from the anxiety that was building inside her. A black woman in a splashy, long African print dress, with gold sandals and big gold hoop earrings, was trying to distract her crying baby. A young, well-dressed Latino man, sat pensively, waiting for a sister, girlfriend, or mother. Another man—perhaps in his late twenties—dressed in a white tee-shirt, his hair slicked back with a greasy pomade with a distinctive smell, sat on the other side of Rachel. His constant foot tapping annoyed her, and she had the urge to tell him to stop it.

Rachel wondered how she was going to explain herself to Santiago's mother.

"What time is it?" Santiago asked, growing impatient.

Rachel checked her watch again. Almost 11:00. *I know Santiago's birthday is coming up,* she thought. *Maybe I'll surprise him with a watch.*

Finally, an officious male guard entered the room with a bullhorn that amplified his voice. "When I call your name, walk into the next room. There's no need to push or shove. Stand and wait for the detainees. They'll be brought in shortly."

A middle-age Indian woman dressed in a lime green sari

asked the guard for further instructions. Tired of answering the same questions day-in and day-out, he grew irritated. "Ma'am, like I said, just head through those open doors, okay. Stand there . . . and wait for the detainees to be seated. Then find who you are looking for. Sit in the cubicle directly across from them."

Rachel nudged Santiago. "This is it, kiddo. You'll finally get to see your mom."

Santiago froze.

"Scared?"

"A little."

"It'll be fine," Rachel said, trying to soothe his nerves, although she was edgy herself.

Chapter 39

Santiago Visits his Mother

S TANDING INSIDE the cavernous room, Santiago's stomach was doing cartwheels. Excitement. Fear. Anticipation. Too many people. Too much noise. His eyes blinked like a hummingbird's wings. Rachel touched his arm gently, but he scooted away. He wanted his mother. He longed to hear the reassuring sound of her soft voice. He wanted to hug her, but most of all, he wanted her to come home. He needed her. After what seemed an inordinate amount of time, a set of metal doors clanked open on the other side of the divided room. Two female guards led a single file line of fifteen women into the vast visitors' hall. Nine women shuffled in before Santiago finally spotted his mother.

"There she is! There she is! There's *Mamá*!"

Santiago never took his eyes off her as the gaggle of women plodded along like kindergarteners being led to the lunchroom. She was wearing an orange jumpsuit and her thick black hair was pulled back in a ponytail—like one of the seventh-grade girls in his class. She looked different. Her deep brown eyes, the color of bark on a rainy day, looked sad.

An officer barked directions in English, but Rosa did not fully understand. Since she never had visitors, she didn't understand exactly what to do. She shadowed the movements of the women ahead of her and took the next open cubicle.

Santiago followed his mother's movements. Ignoring everyone else in the cavernous hall, he dashed to her cubicle screaming *"Mamá! Mamá!"* They were separated by a plexiglass shield. As if in some sort of sick pantomime, Santiago and his mother attempted to match hands and kiss. Sadly, it was the best they could do. And inevitably, they both sobbed so hard their bodies shook.

A mere spectator, Rachel positioned her folding chair slightly behind Santiago's in the small cubicle. At first glance, she thought Rosa looked as vulnerable as a bird with a broken wing. Witnessing such raw emotion, Rachel choked up. She swiped away her tears with the back of her hand. She thought, *there's such an overpowering bond, never to be seen with the naked eye, which exists between a mother and her child. Something that only they could feel.*

Since this was Rosa's first contact with the outside world, a female guard came over and showed her what to do. She placed the phone in Rosa's hands. On the other side of the partition, Rachel tried to hand the receiver to Santiago, but he couldn't speak, he was crying too hard.

She seized the receiver herself. In English—with a smattering of elementary Spanish—Rachel explained that she was Santiago's teacher and that he was doing okay. And for the time being, he was living with Nacho and Yolanda.

Rosa starved for information, tried hard to absorb every word.

Still sniffling, Santiago touched his palm to the scratched plexiglass partition, yearning for his mother's physical touch. Rachel, mindful that they only had an hour for the visit, sensed that Santiago had composed himself enough to talk and handed the receiver back to him.

"*Mi hijo, mi hijo, te amo,*" Rosa cried, her voice strained with uncertainty. "My darling boy. Please, please don't cry. I love you so much. Tell me, are you okay? I have so many questions."

In rapid Spanish, Santiago spoke to his mother. Since Rachel was virtually out of the loop, she had time to round-up her own thoughts. Sitting back, she wondered how many heartbreaking and tragic stories could be told by those in this cavernous room. So much history. So much hope. So many broken hearts. So many broken dreams. From the various cubicles, she heard the din of foreign tongues. At one point, she heard spontaneous laughter and wondered how that could be.

Santiago no longer appeared listless; on the contrary, he was animated and happy talking with his mother.

Twenty-five minutes flew by. Rachel leaned over and tapped him on the shoulder to get his attention. "Don't forget to tell your mom about your brother and his baby?"

In an upbeat mood, Santiago nodded."

"*Mamá,* I've got good news. Javier has a baby girl."

Rosa beamed and laughed, a full, hearty, joyous laugh. A laugh that went from the top of her head down to her toes. "I'm a grandmother! I'm a grandmother! Tell me her name?"

"Annamaria." I brought a picture to show you, but the guard, he wouldn't let me bring it to you."

Watching their conversation, Rachel grew wistful, thinking how little they wanted out of life. She checked her watch. She needed to make sure Rosa understood a few things before they left.

"Santiago," she said, lightly touching his arm, "tell your mom I'm sorry I can't bring you here more often 'cause I teach school. I have to work. Tell her today before we leave that I'm putting fifty dollars in her account. With that money, she can buy a calling card. Then she'll be able to call you."

Santiago repeated the instructions.

Tears welled up in Rosa's eyes. She struggled to find the English words for gratitude. "*Mis gracias más sinceras por su apoyo.*" My most sincere thanks." Rosa was grateful, but embarrassed that a stranger had to make it possible.

"Tell your mom I'm sorry I *can't* bring her anything. It's against the rules. But ask her if she can buy things in a commissary or canteen, whatever they call it?"

"*Sí, sí, señora.* But no can buy a rosary. Please help Santiago to bring my rosary."

Knowing what happened to her precious rosary, Santiago's eyes grew bigger.

Rachel jumped in. "Tell your mom they got lost when you moved."

Looking confused, Santiago knew his teacher was shaving the truth.

"Go ahead," Rachel urged. "Tell her we'll find a way to get her another rosary." She didn't want to sabotage Santiago's visit but had to ask Rosa one more question. "Ask her if they plan to send her back to El Salvador."

Through tears, Santiago managed to ask his mom the most pressing question.

"No one tells to me anything," Rosa shrugged.

With a bullhorn that amplified throughout the entire hall, a guard, adhering to the rigid schedule, announced, "Ladies and Gentlemen, you've got five more minutes. Time to wrap it up."

After their tearful good-byes. Rosa reassured Santiago she would call when she could. Through her son, she once again thanked Rachel for bringing him for the visit. In Spanish she said, "*Este visitacion es mi mundo.* This visit is my world."

When they were forced to put their receivers down, Santiago stood and placed both his palms and his nose against the plexi-glass partition, yearning to touch his mother. His eyes followed her movements as multiple guards herded the female detainees into a single-file line, back the same way they arrived. Rosa turned her head and caught Santiago's eye one last time. She gave him a soulful smile just before she disappeared into a hallway and the metal doors clanged shut.

Walking back to the lockers, Rachel was expecting Santiago

to feel elated. Instead, he felt quite the opposite. He was left with a lingering sadness. He felt let down and more alone than ever. Rachel retrieved her purse from the locker and handed Javier's letter back to Santiago. She had one more thing to accomplish. She found the machine that would take her cash and deposit it in Rosa's account. She stood behind ten others who planned to do the same thing. It was quite an emotional day. And by the time it was her turn, she was exhausted. When she couldn't get the money machine to work, a nearby guard stepped in and offered to help.

As they walked towards her car, she tried to take stock of the day. All in all, she rated the visit a huge success. Santiago had a chance to see and talk to his mother. Rosa could see that her son was well-cared for. Rachel had a chance to explain where he was living. And finally, Rosa would have money in her account enabling her to call Santiago or buy something at the commissary.

As the detention center faded from their sight, she commented, "Wasn't that great? You got to talk to your mom. Don't you feel better now?"

In a flat, barely audible voice, Santiago bottled up his angst and mumbled, "No." He looked down at the floor, something he often did when he didn't want to answer or couldn't find the words to express his deep emotions. Now, more than ever, he yearned for his whole family. Intellectually, he knew it was impossible, but couldn't help himself. He wanted to have them all back. *If my father wasn't murdered, he thought, I wouldn't be here, and my mother wouldn't be in detention. We'd be back in El Salvador with Javier.* A string of memories flooded his mind, finally stopping on one special Sunday:

His father had been in an unusually jaunty mood as their family strolled back from Sunday Mass. With his two sons walking beside him, Mauricio had bragged about his soccer prowess.

"After we change clothes, I'll show you boys a few special moves . . . show you what kind of player I used to be."

Javier claimed he had other plans, but Santiago looked forward to spending time with his father. Mauricio and Santiago headed to a flat area that at one time was a magnificent tree-lined park. But the vengeful government had spitefully cut off the water supply. The once lush lawn had deteriorated into a dusty field and the magnificent trees stood lifeless. Some boys' teams were playing on the field. But Santiago and his father carved out a niche a bit farther away. Mauricio picked up the soccer ball and beckoned Santiago to come closer.

"Santiago, pay attention. A soccer player must master the ball. Watch me close. Watch how I stop, pivot, and change directions."

Santiago tried to listen to his father but grew distracted when he heard the faint noise of a helicopter coming closer. The helicopter swooped low, and bullets rained down from the sky, targeting innocent adults and children. With quick thinking, Mauricio shoved his son against the trunk of a nearby tree. He flung himself over his son until the shooting stopped, risking his own life.

When Rachel glanced over, she recognized the mournful expression on Santiago's face. Eventually he turned to her, still hesitant to call his teacher by her first name. "Ms. Roth, what I do about my mother's rosary?"

"Don't worry," she responded, trying to act confident. "We'll figure something out. Do you go to church with Yolanda and Nacho?"

"Sometimes."

"Is there a little shop inside the church? Maybe they sell rosaries?"

"Maybe. I never look."

"Okay, I'll ask Yolanda. We'll work it out."

"When will my mother be home?"

"I don't know. I hope soon, Santiago. I hope soon."

Silence is a generous gift that shrouds doubts and fears. They both needed quiet time to reflect on the *what ifs* that persisted like weeds sprouting up in the garden of their minds.

Fortunately, Yolanda was home with her girls when Rachel

brought Santiago back to the apartment. In the most general way—so as not to further traumatize him—Rachel tried to explain how their day went.

Chapter 40

Lifestyles of the Rich and Famous

Twin Palms Resort and Spa

B Y THE TIME RACHEL drove back from the detention center and dropped Santiago off at the apartment, she felt like a limp rag doll. The heavy-duty emotions got to her. Out of curiosity and a sense of responsibility, she swung by Benson Middle School to see how her substitute survived. The sub's notes indicated it did not go well. On a sheet of binder paper, the sub had printed in bold letters:

THE STUDENTS WERE UNRULY AND UNCOOPERATIVE

Rachel figured as much, as the restless class tended to be unmanageable unless someone stayed on top of them every minute. She tried to do right by everybody, and none of it seemed to be working out. She dragged herself home, not sure whether she stirred up more problems than she solved by taking Santiago to the detention center to see his mother.

The first thing she did when she closed the door to her condo was kick off her uncomfortable flats and change into khaki walking shorts and a sloppy, loose-fitting navy-blue tee-shirt. From the tension of the day, she needed to reward herself with something naughty. Rachel poured a Coke and grabbed the bag of potato chips that were on the top of the refrigerator. She opened the French doors and checked to see if it was too hot to sit outside. Thank goodness a warm, gentle breeze cooled the air. She carried her pick-me-up outside and sat in the shade under the trellis covered in purple wisteria. In addition to the rush of sugar, salt, and fat, she needed time to decompress and sort out the cluttered thoughts bouncing around in her head.

The modest but private garden—her safe-haven, her sanctuary from the ravages of everyday life—consisted of a brick patio with two chaise lounges and a low-slung table. Beyond was a small patch of grass, and a palette of colorful plants: bottlebrush, lantana, and red bougainvillea that crawled over the dull gray slump stone fence. In the far corner, she had personally planted a small lemon tree, something she had always wanted. It hadn't produced any fruit yet, but Rachel treated it like her baby, inspecting its growth weekly.

Between chips, Rachel compared her birthright—the peaceful, sweet freedom that she so much enjoyed—to Rosa's bleak, pathetic life. She saw first-hand how the detention center ripped apart hopes and dreams and sucked the joy out of life. In a contemplative mood, she realized just how unfair life was.

What came to mind were several Greek myths from a unit she taught back in Reno. One was about a phoenix that rose from the ashes of a fire: *Out of despair, hope must rise.* But just as quickly, a darker myth came to mind. One about Sisyphus, who was confined to rolling an immense boulder up a hill, only to watch it fall back, and having to repeat his actions for all eternity. *"I'm not sure which is more suited . . ."*

Rachel's mind was on fire. *What I'm teaching has no relevance for Santiago . . . or the other stressed-out kids in my class. Most of them are carrying around baggage so heavy, it's a wonder they can make it to school. Most are raised by a single parent or grandparent. Gangs, prisons, and drugs filter their reality. Adults come and go. And those that are there, are struggling to put food on the table and pay the rent. Some, like Santiago, stay home to baby-sit younger brothers and sisters while their parents' work. It's a fantasy to think these kids have a quiet place to study.*

What made it worse, Rachel seethed, *is the inept educational system that pretends every kid will go to college. In fact, most of my class will not. What about them? How are we preparing them to live in a complicated world? We shove these poor kids onto a conveyor belt, push them along, knowing full-well they're ill-prepared for life. The 'standard' curriculum has relevance for suburban kids, but not the kids I'm teaching. They're simply 'marking time,' counting down days until they can drop-out. Half wouldn't even finish high school. These kids aren't failing us; we're failing them. We're not preparing them for life's contingencies.*

Rachel foraged for ideas, trying to reframe her thoughts. *What would it take to make their time in school more meaningful? Santiago has huge learning gaps . . . especially in language and reading. And he isn't the only one. They all lack self-confidence, curiosity, and problem-solving skills. They have so little from which to draw.*

She snapped out of her reflective mood when she heard Stuart whistling as he opened the front door. He frequently whistled when in a jubilant mood.

"I see you got home in one piece," he shouted through the open French doors. "How'd it go today?"

"I'll tell you when you come out here," Rachel replied.

Stuart poured himself a glass of wine. "Want me to bring some olives out?"

"Yeah, fine," Rachel snapped. "And would you pour me a glass of wine? This Coke's not doing it for me."

"The Chardonnay or the Sauvignon Blanc?"

"Doesn't matter. Just bring some wine."

"That bad, huh?"

"Not a stellar day, if that's what you want to know."

As Stuart put down the bowl of olives and handed Rachel the Sauvignon Blanc, he paused, "Well?

She sipped the wine and rubbed her forehead. Then her frustration poured out like water from a pitcher. "It's been a shitty day. In the first place, the detention center isn't in Apple Valley. It's on a crappy road filled with potholes in the middle of nowhere. Twice I had to stop and ask someone for directions. Oh God, Stuart, the place is a prison . . . complete with high fences, watch towers, and enough security to protect Fort Knox. It's an institutional hellhole."

"What'd you expect? A country club? Did Santiago get to see his mom?"

"Yeah. It was sort of pathetic. She had to talk to him over a phone. A plastic partition separated them. Poor thing, she was like a fish in a fishbowl. Frankly, I'm not sure whether it made him happy or sad to see her like that."

"Rachel, the government's not playing around. In their eyes, she's illegal."

"I know that!" she fumed, raising her voice. "But she's not a thief or a murderer. She never harmed a soul in her life. She just had the misfortune of being born in El Salvador . . . in the middle of a civil war. She's just searching for a better life. What's wrong with that? What would you do if you were in her shoes?"

"Well, at least you tried," he said, brushing her off. "You did a *mitzvah*, a good deed. Wanna hear about my day?"

"Only if it was better than mine."

"Mine was pure platinum."

"Goody for you. Tell me, what was so great?"

"I'll tell you over dinner. Judging from your mood, you could use a night out." Stuart loved teasing Rachel. He knew that once he piqued her interest about something, she would dog it until he told her. "How 'bout Johnny Costas? I feel like some good Italian food. If you change your clothes, we can leave right now. We won't need a reservation."

"Whatever," she said, feeling morose. "First I'm going to finish my wine. Why waste it?"

As soon as they opened the restaurant door, the aromatic smell of spices smacked them in the face. Johnny, who usually was in back cooking, greeted them in his unpretentious, hole-in-the-wall restaurant. "I'm gonna give you two lovebirds the best seats in the house," he joked, as he led them over to an empty table with the red and white checkered tablecloth.

"Hey, Johnny, what's good tonight?" Stuart asked. "Any specials?"

"If you want something out of this world," Johnny said, making a circle with his thumb and index finger, "try the osso bucco. You're gonna love it."

"Umm. Sounds good."

Before Rachel looked at her menu, she begged Stuart to tell her what made his day so special.

With a flair for the dramatic, Stuart stalled. "Patience, princess, patience. First, let's order. I'm going with Johnny's recommendation. Osso bucco, a little red vino and garlic bread. What'd you want?"

As soon as Johnny took their order and worked his way back to the kitchen, Rachel prodded Stuart. "Now . . . will you tell me what's so great about your day?"

"Okay, okay. Around 2:30 this afternoon, a man called and said he was a producer from the television show *The Lifestyles of the Rich and Famous.* Got that? *The Lifestyles of the Rich and Famous.* You know . . . Robin Leach. He does that show. We watched it a couple of times. Anyway, he wants to do a segment on the resort. Can you believe it?"

"That's better than great. It's fantastic! How'd that happen? Do you suppose your PR guy, what's his name, arranged it?"

"Of course. How else would they know about us? That reminds

me, first thing in the morning, I'll call and thank Alain. Wait 'til Banning hears about this . . ."

"Well, my hat's off to you. The three of you have really turned shit into sugar. Between Banning's money, Alain's contacts, and your attention to details, you've put the resort on the map."

"I still can't believe it. Geez, Alain's worked miracles. We're becoming the number one spa in the country," Stuart bragged. "I'm getting calls from as far away as New York. Recording people, movie stars, people begging to stay here. Even international magazine and newspaper travel writers."

"The resort's a soap opera."

"You're right. It's the best job I've ever had."

"How about trading jobs?" she asked, feeling the effect of the wine.

For a moment, Stuart succumbed to guilt. He was so upbeat and happy about his job and knew Rachel was down about hers. "Enough about me and the resort. Tell me about Santiago?"

"It was bittersweet. Santiago's mother was thrilled to see him, but with the partition separating them, they couldn't even hug. Santiago wanted to show his mother the letter and photograph of his brother's baby, but the damn security guard insisted he put the letter back in the locker. How rigid can they be? It was just a piece of paper and a photo of a baby?"

"Did you find out if she's going to be deported?

"I asked, but she's got no idea whether she'll be sent back to El Salvador or rot in that hellhole forever."

"Look, you've done everything you can. Don't let it get to you. It's a crazy system and you're not gonna change it."

"I know. But I've been thinking, maybe we can help her. Obviously, Alain's worked miracles for the resort. Didn't he tell us that he worked on the governor's election campaign? Maybe he's got connections. Knows someone who can get Santiago's mother out of there."

"Don't tell me you want to involve Alain. No way. Immigration's not his bailiwick."

"But connections are. Give me one good reason why I can't call him?" For the rest of the evening, they argued about involving Alain, but ultimately Rachel persuaded him that it wouldn't hurt to try.

The next day Rachel felt optimistic. At the end of the school day, she drove back to the resort and headed straight to Stuart's office. As agreed, Stuart would place the call and talk to Alain first. Stuart thanked Alain profusely for putting the resort on Robin Leaches' radar. "You are fantastic. That was quite a coup." When done, he said, "Hold on a minute. Rachel wants to ask you something."

"Alain, I'll get straight to the point. I need a huge favor." She explained Santiago's plight and her day at the detention center. Appealing to his ego, she said, "You're the guy with connections. You know the governor. Maybe he can pull a few strings and spring his mom."

Alain listened to her diatribe, but in the end said, "I don't know enough about it. I'll do some research and get back to you."

When she didn't hear back right away, Rachel grew impatient. Two weeks later Alain called back. "Rachel, here's what I found out. The governor can't do anything. The feds, not the state, deal with illegal immigrants. INS and the Customs and Border Protection Agency handle it. But here's the upshot. I asked around and found an immigration attorney, Alex Villareal. I'm told he's the best in Southern California. Want his number . . .?"

As soon as she could, Rachel called the attorney's office. She got as far as his secretary, who quoted his fee. As much as she wanted to help Rosa, it was out of the question. It seemed like another dead end.

Chapter 41

Computers and Curiosity

THE NEXT EVENING Rachel and Stuart were driving down Palm Canyon Drive in Palm Springs for a quick dinner at Hamburger Hamlet. They had been rehashing the news of the day when out of nowhere Stuart remarked, "Oh, I forgot to tell you I got a call from Jonathan . . .

Before he could complete the sentence, Rachel interrupted. "Who's Jonathan?"

"The company's new tech guy . . . up in Reno. Everyone's getting a new computer. That way if we've got a problem, he can help us out. He said he made a sweet deal with Dell." Even though Stuart wasn't clairvoyant, he had been married to Rachel long enough to know exactly what came next.

"What are you doing with your old computer? Can I have it for my classroom?"

"I knew you were going to say that. You're so predictable. Yes, you can have the old one. I'm also getting a laser printer."

Thinking ahead, Rachel asked, "What about your secretary?

Is she getting new stuff, too?"

"Uh-huh. And yes, Rachel, you can have hers too."

"You've got no idea what the computers and printers would mean for my kids."

"Your kids?" Stuart challenged. "Since when did you become so possessive?"

"You know what I mean. I don't know any kid that isn't fascinated with computers. Kids think they're toys. Listen," she said, getting more and more animated, "There's dynamite software. I see it advertised in *Scholastic Magazine* all the time. Math and grammar drills. Plus, there's a whole encyclopedia on a disk. The kids think they're playing; they don't realize they're also learning."

Not exactly a techie, Rachel asked one of the other teachers for help in setting up the two computers and printers on a banquet table she borrowed from the resort. Rachel, always gung-ho for making charts, labeled one COMPUTER TIME. Not long after the computers were installed, Damien, who usually had attitude, surprised her when he asked, "Can I use one of the computers at lunchtime?"

"Sure," Rachel smiled, knowing how addictive the computer could be. *It's the best toy/teaching tool . . .*

"What about after school?" one of the girls asked. "Can I use the computer?"

"Absolutely, but only for an hour. And you'll have to work quietly. That's when I correct papers and do lesson plans."

The next day, Rachel segued into her planned lesson. First, she propped a stuffed monkey with a red hat on a shelf. "Does anyone know who he is?

"Curious George!" someone shouted.

"Right!" she said, thinking this was a teaching moment.

Santiago's attention suddenly shot up. He recognized the stuffed monkey. Yolanda's daughters had given him a stuffed monkey just like that to sleep with.

In large letters, Rachel wrote CURIOUS on the blackboard.

"Does anyone know what that word means? When no one responded, she asked, "Do you ever wonder about things? For instance, sometimes I wonder why the sky is blue? Do any of you know why?" When no one answered, she explained the word curious. "Take out your journals. Write the word *curious* and underline it. For homework tonight, go home and write down one thing that makes you curious. If you can think of one thing, just one thing that you're curious about, you can use the computer to look it up."

The following day Rachel was disappointed when only two students came back with questions.

Angelina, who usually didn't say much, raised her hand. "I wrote something. How far away is the moon?"

"Great question. I don't know the answer. But with curiosity, we can find the answer to lots of things in books and especially on the computer. What's in this little box is called software." She pulled out the small disk and demonstrated how to use it. "Just think, a complete encyclopedia, A to Z right here on this disk. Imagine that. One small disk that has as much information as a complete set of encyclopedias."

"Angelina, if you want to find out, come in at lunch and use one of the computers."

Pleased with herself, Angelina broke into a big smile.

LaToya popped up. "I gots a question."

"Great. Let's hear it."

"How do eyes work?"

"Great question. How can you find the answer?"

"The computer," several kids shouted out. "That's right. LaToya, you can come in at lunchtime also and use the other computer.

The rest of the class, including Santiago, looked blank.

"Take out your notebooks," Rachel ordered. She reviewed the vocabulary she used the day before. *Curious*. Then she added *Who, What, When, Where, and Why*. "Think about these words," Rachel challenged. "Who can make-up a question starting with the word *who*?" With a carefully thought-out plan, she was pivoting from passive learning—where her students could tune out—to active involvement.

She felt like she was on a roll. That evening—without shame—Rachel composed a letter to some of her friends, pleading for money for her classroom.

> Dear Friends,
> I have always wanted to be in the Peace Corps but never quite made it. But if I had been stationed in some poor country, and asked for your financial assistance, I know that you would do what you could to help. Now, however, I find myself teaching in a brand new, low-end, no frills middle school in Southern California. With the state's limited budget, I don't have what is needed to engage my students. Many of their parents are first genera-tion Americans, mostly non-English speaking and poorly educated. They do not have the where-with-all or resources to contribute to their children's well-being. If you can find it in your heart to make a modest contribution, I would very much ap-preciate it. I intend to buy books and enrichment materials that are more suited to the individual students' reading interests and abilities.

Several weeks later, a blustery Santa Ana wind blew in from the east as Rachel was leaving school for the day. She hugged the papers she needed to grade and her purse with one arm. She had trouble opening the school's heavy courtyard door leading to the parking lot and wondered if they were bullet proof. Before going back to the condo, she swung by the post office to pick up the mail. There were several envelopes addressed to her. As soon as she got back into her car, she ripped them open. Two more checks from friends. Donations for her class. One for a significant amount. At first glance, she thought it twenty dollars, but on a second look, realized it was for two hundred dollars.

Rachel couldn't wait to tell Stuart when he came home that night.

"What are you going to do with all that money?" Stuart mocked

"You're kidding, right? I can buy books about sports and animals. Airplanes and boats. Puzzles. Software. But first I'm going to buy the whole class subscriptions to *Scholastic News*. It's got current events and science information geared to their interests. Written at a level they understand. *Scholastic News* periodically inserts a high interest play. If I divide my class into reading groups by ability, those on the bottom rung are uncomfortable reading aloud. They get embarrassed when they don't know a word. But when they rehearse a play, they need to keep rereading their parts. When they miss a word, someone casually helps them out. Also, everyone needs to follow along, so they don't lose their place. They don't think of it as reading. They stand in front of the classroom and are part of an activity. Sometimes I've taken them into the auditorium to practice on the stage. They get a big kick out of it."

"If it's so great, why doesn't the school supply *Scholastic News?* Why do you have to buy everything yourself?"

"I don't know. They just don't."

There was no doubt that the classroom enrichments stimulated her students. Rachel bought a few brightly colored Chinese kites made of cellophane, with extra-long tails. She strung them across the ceiling, cheering up the rather dull, institutional classroom. Her students loved them. She had cajoled the assistant manager where she banked to give her thirty blank check registers. Then she purchased Monopoly money at the supply store for teachers and doled it out as rewards for various student achievements. The last thirty minutes of each day, the students deposited their money with student appointed bankers. With several student volunteers, Rachel organized a lending library. The new high interest books and puzzles could be checked out and shared with their siblings.

Rachel developed a game called *Intellectual Pursuit*. She divided her class into teams of four. Every week she gave the same four questions to each group. They had to do research and answer the questions on paper. Because one question invariably led to another, they needed to add a follow-up question . . . and answer it. Usually the questions were about sports, history, science, and current events.

Her usual homework assignment was simple. The students were encouraged to read to a brother or sister, or to a grown up. "Here's a new deal," Rachel said, trying a different tactic to motivate her class. "Every day that you bring this slip back signed by a parent and dated, you earn five dollars in Monopoly money. When you earn fifty dollars, you'll get an hour of free time on the computer. On the days that everyone, and I mean *everyone*, brings a slip back signed and dated, the whole class gets an extra ten-minute recess.

Chapter 42

Curriculum

RACHEL AND STUART dropped Santiago back at Yolanda and Nacho's apartment after seeing the movie *Dances with Wolves*. On their way back to the resort, Rachel commented, "Too bad there wasn't enough time to discuss the movie with him. It was a terrific story. How a white soldier develops a relationship with the Indians. There's really a lot to talk about. How two cultures learned to respect each other."

"Rachel, listen to yourself. Is everything with you a teaching experience? You're becoming obsessive. Can't you just let it be a relaxing afternoon . . . a simple movie and a box of popcorn?"

"Yeah. Sure. But I'm trying to broaden Santiago's horizon. You know, create a few sparks. Opportunities to teach sometimes come from other sources. Not everything's in a textbook."

"Yeah, you're right, but can't you just relax?"

"I am relaxed."

"Then lay off Santiago and school for a while."

"I just want him to think about something other than his mother."

"Rachel. You did. He had a nice afternoon. That's it. Don't make it into something more."

Rachel always got her dander up when Stuart cut her off. It was as if someone was waving a *red flag.* "Santiago's my personal experiment. You and I are doing things for him beyond school, beyond his problems. Do you think the state legislators have ever tried teaching poor kids? No," she said, answering her own rhetorical question. "Education isn't about comparative test scores. How can anyone compare the test scores of rich kids living in the suburbs to kids living in a barrio?"

"I don't have a clue. But I'm sure you're going to tell me."

"Well, let me ask you another question. And don't rush with an answer. Do you really think these kids need to know about gerunds?"

"What's a *gerund?*"

"Well, I had to look the word up and I'm still trying to figure it out. I'm supposed to teach them beginning algebra and geometry when they don't even know how to add and subtract, multiply and divide. And most of them are still reading at the 3rd and 4th grade level. Some even lower. They've got zero comprehension, zero world experiences."

"Okay, Rachel, mellow out. You take this job way too serious."

Two days later Rachel went to the *teacher store* in Cathedral City and bought fourteen packets of math flash cards. She made a chart and bought a bunch of Hershey bars—not the small ones but the big ones—to give away as incentives. She also bought a case of tennis balls to hand out one by one. When each student showed their proficiency in multiplying through their 12's, they could choose their reward.

At the end of the day, bribery worked.

Monday morning Rachel stood by the open homeroom door to greet her students. She was still trying to teach them to make eye contact, smile, and say *good morning.* She felt deeply satisfied when Santiago passed through the door wearing the black

Dances with Wolves tee-shirt she bought him.

"Good morning," he responded, with a trace of a smile, as if to say, "see what I'm wearing." His eyes told the story without any dialogue.

During homeroom Rachel grumbled inwardly as she read the teacher's bulletin—another teacher's meeting after school. In capital letters, the notice read: PLEASE NOTE THE TEACHERS' MEETING WILL BE HELD IN ROOM 14 INSTEAD OF THE LIBRARY. When the final bell rang, she had just enough time to clean her blackboards, gather her things, and head for the meeting. For a change, the principal was on time, waiting for the usual laggards to get there.

"They probably forgot where the meeting was," one of the teachers said to no one in particular.

Ms. Webb finally looked at her watch and said, "Okay, let's get started. We've got a lot to cover. I need to update all of you on a few things. But for those of you who haven't heard, the school was broken into over the weekend. The library was ransacked."

From the buzz, not all the teachers knew.

"Two of our boys were responsible," Ms. Webb sighed. "Apparently they had anger issues and were hell-bent on wrecking our beautiful new library. They tossed almost every shelved book on to the floor and messed with the card catalog and reference books. They destroyed quite a few things."

"Who did it?" several teachers asked at once.

"I can't discuss it now. It's been turned over to the authorities."

The staid history teacher, who always wore a tie, raised his hand. "Do you need some help cleaning up?"

"No, thanks. Mrs. Hymes and I spent all day Sunday putting things back where they belonged." Then Ms. Webb moved on to the next thing on her agenda. "The district has adopted the DARE program." She picked up the chalk behind her and wrote the letters D.A.R.E. on the blackboard. Looking at her notes, she repeated the words. "Drug Abuse Resistance Education. Beginning next week, a police officer trained in the program will be here.

Those of you who teach social studies needs to block out two one-hour periods a week, for ten weeks. Mondays and Wednesdays. I just wanted to give you a heads-up."

Rachel groaned. It's always something, she thought. *Between the Smile Mobile, the hearing and eye tests, assemblies for self-esteem and fund-raising, Jump for Your Heart, speech therapy, special ed., fire drills, and mock lock-down drills, there's hardly any teaching time.*

One of the science teachers reached his limit. "Is this part of Nancy Reagan's whacko 'Just Say No' program?" he asked. "Because that's simply not going to work."

Rachel didn't say a word, but sat in disbelief, thinking the entire system was crazy. *The U.S. Department of Education, the State Department of Education, the county Department of Education, the district office, and the principal, they all have input about the curriculum. Everyone but the teachers. The ones who know the students best. Oh, she thought, how can I leave out the religious zealot that just complained to the principal about me teaching the poem Invictus, especially the part:*

> *I am the master of my fate,*
> *I am captain of my soul.*

Ms. Webb continued. "We've got ourselves a new student, Tomás Zelaya. He transferred from San Bernardino County. For those of you unfamiliar with the area, San Bernardino is gang infested. You might have seen Tomás. Some of you might even have him in your class. He's in the eighth grade, and quite big for his age. He's the one wearing a hairnet."

A few of the young teachers started to giggle.

"It's no laughing matter. The hairnet's a sign of gang membership. I've got no legal recourse to expel him or to tell him to take the damn hairnet off. From what I hear, the two rival gangs—the Crips and the Bloods—are moving into this area. We can't deny him the right to go to school, but I want to make sure you watch him carefully. I don't want any trouble and he looks like trouble."

Officer Stenson—dressed in a non-threatening but obvious police uniform complete with an official badge—entered Rachel's classroom. Part of the D.A.R.E. concept was to make the police a less threatening part of the community. He introduced himself and asked the students their names. They were enthralled when he handed out some slick D.A.R.E. stickers and colorful workbooks. He immediately started talking about drugs and gangs. Rachel listened while correcting papers in the back of the room.

"How many of you know people that are in gangs?" he asked.

Almost a third of the class raised their hands.

"Okay," Officer Stenson said, not appearing to be shocked. "How many of you know people that are in prison for one reason or another?"

Rachel's ears perked up. She was stunned that so many of her class raised their hands. She glanced over at Santiago who appeared perplexed by the question. She understood his confusion. In his mind, he was trying to determine if detention was considered a prison. She wondered how many more have family in detention centers that weren't raising their hands?

Officer Stenson pulled out seven snapshots of young Hispanic boys and passed them around to the class.

"Take a good look at these guys," he said, hoping to shock them. "They were all gang members in this area. Not one of them lived to the age of twenty-one."

Several weeks zipped by. Rachel had almost forgotten about the gang situation. One day while in the teachers' room eating a slice of leftover pizza, she heard an unusual request over the P.A. system. "All teachers are invited out to the playground NOW," with an emphasis on the word now.

"Crap, that could only spell trouble," someone said knowingly.

Without enthusiasm, Rachel hustled out to the playground with the other teachers. Usually the students ate their lunch, then played basketball or soccer, handball, or tetherball . . . or just hung around talking.

By the time she got out there, a few teachers who had yard duty were surrounded by a group of boys. A short little man with a red beard and mustache, who looked more like a Bavarian elf in lederhosen than a music teacher, was shooing away the busy bodies who loved to watch fights. Rachel was aghast when she saw Santiago in the middle of the ruckus, with his hand holding a big gash across his chin. Apparently, Tomás Zelaya, the new kid and a few of his followers, began to push and shove the boys who were playing soccer. When Santiago refused to give up the soccer ball, Tomás whacked him across the face with brass knuckles. Worried about contracting AIDS, most of the teachers did not touch Santiago. He stood by himself and cried softly.

Shocked that no one tried to stop the bleeding, Rachel asked, "Does anyone have a handkerchief?"

Reluctantly the music teacher forked over his. Rachel handed it to Santiago to stop the bleeding. She hustled him to the nurse's office only to find it wasn't her day to be there. As Rachel tried to calm him down, the school secretary—who was acting as the surrogate nurse—came in and helped patch him up. Several male teachers marched Tomás, who still had a defiant snicker on his face—and his posse of bullies—to the principal's office. It was unfortunate that Santiago bore the brunt of Tomás's aggression. However, brass knuckles were considered a weapon, giving the principal latitude to expel Tomás.

Chapter 43

Evaluation

ONE MORNING as Rachel was teaching her lesson, she heard the click of the classroom door. With her back to the door, she swung around to see who was there. Ms. Webb, her principal breezed in carrying a black binder and pen. She caught Rachel's eye and nodded slightly. Knowing another observation was taking place, Rachel returned to the task at hand, helping five students at the chalkboard who were having problems with long division.

Several months earlier, Rachel had rearranged her classroom. Instead of the students' desks lined up in straight rows, they were arranged in clusters of six—two on each side facing each other with one desk on each end. Not only did it save space, but it gave the students an opportunity to work as a team, sharing supplies, and collaborating when appropriate. Ms. Webb sat in an empty chair at a student's desk. The boys and girls at each cluster, intimidated by the presence of the principal, suddenly did their math drill silently.

The principal observed two girls at an odd table that was pushed against a side wall. Rachel had lifted the table from the resort's storeroom. The girls were intent on a puzzle of the United States. In the back of the room a boy and girl were staring into computer screens, both doing research. A few students, talking softly among themselves, were drilling with math flash cards.

The principal crinkled her brow. She couldn't figure out why Rachel had written DRACULA'S MOTHER SUCKS BLOOD in big, bold letters across the board. She jotted the phrase down, planning to ask her about it later.

When Rachel turned around again, she could see her principal's head down, scribbling furiously. Twenty minutes later, Ms. Webb heard Rachel say, "Put your things away. Let's get ready for recess. Congratulations! You did it again today. You've earned ten extra minutes outside after the recess bell rings."

Loud cheers went up.

As they waited for the recess bell, Rachel did mental math with her students. "If you know the answer, raise your hand. Don't shout it out. "What's five times five, plus five, divided by six. Who knows?" Hands flew up and she called on Santiago. "Five," Santiago blurted out.

"Right. Go stand by the door. You can be line-leader today." Although she tried to treat everyone fairly, she reserved a special place in her heart for Santiago. Rachel understood why he was so introverted and lacking in self-esteem. She tried hard to nurture his self-confidence and provide opportunities for him to get actively involved in the learning process. She hoped that eventually he would begin to feel more successful in the classroom, in sports, and with his classmates.

She threw out more mental math problems. And each time someone gave the right answer, they got to line up at the door. When the bell rang, she let the remainder of the class line-up.

Luther asked. "It's my turn to use the computer. Can I come in at lunch?"

"Me, too," Armando said. "I get to look up my question."

The two girls that were doing the puzzle asked if they could come in.

When the students finally scooted out, the principal thanked Rachel and left without commenting. Rachel sighed, wondering what her evaluation would be like.

Two weeks went by, and the principal said nothing. Finally, one morning there was a note written in pencil in her box.

See me after school today.

In the principal's office, Rachel glanced over her copy of the evaluation. She told herself to relax. It was just another meaningless form, never very helpful.

> *Mrs. Roth's room is cheerful with several colorful kites strung from the ceiling. In addition to many charts, her room is decorated with the students' writing and art. With a few exceptions, the students were working quietly.*

Yeah, Rachel thought, *I had to buy the kites and charts on my own.* Besides, who cares about *decorating* a classroom. It should serve a purpose; it's not a staged house for sale. It's about connecting with the students. Her immediate urge was to fix the principal's collar in the back. It was sticking straight up.

Under the self-improvement section, Ms. Webb had written: A parent reported that Mrs. Roth was using the "F" word in class.

"Really? A parent called you about that?" Rachel covered her mouth with her hand to stifle a giggle. "Guilty as charged."

Ms. Webb, who had a habit of frowning when perplexed, couldn't believe Rachel's cavalier attitude.

"Want to hear the story about the "F" word? I told my class I'd teach them the "F" word. It worked. It got their immediate attention, just like it got the attention of that parent that called you. I pointed out that the "F" word was FOCUS. The students need to *focus* when I introduce a new concept."

"Sorry," Ms. Webb said, breaking into a begrudging smile. "I didn't know what to think when I heard from that parent. I should have checked with you before I wrote it on your evaluation. Okay. So, tell me about **GEEK OF THE WEEK**. I saw that written on the chalkboard . . . under the date."

"Oh that . . . well, I never actually put any names there. I chide them about it. I always say, 'Don't make me write your name down for being the *Geek of the Week*. They just laugh. It's our little classroom joke."

"Frankly, I wouldn't do that if I were you. It might intimidate some of the students and I can see why some parents might get upset."

There goes our humor.

Ms. Webb's evaluation continued. She read aloud, "Mrs. Roth's board had another highly unusual saying: **Dracula's Mother Sucks Blood**. What's that about?"

There's a legitimate explanation. When I'm teaching long division, the first letter of each word, D, M, S, B . . . gives the students a roadmap. The D stands for divide, the M for multiplying, the S for subtracting, then the B for bringing down the next number. It's just a way for the kids to remember what to do. If you've got a piece of paper, I can show you?"

Once Rachel convinced the principal that the saying was legit, Ms. Webb continued with her evaluation. "Mrs. Roth had her back to the class."

Rachel thought the comment ridiculous. *If I had the overhead projector that I requested at the beginning of the year, there'd be no problem. But I'm still waiting. Oh, well.* She had to do her evaluations. *But we both know that it's all a pointless charade.*

"Rachel, I must say, you run an unconventional class. I noticed some kids playing a computer game on a table not sanctioned by the school district. And you weren't using the regulation text."

"What's the use of going forward until they've mastered the basics? Some of these kids aren't ready for fractions and decimals."

"But we have approved curriculum."

"These basic drill sheets work for me. Not everyone's on the same page at the same time. Their abilities aren't all alike."

"Just out of curiosity Rachel, where did you get those worksheets?"

"At the teacher store. . . from a workbook with lots of drill. And I made copies."

Ms. Webb honed-in on that like a bee sucking honey. "You know there are copyright laws."

"You can't be serious? I'm just trying to teach. I'm not trying to resell the workbook. Most of my class is behind. They need to grasp one skill before they go on to the next. Not a new concept every day. That doesn't work. This way, if they don't understand, I can work with them while others work at the computers or on enrichment. I don't see why we've got to teach to the tests. No child left behind means just that. They have plenty of time to get algebra and geometry."

Just then a phone call came through. Ms. Webb picked it up. It was from the district office. Something about a school bus driver and an unhappy mother. Ms. Webb smiled at Rachel and raised one finger pointing to the phone. She indicated that Rachel was excused, at least for now.

Rachel couldn't get out of there fast enough. She thought the evaluation an exercise in futility. She wondered how the principal could possibly know what goes on in her class from a twenty-minute observation? *It's like judging the entire ocean from one rocky tide pool.*

Chapter 44

The Boys' and Girls' Club

W ITH THE MONTHLY STIPEND Stuart gave Yolanda, she enrolled Santiago in the Boys' and Girls' Club.
The after-school program was the best thing that ever
happened to him. Without the looming dangers in El Salvador,
and without the responsibility of babysitting, Santiago broke
free. The Boys' and Girls' Club offered games, help with homework, ping-pong, basketball; they even had a swimming pool
that opened in the summertime. But what drew Santiago in was
playing soccer. He made friends. Most of all, he idolized Coach
Ruben, who had an outgoing, fun-loving personality and knew
just how to handle Santiago. A freshman at College of the Desert,
he coached the boys' team three times a week. In addition, he organized competitions on Saturdays, enabling the parents to attend
the games.

Even though Rachel and Stuart didn't know one soccer rule
from another, they often drove over to the field to see Santiago
play. As they watched him interact with his teammates, Rachel

commented, "Did you notice how much more outgoing Santiago is? What a transformation."

"Yeah, he's doing good," Stuart conceded, wondering why the ref blew the whistle again.

After the game ended, the boys went through the line, touching their opponents' hands, a token of good sportsmanship. Afterwards, Santiago, still red-faced and sweaty, walked over to Stuart and Rachel. "Did you see the whole game?"

"Almost," Rachel admitted. "Good game."

"Hey Buddy," Stuart said, "you played great today."

Santiago beamed.

"One of these days you'll have to teach us about the penalties," Stuart said. "You know, I never played soccer. Half the time when the ref blows his whistle, I don't know why. By the way, I found this great little place. They specialize in hot dogs. Wanna try it? Maybe you can explain the penalties over lunch."

"Okay. But I gots to ride my bike back to the apartment. Yolanda likes to know where I go." Santiago had grown comfortable around Rachel but was still a little stiff with Stuart.

Rachel and Stuart sat in the car outside the apartment, waiting for Santiago. "Giving him that used bike was a stroke of genius," Rachel said.

Stuart shrugged. "What the heck. We bought a couple of new bikes for the resort. What else was I going to do with the old ones?"

"I think you bought a few new ones, just so you could give Santiago one of the old ones."

The corners of Stuart's lips edged upward. "Teenagers need wheels. It's empowering."

At seven o'clock the following Wednesday, the Desert Oasis City Council meeting was called to order. The town council had a bad reputation, long on self-dealing, short on common sense. Three of the five members were small-minded and pumped up on their own importance. Adding to the town's dysfunction, the city manager—who received an obscene compensation package considering his experience, the size of the community and the financial shape they were in—was content with his job and preferred not to rock the boat.

The public meeting room was packed with angry citizens. The projected budget for the next year was being reviewed. Everyone listened as the council members dispassionately discussed bankruptcy. It was the result of a lawsuit that went on for more than seven years, involving a trailer park proposed at the far end of town. In reality—if it got built or didn't get built—it wouldn't have changed the complexion of the town one iota. Wise people had advised them to settle the case. But the council members, who listened to their attorney, let the lawsuit drag on from court-to-court, throwing away good money after bad. If they had the slightest vision for the town, that money could have been used in so many more productive ways. Sidewalks. Streetlights. Stop signs near schools. Fixing potholes. An improved library. In the end, the city lost their case. Not only did they have to pay their attorneys' astronomical fees but those of the opposing side as well. They hocked the town's future. It wound up costing multi--millions that they didn't have and would be paying off for years to come.

Their budget meeting turned contentious. The voices of incensed special interests rose louder. Insults flew. With their coffers depleted, Desert Oasis lost control of their police and fire departments. The county would be stepping in to operate those services. When they announced the closing of the Boys' and Girls' Club, pandemonium broke out. Working parents relied on it to babysit their children after school.

Stuart—who followed the crazy politics of the town—attended the meeting. He was so frustrated when he returned home, he slammed the door. Rachel turned off the television. "Let me guess. Things did not go well tonight."

"You should've been there. It was chaotic."

"You know I hate meetings. What happened?"

"You wouldn't believe it." Then he repeated what happened.

"That's bogus. How can they close-down the Boys' and Girls' Club? Isn't it funded by United Way?"

"Well, they just did. Apparently, the city owns the land and the building and contributes a lot of money to its operation. But the town's flat-out broke."

"God, Santiago will be devastated. He loves it there. I've noticed a real change. He seems so much happier. Even his English has improved."

"What can I tell you?" Stuart said, rubbing his forehead as if he had a major headache. "Hell, the council's dumber than shit. With all their shenanigans, it only took five people to single-handedly destroy this town. Not to change the subject, but what do you have to eat? I'm starved."

The next day Rachel was in the teachers' lunchroom complaining that the city council was closing the Boys' and Girls' Club. "Santiago—that kid in my class that was living alone—he really loved going there. His whole life revolves around soccer."

One of the science teachers overhead Rachel. "Hey, there's always A.Y.S.O."

"What's that?"

"American Youth Soccer Organization. It's a competitive soccer organization for kids."

"How come I've never heard of it?"

"Cause you're old," he said and winked. "You're out of the loop. It's kinda new around here. The fee is pretty steep, but it's worth it. They supply uniforms and trophies. They may even provide insurance, but I'm not sure about that. My nephew is on a team that has a sponsor."

With the word *sponsor,* Rachel's wheels began to spin. She wanted to find out a little more about it but felt positive she could convince the resort to sponsor a team.

Stuart thought it a great idea. "Good P.R. But I'm going to run it by Banning, just in case. I need to call him anyhow and tell him about the disastrous city council meeting."

When Stuart approached Banning about sponsoring an A.Y.S.O.

soccer team, he said to go ahead and do it. But he reminded Stuart, "Don't give the bills to accounting. You know how goddamn tight they are. Send the bills directly to me."

In his element, Santiago was a transformed kid. He had always dreamt of being on a real soccer team, with uniforms and trophies. Along with two other players, he excelled. Without realizing it, he was becoming a leader. He showed some of the less experienced members of his team the moves his father taught him. During the practices and games, he was totally focused. He didn't worry about his mother or anything else. When it was his turn to provide refreshments, Rachel volunteered. She brought cut-up oranges, the team's favorite pick-me-up. When she and Stuart stood on the sidelines, Santiago played even harder, glancing over every now and then to see if they caught his moves.

Chapter 45

Bumps in the Road

BANNING CONTINUED to lead "the good life." With all his money and his flamboyant lifestyle, he attracted beautiful women like paper clips to a magnet. Frequently he joked, "I don't know what to do with them all." He stashed them everywhere—at the time-share hotel in Reno, at the Twin Palms Resort and Spa, and the other small motel he owned in Desert Oasis. Without hesitation, he humored the women, keeping them on a string—giving them low paying jobs—so they would be at his beck-and-call.

With multiple businesses running smoothly—and bags full of money rolling in daily—he indulged in drugs, women, and partying. Years earlier he got burned in a big L.A. lawsuit. Now he made it his policy to settle any disputes out-of-court. Not surprising, every now and then, his wild lifestyle hit a bump in the road. Two of his lady friends found themselves pregnant and threatened paternity suits.

He had hired Jeanné, who possessed striking features and

an effervescent personality, to work at a time-share booth out-side a downtown casino in Reno. At twenty-three, she possessed a razor-sharp mind, and an intoxicating French accent. Her job was to entice greedy tourists to stop-by for a *free* roll of nickels—worth two dollars. When they claimed their *freebie,* she tempted them with an even larger prize—a television set or boom box—if they signed-up to attend a time-share presentation at his hotel. Banning accrued a fortune playing off people's naivete and greed. From previous experience, he knew the smooth-talking, high-pressure, slick salesmen that he brought from L.A. could convince a certain percentage of those *listeners* into buying a week or two of time-share.

He fell head-over-heels for Jeanné's effusive charms. He couldn't leave her alone. There was only one drawback, she had a *sham* marriage to get into the U.S. It didn't take long for her to get swept away with Banning's grandiose lifestyle. Jeanné was no fool. When she got pregnant, she insisted on keeping the baby. In her wily way, she persuaded Banning to buy her a place in San Francisco. In addition, he paid up-front for the baby's education at the expensive French School on Balboa Street. She demanded—and he set aside—a bank account to fund the baby's college tuition.

Since Stuart was originally from San Francisco, Banning as-signed him the task of finding her a home. Not just any home, but a substantial one. Stuart found out about an auction of ocean front condominiums that had replaced Playland-at-the-Beach when it was torn down. Banning and Stuart flew down to the city on the day of the auction. Jeanné wound up with a mortgage-free penthouse overlooking the Pacific Ocean.

There were always others. For the busy summer months, the human resources department at Harrah's Casino in Reno, Nevada, imported temporary workers from Europe. Most nights Banning and his entourage sauntered over to the hotel for a late-night sup-per. They usually hung around, had a couple of drinks, and caught the lounge show. Marina, a curvaceous twenty-one-year-old who spoke English with a thick guttural accent was quick-witted. She dished out the repartee as fast as the guys handed it to her. She, too, recognized Banning's potential . . . especially his lavish tips and lifestyle. She soon became one of Banning's favorites. He frequently invited her to party after her shift ended. It didn't take long before she became a regular at their private soirees. And, not by accident, she too got pregnant.

In Banning's world, wild ideas frequently percolated up in the wee, small hours of the morning. With all the mineral water that flowed through the property, he decided he could bottle it and one of his lady friends could sell it at the resort. The Friday after this new idea popped into his head, Banning flew down to the desert and set-up a late afternoon meeting with Stuart. He hit him with his latest idea. "I think we should get into the cosmetic business."

"You're kidding, right!"

"No, I'm serious."

"I'm not sure that's such a good idea," Stuart said, thinking this was over the top. "What do we know about cosmetics?"

Banning ignored Stuart's reservation. "Think about it. We've got so much goddamn mineral water right here in the ground. It costs us nothing. We might as well profit from it. Put it in spray bottles. Have one of the good-looking gals walk around the resort spritzing everyone, touting it as a healthy way to cool off. Good for the skin. Then we can sell the hell out of it in the boutique. People don't know what they want until we tell them . . ."

"Frankly, I know *borsht* about cosmetics. I'm not sure I could be much help."

"Sure, you could. You just need to do a little research. Find out about bottling. I want our name and logo on the bottle. Price it all out. Take my word for it; it'll work."

Stuart was completely out of his element. He just had a knack for zeroing in and getting things done. He was convinced it was a real bird-walk from his field of expertise; yet deep down he found it intriguing. A new challenge.

Twin Palms Resort and Spa—which had developed a high-end clientele—merchandised the natural mineral water. At Banning's direction, Birgitta, another one of his attractive lady friends, flew down from Reno and hung around the resort. After lunch, when the outside temperature climbed, she meandered from the spa to the swimming pool *spritzing* mineral water on the faces of over-heated sun-worshippers. Then, with her Scandinavian accent, short blonde hair, and long legs, she dazzled the clientele with a perfect sales pitch.

Banning's success in selling the plastic spritz bottles with mineral water was just the beginning. Six months later he pushed his idea even further. "You know," he said to Stuart at another meeting, "We've got plenty of mud. Let's bottle it up. We can sell the crap out of it."

Stuart—used to Banning's cock-a-mammie schemes—now had a contact in the bottling world. He ordered cases and cases of round, opaque milky white glass jars. Willy, Banning's chauffeur and jack-of-all-trades, flew down on the jet. His instructions were to fill the jars from buckets of greenish-gray mud pulled from the well, wipe the jars clean, and slap on the Twin Palms Spa and Resort labels. Using resort guests as guinea pigs, Birgitta offered to slather the mud on the guests faces for a quick facial. No one thought it unusual to see the guests looking a bit like circus clowns in bathing suits strolling around the grounds of the resort with caked mud on their face.

Alain, the PR guru was called in and told to bring a photographer. Not long after that, articles appeared in the *New York Times* and *Los Angeles Times* about the Twin Palms Resort and Spa *clay* facials—no longer called mud. Word spread, and the story ran in many up-scale magazines and in the travel section of newspapers. The hip clientele, always anxious to be in on the cutting edge, clamored for all the clay they could get.

Once again Banning flew down from Reno. This time to discuss his desire to go full force into the cosmetic field. In the small banquet room where he and Stuart always met, Banning—oozing confidence in his ability to sell anything—leaned back in his chair, folded his fingers together, and stretched out his legs. "I've no doubt that we can take the cosmetic industry by storm. Stuart, all you need to do is find a chemist. Work with him. Assign him the task of developing a full line of products. You already found the bottler. Once we get some formulas, we'll put it all together and market the whole shebang—the mineral water *spritzes,* the clay facials, and the cosmetics to up-scale department stores. Then my lady friends would have something to do. They could work the counters in those stores."

Still hesitant, Stuart's mind was doing cartwheels. "It's one thing to sell the mineral water and mud right here at the resort. But frankly, what do we know about the cosmetic industry? Multinational companies have saturated that market. Go to any drug store or department store and you'll see an array of Revlon and Este Lauder products."

"So what? My friend Donavan grew rich selling the hell out of hair products. Believe me, he didn't know diddly squat about them before he started. The guy was a hairdresser. Look, the whole goddamn cosmetic business is all about marketing." Banning took the last swig of his beer and winked at Stuart. "It'll be a cinch." A master of persuasion, it didn't take Banning long to convince Stuart that they were on a roll.

When Stuart returned to the condo at the end of the day, he fumbled around in the kitchen trying to make guacamole with a couple of avocados one of the housemen brought back from Mexico. As Rachel handed him the potato masher, Stuart laid it all out. "Can you believe it? I'm going full-swing into the cosmetic business."

"From restaurants, hotels, and time-share . . . Wouldn't you say that's a pretty big stretch? You don't know the difference between a lipstick and an eyelash curler. For God's sakes, you don't even know the difference between your eyebrows and eye lashes," and she started to laugh.

"Don't remind me. All I've got to do, so I'm told, is find a chemist who can stir up the right ingredients." Trying to convince himself, he added, "It's a lot like making this guacamole. Just add a little of this . . . and a little of that, until you find the right balance. Women are so gullible."

"Truth be told," Rachel added with a devilish smile, "some women make cosmetics from household foods like eggs, coconut oil, even cucumbers . . . but don't tell Banning."

It took some searching, but Stuart eventually found Sing Li, a young chemist and charged him with the task of concocting a distinctive line of cosmetics. No one had to tell him, Stuart just knew that he would be the one that had to convince the upscale department stores to carry their products. It was going to be one giant leap.

Chapter 46

Seeking Asylum

Apple Valley Detention Center

ROSA FOUND HERSELF stuck in a vacuous hell hole filled with meaningless routine. The only things she looked forward to in her day was walking outside in the courtyard and Sunday Mass with Father Cabedo. She continually cursed her dead husband for getting involved with the insurgents. *If only Mauricio wasn't murdered, I'd still be in El Salvador among my own people.* Stripped of everything she held dear, she felt discarded and forgotten by a society that despised her for just living amongst them.

She worried constantly about Santiago. *What does he do all day? Is he lonely? Are people taking advantage of him?* She lived for his visits. Yolanda and Nacho—who were forced to buy another van after their minivan had been impounded on the night of Rosa's arrest—drove Santiago to see her several times, but mostly it was Rachel that made the connection.

In the detention center, Margarita, a new detainee, was assigned to the same pod as Rosa. At the age of eight, she had snuck across the border with her mother. Now a street savvy woman in her late twenties, she spoke Spanish and English fluently. Before getting busted for smuggling marijuana into the country, she spent three years working for a group of immigration attorneys in Phoenix. With nothing but empty days and an abundance of energy, she offered to teach English to any of the idle women that wanted to learn. Rosa was proud of herself as she began to learn rudimentary English.

Margarita, the only detainee there with knowledge of the legal system, also took it upon herself to advise them on their legal rights. She frequently urged the women to fight back. "Learn the word *ASYLUM*. Remember that word," she said over and over. "It means you get a day in court to plead your case. The judge will decide if you can stay in the U.S. Don't be afraid. Ask for asylum. Every one of you has the legal right to seek *asylum,* to tell your side of the story."

The women, including Rosa, listened with both ears.

Margarita preached. "Don't sit back and let them deport you. FIGHT BACK. The first thing you'll have to do is fill out forms requesting *ASYLUM.* You and I both know that you can't afford a lawyer. And so does the government. They take advantage of that. But there are volunteers. Nice, kind, people. They'll help you fill those forms out. The volunteers work for nothing. *Nada.* And when you get your asylum hearing, don't be afraid to insist on a TRANSLATOR if you're not comfortable speaking English. They'll explain what's happening."

Barely out of her teens, a timid young woman from Tepec, in Mexico, asked the obvious question. "How can we do all that? No one listens to us."

Several months passed before Irene Schneider, a young idealist, born with a strong spirit of social justice, connected with Rosa. They met in a sparsely furnished, bare bones conference room. Ms. Schneider, who spoke Spanish fluently, explained, "Once a week I volunteer to help people like you file for asylum."

Rosa crinkled her forehead and nodded, as if she understood, but it was all rather vague and confusing.

"I know how hard it is to be locked up. But before we go ahead, I want to explain what happens if you file for asylum. You'll be here much longer than if they simply deport you. It can take many months, maybe another year, before you get a hearing. And, in the end, there's no guarantee. Requesting asylum and getting it are two different things. If the judge doesn't give it to you, you'll be right back where you started. Deported. It's a huge gamble. Rosa, I can't make this decision for you. But if you decide you want to push for asylum, you'll need to sign this paper. It gives me permission to help you. Think it through very carefully."

Rosa tried her hardest to understand the ramifications of Ms. Schneider's explanation. But being incarcerated changed her. She no longer trusted people or the system. *On the other hand,* she reasoned, *it was the first time anyone showed any interest in her or her case.* She weaved the fingers of both hands together and raised them to her chin. Then she bowed her head and prayed silently.

Ms. Schneider, who was sitting directly across from her, heard the minute hand on the big wall clock jump several times.

Struggling for an answer, Rosa uncurled her fingers and kneaded her furled brow. After an abnormally long pause, she replied softly, "*Sí,* I sign the paper."

Ms. Schneider smiled. "Okay, then. Let's get to work. I'll help you fill out these forms. How many months have you been here?"

"I'm not sure. Maybe ten or eleven months," Rosa said, digging into her scrap of memory. "Maybe longer."

Hour-by-hour, day-by-day, the only thing that kept Rosa going was the thought of her asylum hearing and the chance to go free. But as one month drifted into another, she began to think she had been abandoned, lost to the outside world. Her sagging spirits were lifted once again when she finally got word that her case would be heard.

Ms. Becker, a second-year law student at the University of

Southern California, had lived in Spain for four years growing up and spoke fluent Spanish. She volunteered at the detention center part-time as an interpreter and advocated for women in the courtroom. She knew there was too little preparation time, but felt her help was better than nothing. Seeking asylum was always a hit-or-miss thing.

She and Rosa sat together in a conference room. "In an hour or two, your petition for asylum will be heard in court. I'll be there to help you get through it, but I need to know your background." Ms. Becker needed to flush out the details. "Tell me what happened at your first hearing? Why didn't you ask for asylum then?"

Rosa was nervous as she began her disjointed explanation. "I was scared. I didn't understand. Everything was in English. When a man asked me to sign a paper, I did. I thought I was being helpful. No one told me about asylum."

Ms. Becker laid her thick, round glasses on the table, rubbed the bridge of her nose, and started to take notes on a yellow legal pad. *It's the same old story,* she lamented.

When her name was finally called, Rosa, still in her orange jumpsuit and clogs, entered the modest courtroom. She felt as confused and unprepared as the first time even though she had Ms. Becker acting as her advocate. Rosa still did not understand what the judge expected or how it would play out. And the stakes couldn't be any higher. All she knew was that she could very well be sent back to El Salvador and never see Santiago or Javier again.

Judge Bartlett, his reddish face sculpted in a perpetual scowl, was not the most sympathetic judge to draw. Monday through Friday for the past twelve years, the hard-edged judge commandeered this courtroom. If he had to, he couldn't count the number of illegal immigrants he had seen in that time. Unbeknownst to the detainees who had the misfortune of landing in his court, Judge Bartlett only saw things in black and white. From his point of view, he looked upon most of them as common criminals, people who had broken the law. On most days, the judge tended to adjudicate his caseload as quickly as possible so that he could hustle out to the golf course. Over drinks with his cronies, he said more than once, *as a nation, we can't save everyone.*

When she took the stand, Rosa tried to keep her hands from shaking. From nerves, her voice cracked as she tried to explain why she fled El Salvador . . . about the death squads, the random shootings, the dead bodies, and the mortally wounded left in the streets to die. She recoiled as she relived the horrific scene when she discovered her husband's mutilated body in front of her house.

There was a long pause. "Take your time," Ms. Becker, her translator, advised. Once Rosa had collected herself, her well-meaning advocate made the mistake of asking her if she could explain the psychological trauma she was feeling.

There was nothing unique about her story. Judge Bartlett had heard it all before. Over the years, he had developed a Machiavellian technique for cutting his hearings short. "Hold on a minute," he said gruffly. "Mrs. Lopez may *not* speak about *psychological* trauma, unless she is qualified as an *expert* witness." Then he threw a few questions at her. "Mrs. Lopez, how many years have you gone through school?"

"Six years."

"Mrs. Lopez, have you ever lectured on psychology professionally?"

Jesus, where's he going with this? Ms. Becker wondered. After she translated the question and explained it, Rosa shook her head, indicating no.

"Let the record show," the judge said for the benefit of the court reporter, "that Mrs. Lopez has never lectured professionally on psychology."

Judge Bartlett glanced down at his calendar. He had two more cases to hear and was in a hurry to move on. He didn't hold back. "Since Mrs. Lopez has never lectured in a university or on a professional level, and I am assuming she has never written any professional journals, she can only speak as a lay witness but *not* about psychological problems."

Rosa did not completely understand the judge's words, but the tone of his voice sounded ominous. Ms. Becker understood all too well from the judge's confrontational style that Rosa had just been shafted.

In less than half-an-hour, Judge Bartlett adjudicated her case. "Rosa Lopez does not meet the credible fear threshold for asylum. I hereby order her deported."

Chapter 47

Angel Island

STUART, WHO NEVER HAD A MASSAGE in his life—
and didn't plan to have one in the future—had been thinking
that the resort needed something new and different. Some
more fodder for the travel writers. Perhaps some alternative treatments. One rainy Sunday on the way to see *Schindler's List*, he ran
an idea past Rachel. "What'd you know about mud baths?"

"Nothing, why?"

"Linda, one of the gals that works in the spa, was telling me
that the Indians used natural mud and mineral water for healing
purposes. I want to find out more about it. I've been thinking of
putting in a couple of mud baths. My grandma used to go to
Calistoga just to sit in the mud. Claimed it helped her arthritis."

"My grandma went to the mud baths, too! Probably for the
same reason."

"No kidding. Maybe we're on to something. Want to take a
long weekend? We could drive up to Calistoga. And *you* could
try out the mud baths. Then I thought we could do a little wine

tasting in Napa."

"Whoa! Why won't *you* try them?" Rachel asked.

"I'm not going to put my *tush* in that mud. You know how squeamish I am. All I want to know is how to build and maintain them."

"Coward. How do you expect your guests to try it, if you won't do it yourself? But if you're too chicken, I'll give it a try."

"Really. You'll sit in the mud?"

Rachel—who thought negotiations were one of the pillars of a happy marriage—retorted, "Yeah, if we can spend a few extra days in *the city* on our way up to Calistoga."

Several weeks later, Stuart and Rachel drove up to San Francisco. Since they were both born and raised there, they simply referred to it as *the city*. As they crossed the Bay Bridge, Rachel commented, "The skyline is gorgeous. I really miss it."

It was four-thirty by the time they checked into the Kimpton Hotel, an old hotel on Powell Street that had been completely gutted and remodeled. As soon as they checked-in, Stuart—the practical one who was always concerned about his next meal—brought up dinner. "We need to make reservations. If we don't get a reservation, we'll have to wait for hours. You know I'm a bear when I get hungry. Let's try Kuleto's? It's right downstairs. We can pop in, make a reservation, then kill some time walking around."

Kuleto's, a traditional, old style San Francisco restaurant, had dark wood paneling with black and white tiles on the floors, set like an intricate mosaic. A wrought iron pot-rack extended the full length of the bar. It reminded Rachel of a still life painting. Italian salamis, wrapped cheeses, and blanched straw-wrapped Chianti bottles dangled from the rack.

A regal looking Eurasian hostess, with a long neck and perfect posture, scanned the reservation book. "Sorry, sir, we're booked solid from six through nine-thirty. But I could seat you at five-thirty. However, you need to promise me you'll be here on time."

"Fine. Put us down. We'll be back."

The tumult of the big city felt exhilarating. Stuart and Rachel meandered across Market Street, shocked to see that the

Emporium Department Store had all but disappeared. The huge building had been made into another Westfield Center . . . with specialty shops, a basement food court, and a multiplex theater.

"God, things are so different!" Rachel exclaimed. As they strolled through the center browsing in the windows of the up-scale boutiques, she continued. "You know, I can close my eyes and still picture the fourth floor. In the sports department there was a large canvas tent set-up with a lantern and a Coleman stove. I would stand in front of that display and dream about camping."

Stuart smiled inwardly. He could see that Rachel was enjoying herself reminiscing. Taking her away from teaching, Santiago and his mother was the right thing to do.

Thinking back, Rachel said, "You know, growing up here, we were never at a loss for things to do."

Eventually their conversation led back to the resort. Stuart remarked casually, "I forgot to tell you, I finally got the approval to get health insurance for our full-time employees. I'm not sure what suddenly changed Reno's mind. My bet is Banning wanted it for his girlfriends. At any rate, it'll help us retain our employees."

The next morning Rachel and Stuart stood at the foot of Market and Powell Streets, shivering as the cutting wind reminding them that they should have brought warmer jackets. They watched intently as two conductors swung an empty cable car around on a turnstile. As soon as one of the conductors signaled it was okay to board, an excited teenage boy elbowed Stuart in his haste to take an outside seat.

"It's still chaotic boarding one of these," Stuart laughed. "Nothing's changed."

With a little aggression of their own, they managed to seize the last two outside seats. The legendary Powell-Hyde Street cable car frantically clanged its distinctive bell. *Get out of the way; get out of the way*—a warning for any person or vehicle that dared to move onto their tracks.

As they sat there, they could feel and hear the vibrations of the cables rolling beneath the street. The cable car seemed to struggle up the steep hills and then carefully claw its way back down. Rachel—more cautious now than when she rode the cable car as a child—didn't want to think what would happen if the cable broke. They hopped off at Ghirardelli Square, the end-of-the-line. Half a block away she caught sight of the sailboats, their multi-colored sails tacking in the wind. Walking towards Fisherman's Wharf, she stopped to watch as the seagulls swooped down and landed on the old fishing trawlers. Her heart practically sang *Ode to Joy*. She was home.

Stuart had been unusually quiet until he inhaled the pungent smell of crabs cooking in the large cauldrons in front of Alioto's Restaurant. "Now I feel like a San Franciscan again. I can practically taste the fresh crab . . . with some good sourdough bread."

Playing tourists, they traipsed in and out of a string of souvenir shops—all more-or-less with the same merchandise. Knick-knacks. Seashells and tee-shirts. Mugs. Rachel picked up a small statue that looked like a carved sea captain in a bright yellow rain slicker and matching hat. "I'm buying this for you."

"What for?"

"You're like the old sea captain that's weathered many a storm."

"Save your money. I don't need another *chatzka*."

The sun broke through the shroud of gray fog just as they walked out of Alioto's Restaurant. Rachel exclaimed, "This has been so much fun." Just then, she noticed people lining up to get on the ferry to Angel Island. "You know, in all the time we lived here, I've never been to Angel Island. Have you?"

"No. What's on Angel Island? Angels," Stuart quipped. "Don't tell me you're looking for another miracle?

"Very funny. Tomorrow let's take the ferry over there. I think there are some trails, and we can hike around."

As usual, the next morning fog enveloped the city. But they buttoned up, headed to the pier, and took a ferry to Angel Island. They planned to explore on their own, but as they disembarked, a cluster of tourists gathered around a young, clean-cut park ranger.

"Let's hear what he's got to say?" Rachel asked.

They scooted in behind a crowd of Asian tourists with cameras slung around their necks.

"Can you hear me in the back?" the ranger asked through his amplified bull horn.

They nodded.

The ranger explained that they were about to enter an immigration center.

Obviously unhappy, Stuart said, "I thought we were leaving Santiago and the immigration issue behind. I planned this weekend, hoping you could forget all that . . . and just relax."

"Honest to God, in all the years that I lived in *the city*, I had no idea anything like this was here. I thought it just had some hiking trails. But since we're here, let's take the tour."

The ranger led the group to the Angel Island Immigration Center. As everyone gathered around the entrance, he began to explain, "This place has an illustrious past. Angel Island was known as Ellis Island of the West. But there was a difference. The immigrants that passed through here were from Asia, not Europe. It was built in response to the Chinese Exclusion Act of 1882."

Rachel couldn't contain herself. She nudged Stuart. "Did you hear that?"

"Rachel, be quiet. I'm trying to listen."

She was pleased that the ranger had his attention.

"The Chinese were viewed as a threat," the ranger continued. "The U.S. was experiencing serious unemployment problems that resulted in increased discrimination. The Chinese were targeted as *unsuitable Americans* due to their appearance and low social status. Many were stopped and held here for extended periods of time, until they could be sent back home."

As they toured the buildings, the ranger pointed out heart-rending poems that were carved into the wooden walls or floorboards. "These poems," he said loud enough for everyone on the tour to hear, "are immensely important to our history. They are physical remnants that tell the heart-breaking story of this first wave of Chinese immigrants."

For a few minutes, the group stopped and lingered. Rachel scanned a few of the poems that had been translated into English, enlarged, and framed on a nearby wall. She couldn't help relating their anguish to Rosa's plight.

> *America has power, but not justice.*
> *In prison, we are victimized as if we are guilty.*
> *Given no opportunity to explain,*
> *it is real brutal.*
> *I bow my head in reflection,*
> *but there is nothing I can do.*

Another read

> *I thoroughly hate the barbarians because they*
> *do not respect justice.*
> *They continually promulgate hard laws to*
> *show their prowess.*
> *They oppose the overseas Chinese and*
> *violate treaties.*
> *They examine for hookworms and practice*
> *hundreds of despotic acts.*

Returning to San Francisco, the wind had picked up again and the ferry swayed with the churning waves. With sad eyes Rachel turned to Stuart and said, "You know, even though The City has changed, our government hasn't. Can you see the similarities? We're still doing the same thing , locking up foreigners that just want to work, to have a better life."

"Rachel, let's not talk politics. Could we just enjoy the day? Look at the view. From here you can see all three bridges."

Rachel knew she was being patronized and grew frustrated. "I'm not talking about the view. I concede. It's fabulous. I'm talking about our government. You know, sometimes when I recite the Pledge of Allegiance with my class, I choke up on the phrase . . . *and justice for all*. There never has been justice for all. We claim America's a big melting pot, but it isn't. It's an illusion."

Stuart sighed. "It's an ideal. Something we strive for."

"No. It's pure propaganda."

"Rachel, it's Sunday. Give it a rest. We can't do anything about it."

The next day they drove up to Calistoga to research the mud baths. While Rachel ranted on and on about America's rotten attitude towards immigrants, all Stuart wanted to do was check out the mud baths, eat a few good meals, and go wine-tasting.

Chapter 48

Soccer Celebration

Desert Oasis, California

LATE ON THURSDAY the sun had just dropped behind the San Jacinto Mountains, as Banning's jet landed at the Palm Springs Airport. As prearranged, a limo picked him up and drove him to the resort. Lately he had been tossing around the idea of building some additional units at the resort, possible turning it into a time-share. He had scheduled a meeting the next day with Stuart, Tom Akins, an engineer familiar with the Twin Palms property, and a well-known L.A. architect.

He caught up with the men on Friday at eleven o'clock—early for him—and they slogged over the sandy dunes. He intended to give the architect and the engineer a sense of the acreage and his vision for future development. After familiarizing them with the large expanse of land, they had a few platters of food brought into the private banquet room. When lunch was cleared, Stuart pulled out the plot and topography maps and spread them across the large oak table. The men hammered out multiple possibilities.

As the meeting wound down, Stuart excused himself and returned to his office to take care of some issues that had popped up. He lost track of Banning until breakfast Saturday morning. "I thought you were flying back to Reno last night."

"No, something came up," Banning said, giving Stuart a knowing wink.

Stuart suspected—but really didn't want to know—if Banning met his courier/girlfriend and was planning to fly back to Reno with a stash of cocaine. "What's on your schedule for today?"

"I told the pilots to have the jet ready around five. I thought I'd just mosey around. See for myself how things are going." Banning said. "Why? Got something in mind?"

Stuart hesitated, debating whether Banning would be interested, but then decided what the hell, he'd invite him anyway. "You know that soccer team you're sponsoring? Well, they're going to be playing at noon. The park is nearby. Rachel volunteered to bring refreshments, so I'm tagging along. Wanna see what you're paying for?"

Banning—by no means a suburban father—had never done anything this wholesome. He immediately noticed the boys wearing their soccer shirts emblazed with Twin Palms Resort and Spa across their backs. It filled him with pride. In a generous mood, he whispered to Stuart, "They look good. Invite 'em all for pizza after the game. My treat."

"Really? You sure you want do this?" Stuart was floored by Banning's unexpected interest.

"Hell yeah. Watch them. These guys play their hearts out. I like that spirit."

Happy about winning their game and jazzed about this unexpected treat, the team and their families overwhelmed the small pizza restaurant. No one could hear above the clamor as they sat at the picnic tables and chatted with their families. All except Santiago. He sat alone. Usually, Stuart and Rachel stepped in as his surrogate parents. However, Stuart was preoccupied with

Banning and Rachel was preoccupied with the families.

"What's with that kid?" Banning asked, pointing towards Santiago. "Why is he alone?"

"It's a long story," Stuart said. "Ask Rachel. She's pretty involved with him. She's over there schmoozing with some of the parents. I'll get her. She's the resident expert when it comes to Santiago."

"What's up?" Rachel asked, when Stuart nudged her back to his table.

"I'm just curious. What'd you know about," and Banning paused, ". . . what's that kid's name again?"

"Santiago," Stuart interjected. "Rachel, Banning wants to know why Santiago's sitting by himself."

"Well . . . how can I sum it up? He's in my class. A good kid with some bad breaks. His mother is in a detention center. I found him living alone."

"Where's his father?"

"Dead. Murdered."

Banning wasn't expecting that kind of an answer. "Murdered?"

"Yeah, but not here. In El Salvador. Santiago doesn't talk about it, but I researched the country. El Salvador has a corrupt government. They've turned against their own people. Apparently, Santiago's father fought against them. After he was killed, his mother fled with her two sons."

"Where's the other kid?"

"When Santiago and his mother came to California, his brother refused to go. He stayed in Mexico."

Banning started to say something, but with all the racket Rachel could hardly hear him. "Wait, this is ridiculous. The noise is getting out of hand. I can hardly hear you. I'm going to quiet everyone down."

Stuart jumped up. "I'll go quiet 'em down."

"NO!" Rachel snapped. "Stay here. You'll just yell at them. I'm a teacher. I'll quiet them down without yelling." She stood in the middle of the room. She raised her right hand high with just her index finger pointing towards the ceiling and paused. One-by-one the boys and their families stopped talking.

"Thank you everyone. I need your attention for just a minute. Congratulations to all of you. Today's win was spectacular. Let's give a big round of applause to Coach Ruben. He's the best! Maybe he would like to say a few words . . ."

Ruben had coached soccer at the Boys' and Girls' Club before it closed. Now he volunteers his time coaching Santiago's A.Y.S.O. team. Always gracious, he said, "I'd like to thank Stuart and Rachel for coming out to so many games, buying us oranges, and cheering us on. And a big thank you to Mr. Banning. We appreciate your generosity, for sponsoring our team and these awesome uniforms. And of course, for giving us this great pizza party. Boys, let's give them all a big round of applause."

The server nodded to Rachel, indicating the pizzas were ready.

"Okay," Rachel said, "I'm sure you're all hungry. Let's try to keep the noise level down. Remember, there's other people in the restaurant." Quietly she went over to the Zamora family and asked if Santiago could sit with them. Mr. Zamora, a devoted father, worked banquets at the Gene Autry Hotel and was a part-time house painter. Nevertheless, he tried to attend as many games as possible.

"*No problema,*" he said, and urged his son Antonio to make space. He personally went over and brought Santiago back to join his family.

When Rachel returned to the table to join Stuart and Banning, she asked, "Where were we?"

"I'm eating my pizza while it's hot," Stuart said, cheese dripping from his mouth. "You were starting to tell Banning about Santiago."

"Oh, yeah. Santiago's had it rough. He's in my class. That's how I got to know him. He was hardly ever coming to school. Then he disappeared. So, I went to the office to find out about him."

"You don't need to get into the nitty-gritty," Stuart reminded her.

"Okay. Okay. Anyway, I found out he was living alone in an

apartment, babysitting little kids. It's really hard to imagine."

Not particularly interested in chowing down on pizza, Banning tried to follow the story.

"Apparently Santiago and his mother crossed the border illegally. Eventually she got picked up. She's in a detention center . . . about a three-hour drive from here. Know where Apple Valley is?"

Banning chuckled. "Know it well. I developed a tract of land in Antelope Valley. That's about an hour-and-a-half drive from Apple Valley. Jesus, both places are off the beaten track. Is the kid still living alone?"

Tired of hearing about Santiago, Stuart asked, "Does anyone want this last piece of pizza? Banning, how 'bout you?"

"No, thanks. Be my guest."

For the moment Rachel wondered if she should tell Banning the whole story. "I found a place for him to live. Up in Sky Valley. A boys' ranch. But that turned out to be a disaster. Now he's living with some distant relative. Stuart pays the family for his room-and-board. And I'm trying to bring him up to speed at school."

"Stuart, that's damn nice of you. How come you never told me about it?"

"Truthfully, it never came up. I just felt sorry for the kid. He was all alone."

Banning leaned an elbow on the table, sniffed, and wiped his nose with his thumb and finger. Then he gazed out into the distance. There was a long silence. When Banning spoke, it was as if reliving some past experiences. "I don't usually talk about it, but I spent a lot of time in foster care. In a bunch of different homes. And let me tell you, it was the shits. My mom died when I was seven, and, well, my dad moved around a lot. I feel for that kid."

"It must have been rough growing up in foster care." Rachel said. "Did you ever get to see your dad?"

'Yeah, from time to time he would get a new position somewhere in Southern California and he'd come and get me. But then he'd drink, and eventually lose his job. And back I'd go to another foster home. I always had high hopes we'd be together. He was all I had. In the end, the liquor did him in." As if to change the subject, he asked, "Tell me more about Santiago. Does he ever get to see his mom?"

"Yeah, the people he lives with have taken him a couple of times, but mostly I take him."

"When's she getting out?"

"She's not. They're going to deport her, but she doesn't know when. It's hard to get the real scoop. She speaks broken English. From what I gather, she's had a couple of hearings, both fiascos. She really doesn't understand what's going on. And there's no one I can ask. It's not like she has a case worker or something. It's pathetic."

"Anything I can do?"

"Umm, I don't know. It seems hopeless."

Stuart gave Rachel a look, as if to ask permission to talk. "Remember Alain," he interjected, "the PR guy?"

"Of course."

"Well . . . you probably already know this, but he was instrumental in getting the governor elected. So, we thought he might have some juice. You know, some connection. But when Rachel talked to him, Alain told her the governor couldn't do anything. It's not a state issue. It's in the hands of the feds. I think he said the Department of Justice. Anyhow, he suggested some hot-shot immigration lawyer in L.A. Supposedly tops in the field."

"What happened?"

"A while back Rachel called and spoke to the secretary in his office."

"And . . .?"

"He charges a fortune. Way too expensive for our blood. It could run into thousands of dollars. We just threw a wedding for one daughter, and another is in grad school."

"Hell, if you think the attorney can help, call him back. I'll pay the goddamn attorney's fees."

Rachel was euphoric. But her exuberance evaporated a few weeks later when nothing changed. She thought Banning had forgotten his offer. She constantly pestered Stuart, asking him if Banning said anything further. He would shrug his shoulders and put out his arms, as if to say, "What can I do? It's not my money." Just when she thought Banning had forgotten his magnanimous offer, Stuart came home from his office whistling. He dropped an envelope on the living room table.

"If that's your paycheck, don't leave it lying around. It'll only get lost."

"Nope," Stuart said, with a mischievous smile. "It's a cashier's check for the attorney. Fifteen big ones."

Chapter 49

Alex Villareal

RACHEL HAD the fifteen-thousand-dollar check in hand and couldn't wait to call Alex Villareal, the immigration attorney that Alain had recommended. She had called months earlier but dropped the whole idea when she found out how much it cost. Now, with Banning's check in hand, it was more than pie-in-the-sky and wishful thinking. Nevertheless, her stomach did butterflies as she punched in his number. By the time she hung up the phone, she could have danced on the ceiling. She finally got the appointment, although it was months away. That night, when Stuart came home, he could tell she was in a buoyant mood.

"Guess what?" Rachel said, before he could take off his shoes, "I've got some good news."

"I'm not good at guessing, but I imagine it has something to do with Santiago."

"You're right. This afternoon I made an appointment with that immigration lawyer. The appointment is a few months down the road, but it's a start."

Despite days of grumbling about Rachel's involvement, Stuart got swept up in the *cause célèbre*. "Great. Did you tell Santiago?"

"No, I don't want to get his hopes up. I want to hear what Villareal has to say first."

"Listen, Rachel, I'm not too keen about you driving into L.A. Where's his office, exactly?"

"Century City. His secretary said it's a breeze to get there."

"You have no idea where you're going, and the drivers on the I-10 are crazy. I'll drive you."

"Like you're not a crazy driver?"

"No. When's the last time I got a ticket? Besides, fifteen grand is a big number. It would be irresponsible to just fork it over without seeing if this guy is legit. Besides, I've got more experience dealing with attorneys. Sam Mitchell, one of Banning's real estate attorneys, has an office there. I've driven to Century City at least a dozen times. If you want, we can even stop and have a leisurely lunch at Il Fornaio. They've got the best French bread outside of San Francisco."

On the day of the appointment, Stuart spent the early morning checking on things at the resort. Mid-morning, he picked Rachel up at the condo. "Did you bring the notebook with all the info on Santiago and his mother?"

"Yep! Right here next to my purse."

They no sooner got in the car when Stuart slipped in his favorite Frank Sinatra disc.

"God, am I condemned to listen to that music for the rest of my life?" Rachel teased.

"What's wrong with Sinatra?"

"Nothing. Just put in something else for a change. I'm tired of listening to the same old songs."

"What would *my lady* like to hear?"

"Anything but Sinatra. How about Roberta Flack? Better yet, let's talk."

"Fine. But I was hoping for some time to unwind. I've had an aggravating morning. Remember Quinn?"

"Sort of. He's the gardener guy, right?"

"Good memory. Well, he's being a royal pain in the ass. I think he's been drinking again. This morning he pissed-off one of the housekeepers. She came into the office crying. He threatened to have her fired."

"Why don't you get rid of him? He sounds like a bully."

Rachel couldn't get Rosa out of her mind. "I can't imagine doing time in prison. You and I are both softies. We wouldn't last a week without our creature comforts. You couldn't stand it without pizza and Sinatra. And I'd freak out without my nightly bubble bath."

"Speak for yourself, princess. I'm tough. I could handle it."

"Yeah, right. You've got the cushiest job in the world.

After lunch they drove into the Fox Auto Park closest to Villareal's office.

"You'll never find the car again. This garage is humungous."

"Have I ever lost a car?"

"Not yet but pay attention to where you park."

"Rachel, mellow out. Stop worrying about everything."

On the directory near the elevator, she spotted the attorney's name and floor. As they rode up in the elevator to the ninth floor, she whispered, "This isn't the easiest place to get to."

"Patience, my dear, patience. By the way, where'd you get that blazer? I've never seen you wear it before?"

"God, I've had it for years. Since we moved from Reno. I haven't had any occasion to wear it. It just sits in the closet. Today I just wanted to spiff up my professional image."

"You should wear it more often."

As they entered the lawyer's suite, Rachel glanced around, expecting a luxurious office. She was disappointed. The small reception area had no magazines and the western artwork looked pedestrian. A receptionist-secretary came out of her office when she heard the door open. "Have a seat. Mr. Villareal will be with you in a moment."

After she disappeared, Rachel turned to Stuart and said, "For a high-price lawyer, this place isn't very impressive."

"Don't be obnoxious! Do you have to comment about everything? You can't judge a lawyer by his office furniture. At least, hear him out."

"Yeah, but I've read about shyster lawyers that prey on immigrants. They charge exorbitant fees, make all kinds of promises, and never do a damn thing."

"Stop nitpicking. You're the one who couldn't wait for this meeting. So far, Alain's been right about everything. Give this guy a chance. And for crying out loud, lower your voice. Everyone can hear you."

Shortly after their private exchange, Alex Villareal, a tall man with an athletic build and a pale complexion appeared. He was wearing gray slacks, a long sleeve, white shirt, tie, and well-polished black wing-tip shoes. "If my secretary got it right, you must be Mr. and Mrs. Roth."

He personally led them down a short corridor—framed with certificates of merit meant to impress his clients—to his unassuming office. The wall separating his office from that of his secretary held two sets of floor-to-ceiling bookcases, all lined with volumes of law books, a few family photos, and several trophies. Two huge windows behind his desk overlooked the surrounding neighborhoods. In the far distance, one could barely make out the San Gabriel Mountains, encased in a grayish-brown smog.

"Can I get you folks something? Water, a soft drink, coffee?"

"None for me," Stuart replied, "We just ate a huge lunch."

"Nothing for me," Rachel added, suddenly polite. "Thanks anyway."

"Do you mind if I pour myself a cup of coffee? Actually, I think better with a shot of caffeine."

When Mr. Villareal left his office, Rachel couldn't contain her thoughts. "He's got a Spanish name, but he looks American."

Stuart gave her one of his infamous looks. *Enough!*

When Mr. Villareal returned, he placed his coffee mug that said *Dad* on his desk and sat down. "I couldn't help overhearing the last bit of your conversation. And yes, I'm Hispanic. My lineage goes all the way back to Spain. Somewhere along the line, parts of the family migrated to Mexico. Eventually my family landed in California. I'm native born. Grew up in Boyle Heights."

"I apologize. That was very rude," Stuart said, taking the blame for Rachel.

Alex smiled. "I don't think anything of it. People have a crazy notion that all Hispanics are short with dark skin. I guess I'm unusual in Southern California. By the way, sorry I couldn't see you sooner, but we have a little cabin up at Lake Arrowhead. A nice retreat from the daily grind. When the kids get off school, we head up there."

"We've only been up there once. But we loved it," Stuart remarked. "We're relatively new to this area. We're still exploring the highlights."

Mr. Villareal leaned forward, planting his elbows on his desk. "Over the years, L.A.'s changed. When I was growing up, Century City didn't exist. Tom Mix and 20th Century Fox owned this land."

"Oh, my God!" Rachel popped up, "Tom Mix. I haven't heard that name in years. Growing up, he was my favorite cowboy hero. I think his radio program came on at five o'clock."

"Well, I haven't heard anyone talk about radio programs in years," Mr. Villareal chuckled. A master at handling people, he quickly brought the conversation back to center. "Tell me, what brings you here?"

Stuart took charge. He handed the attorney his business card. "I run a resort in the desert and Rachel teaches school. Somehow, she connected with a boy in her class and discovered him living alone."

Overanxious to get it all out, Rachel interrupted. "His mother's an *illegal immigrant* from El Salvador."

"Whoa," Mr. Villareal said. "Coming from El Salvador *illegal immigrant* is not a phrase I would use. It's a loaded political phrase, denoting criminals, not the hard-working nannies, gardeners, and farm workers you and I know. El Salvador's a mess . . . chaotic, lawless. In the midst of a brutal civil war. Think about it. Let's just say she's a *refugee, an undocumented worker.* I don't mean to lecture you, but I've spent my entire career fighting against the use of the phrase *illegal immigrant.* Why would anyone leave their home, family—everything they value, everything that is familiar to them—if they were not desperate?"

Rachel had a flashback.

She remembered that night in the resort dining room when Alain, the P.R. guru, explained the power of words. That was his job. He too got paid big bucks to play with words. Create images. Rachel immediately caught on. She had to rethink what she was about to say. "I see your point. Anyhow, INS picked Santiago's mother up in National City for driving some . . . some *undocumented workers.* She's been stuck in a detention center ever since."

"Where?"

"Apple Valley. She's been there over a year. Maybe two. I'm not really sure. I've no idea what's really going on. For all I know, she could be deported tomorrow."

Mr. Villareal picked up a yellow legal tablet.

"Okay. I'll need some basic facts. What's her full name?"

"Rosa Lopez."

"Umm, that's a common name. Have anything more to go on? Perhaps a middle name or some other way to identify her?"

"I have her alien number. Will that help? It's right here . . . in my notebook."

"Perfect."

She read the numbers off to him.

"What about children?"

"Two," Rachel said. "The older boy, Javier, lives in Mexico. Santiago, the boy in my class, was the only one living with his mother when she got picked up. Can you imagine, he was left alone? The government could care less."

"It's common," he said. "How old's the boy?"

"Fourteen. He's living in Desert Oasis with some relatives."

"Hold on. Not so fast. I'm trying to jot this all down."

"Okay. Sorry."

Before Rachel got on her high horse, Stuart interrupted, hoping he could stay on message. "Rachel's been running interference for him."

Mr. Villareal stopped and sipped his coffee. "Help me out. Is Santiago still living alone? I thought I heard you say he's living with relatives."

"He was living alone," Rachel explained, "but now he's living in an apartment with some relatives and their three kids."

There were more questions and answers as the attorney tried to piece everything together.

Finally, getting to the business side, Stuart added, "We found someone willing to foot the bill for your services." Stuart unzipped a black leather pouch, pulled out an envelope, and handed it to Mr. Villareal.

Not shy about money, Mr. Villareal put on his wireless glasses before opening the envelope. He glanced approvingly at the numbers. *A retainer of fifteen thousand dollars.*

Confident that he had Mr. Villareal's ear, Stuart continued. "That's a cashier's check. Mr. Banning, my boss, is the sole owner of TRB World Holdings. For him, this issue's personal. He's committed to paying any-and-all expenses incurred in reuniting Santiago with him mother. If you want, you can check him out with Dun and Bradstreet. But I can tell you right now, he's good for it."

Looking pleased, Mr. Villareal stared at the check one more time; then he slid it into the top right-hand desk drawer. "May I speak candidly? The only promise I'll make today is that I'll search the records and review Mrs. Lopez's case. Then I'll set-up a meeting with her. And rest assured, I'll fight like hell for her release."

Rachel thought, *for fifteen thousand bucks, you damn well better fight hard.*

"I've got a pretty good track record, but I want you to know, there's no guarantees. You've got to understand," Mr. Villareal continued in a professorial tone, "the system is rigged. There aren't enough immigration judges and they're always rushed. They've got no time to research a case and gather facts. They're forever backlogged. *Due process* isn't a given. It's a Potemkin village."

Neither Rachel nor Stuart understood that phrase, but let it go.

"It's set up to look like justice, but that's an illusion. It's the furthermost thing from it. And to make matters worse, the detention centers are privately run operations. They're owned by several international corporations. They answer to stockholders. For them, it's all about profits and dividends. It's business with big-time lobbyists in Washington, D.C. Congress gave the corporations a sweetheart deal. They're reimbursed big time for every occupied bed. Obviously, the corporations aren't in a big hurry to release the *undocumented workers*." He paused, to let it all sink in. "Just the other day, I heard about a senator that held stock in one of the corporations."

Rachel blurted out, "Isn't that illegal? You make it sound hopeless."

Embarrassed that his wife was so blunt, Stuart tried to tone her down. "Why don't you let Mr. Villareal finish what he was saying, DEAR."

Rachel did not appreciate being silenced. "Well, it's sounding pretty dismal. And I'd like to know what Banning is paying for."

Stuart shot daggers at Rachel, an indication she needed to shut up.

Trying to appear earnest, Mr. Villareal continued his spiel. What he had to say had been repeated to his clients so many times that he could almost say it by heart. "There are no guidelines. The interpretation of immigration laws varies from state-to-state, court-to-court, even judge-to-judge. Without exaggerating, it's a three-ring circus. Here's the problem in a nutshell. In the judicial pecking order, an immigration judge isn't particularly prestigious. They're appointed by the Justice

Department without senate confirmation. The process is supposed to be apolitical, but it never is. Over time, some judges are selected by liberal regimes. Some by conservative regimes. So, it should come as no surprise that the judges, depending on their politic leanings, think one way or the other. Some are as biased as hell. Others can be soft-hearted and lenient. And just so you realize the inconsistencies, it also depends on the politics of the state. In Texas, for instance, only a small percent of judges give asylum. Here in California, it's much more lenient, but it can still be arbitrary."

Just then Mr. Villareal's phone rang. "Excuse me for just a sec." He picked up his phone. "Is it an emergency?" he asked, annoyed at the interruption. "I'm meeting with clients. Tell her not to worry. I'll pick George up from swim practice today."

He sighed. "Sorry. Where was I?"

"About the odds," Stuart reminded him. "You were explaining how the system works."

Mr. Villareal smiled. "There is hope. There are a couple of ways to skin the cat. If we're very lucky, we'll get a sympathetic judge. Another tactic is to keep petitioning for hearings . . . until we beat them down. The overworked immigration judges handle three times the number of cases as federal court judges. And their staffs and budgets are much smaller. When an attorney like me—from outside their system gets involved—sometimes, but not always, the judge will dismiss the case just to get rid of us. Essentially, they're running legal assembly lines. Time is of the essence. They simply aren't equipped, or don't have time for any lengthy hearings with witnesses and testimony." Mr. Villareal took a sip of his coffee, then continued. "If you're an odds player, detainees that have an outside attorney have a much better record of winning asylum cases." Then to protect himself, he added, "But it's not a given."

Chapter 50

A Turning Point

Apple Valley Detention Center

IN A BUOYANT MOOD, Rachel took Santiago to McDonald's, before driving him to Apple Valley Detention Center to visit his mother. As they pulled into the restaurant parking lot, a carload of giggly girls wearing soccer uniforms were leaving. Rachel smiled inwardly, as she watched Santiago coyly look them over. She wasn't sure if it was the girls or the soccer uniforms that interested him most. Once inside, Santiago offered to clear the napkins from an empty, but not quite clean table, while Rachel placed their usual order.

As she distributed their food she asked, "What's up, Santiago? You seem so happy today."

He pulled the wooden rosary from his pocket and laid it on the table. "Think I can give this to my mom? Yolanda bought it for her."

Rachel cringed. She knew better than to give him false hope.

The guards could be so heartless and for the first time he seemed joyful. She noticed his English was improving. He was better able to express himself. Without answering his question directly, she added her own good news. "There's a lawyer who's reviewing your mother's situation. He's going to try to help her."

"Can he get her out of jail?"

"Well, he's sure going to try." His reference to *jail* rather than *a detention center* did not go unnoticed.

When they arrived at the detention center, Rachel and Santiago were both familiar with the routine. Identification. All personal possessions in a locker. The metal detector. For the moment, the rosary slipped Rachel's mind. Thankfully, it did not set off any alarm. As they assembled in the large room waiting for their turn to visit, Santiago asked, "What should I do with the rosary?"

"You still have it?"

"Yeah."

Rachel didn't know what to say. She didn't want him to be disappointed. "Give the rosary to the guard quietly. When no one else is around. Tell him your mother's name and ask him to give it to her. All he can say is no."

When everyone was called into the large assembly room to meet the detainees, Rachel and Santiago hung back until they were the only ones left. "Go on, ask the guard," Rachel urged, thinking he had nothing to lose.

"Please, sir," Santiago said, clutching the rosary, "will you give these to Rosa Lopez? She's my mother."

Touched by the young boy's innocence and his pleading eyes, the bulked-up guard whispered, "I'll try," and quickly pocketed it. "Now go on in and see her."

Rachel was reminded once again of Rosa's pitiful situation as she watched Santiago and his mother—separated by the plexiglass partition—conversing over the phone. Close, but not close enough. Santiago seemed different, so much more animated when he was speaking with his mother. As time was running out, Rachel tapped him on the shoulder. "Santiago, listen to me carefully. I want you to explain to your mom what I'm about to say, okay? Make sure you tell her word-for-word. It's very important."

"Uh-huh," he nodded, sensing the importance.

"Tell your mom that a lawyer, Mr. Villareal, will be coming to visit her soon. And that he wants to help her get out of detention. Got that?"

"Uh-huh," Santiago said again, and then repeated the essence of it to his mother in Spanish.

Rosa, who had developed a nervous tick, blinked many times. "I no got money."

"Tell her not to worry about the money. It's all paid for. Someone else is paying."

Rosa's face lit up.

In the Volkswagen on the return to Desert Oasis, Rachel could not stop thinking about Rosa. She worried that she may have gotten her hopes up and that Mr. Villareal might not deliver. The picture he painted was gloomy, lowering their expectations.

"Do you think the guard will give the rosary to my mother?"

Rachel's response was vague. "I can't be sure. He seemed like a nice enough guy. We'll just have to wait and see. Santiago, when your mother calls, ask her, okay?"

Chapter 51

Discovery

Apple Valley Detention Center

BEFORE SPEAKING with his newest client, Mr. Villareal set out to fully research Rosa's situation. Always diligent, he understood all too well that lives often hung in the balance, hidden away in little known or forgotten details. Using a research site for attorneys, he located her case number. From there he learned that she had been apprehended by Border Patrol Agent Flores in National City on Wednesday, September 13, 1985. She was charged under U.S. Penal Code 1324 with reckless disregard that aliens had entered the U.S. and attempted transport of illegal aliens.

Mr. Villareal grimaced as he read the words *illegal aliens* He couldn't help thinking that expression was bogus, as if passengers arrived from outer space. The term deliberately lacked a face. A beating heart. A person with major troubles. As he studied Rosa's file, he took copious notes. Within the second hour he found a major error. He read and reread it over and over to make sure he got it right.

The three people that Rosa Lopez had picked up the night of her arrest turned out to be *legal*. All along, they had been carrying *H-2A* visas that gave them the right to be in the United States as temporary migrant farm workers. But at the time of their arrest, neither Rosa nor the Border Patrol agents knew that they had special visas. The Border Patrol agents—playing to their advantage—only spoke English, knowing full-well that the four they were arresting didn't understand a word they were saying. That night the agents had been watching the *stash* house, hoping to crack down on *illegal immigrants* hiding there. The way things came down, they simply made the wrong assumption. They claimed Rosa Lopez was *aiding and abetting three illegal immigrants* and threw the book at her.

Mr. Villareal learned that all four had been transported to the National City jail. All Rosa had known was her assignment—*to deliver the two men and the woman to the strawberry fields in Carlsbad*. In jail, Rosa had lost track of the three passengers. Truth be told, she did not even know their names. When the passengers' belongings were confiscated by the authorities at the jail, they discovered the three did have proper documentation and were **NOT** illegal. Realizing their mistake, the court quickly released them. But during their bureaucratic snafu, nobody thought to drop the *serious* charges against Rosa. She had been tagged and held at the jail until INS, *Immigration and Naturalization Service,* could interview her. Ultimately, they sent her to Apple Valley Detention Center to be held over for trial.

Once Mr. Villareal discovered what happened to the three passengers in Rosa's van, he felt hopeful. He had something solid, something substantial, if only he could get a judge to listen. The next day he called the detention center to schedule an appointment to meet Rosa Lopez, his new client. He doodled little boxes on a notepad as he waited to be connected to the right person.

"Yes, I'm an attorney," he said, "I need to meet with my client as soon as possible. No, I don't want an early morning slot. On a good day it's a two-and-a-half-hour drive from L.A. How about something right after lunch tomorrow. Can you swing it? Okay, then next Tuesday." *He bemoaned the fact that by the time he drove out there to see his client and return, his day would be shot to hell.*

A hefty Tonganese guard—a known predator within the system—came to collect Rosa. Officer Ngata didn't say where she was taking her, and Rosa knew better than to ask. None of the guards bothered to answer the detainees' questions. But Officer Ngata, with her belligerent and bullying attitude, was among the worst. She deliberately referred to the Hispanic women as *wetbacks* knowing full well that it got under their skin. As in "Hey, you, Wetback, I'm talking to you."

Alarmed that she could be set upon sexually, Rosa panicked. She had observed others that had left with Officer Ngata and came back in tears. In addition, just below the surface, she lived with the constant fear that she would be sent back to El Salvador. All she thought about were her two boys. *Suppose I don't have a chance to say good-bye to Santiago. What about Javier? How is he managing? I want to see my granddaughter at least once before I die.*

In handcuffs, she shuffled through the dull gray, windowless corridors until they reached the landscaped patio that separated the detention center from the courthouse. She recognized the three-story courthouse where she had been taken for two previous court hearings: one when she pled guilty and the other when her request for asylum was denied. Once inside the courthouse, she was led through an unobtrusive hallway to a series of small conference rooms where attorneys met with their clients. A strange, ominous man sat at a metal table rereading his notes as he waited for her.

Officer Ngata removed the handcuffs and stood outside the door. Rosa could feel her heart racing as she faced an unfamiliar man sitting alone. Her self-worth had been chiseled down to nothing and she had grown suspicious of everyone. Terrified, she stood there and waited for him to speak. Not a novice at this,

Mr. Villareal immediately sensed her discomfort. In Spanish, he said, "Please, don't be frightened. I won't hurt you. My name is Alex Villareal. I'm a lawyer sent to help you. Are you Rosa Lopez?"

"Sí," she said tentatively.

"Please take a seat," he said, indicating a metal chair directly across the table from him. He waited for her to get settled before he spoke again. "Did Mrs. Roth tell you she hired an *abogado*, a lawyer to see you?"

Fiddling nervously with her hands, she responded. "*Sí.*"

Alex Villareal took off his rimless glasses and laid them on the table. "Well, I'm that lawyer," he said with a smile. "I'm told you have two fine boys. One living in Mexico and one here in California."

"*Sí.*"

"I have children too. Two boys and a girl. I can't imagine how hard it must be, not to see them."

The mention of her boys brought tears to Rosa's eyes.

He patted her hand lightly. "Rosa, I believe I can help you. But first there are a few things I must say."

She had forgotten what the human touch felt like and pulled away.

"From what I understand, you're scheduled to be deported. I'm not sure when. Frankly, I'm not sure anyone knows exactly. However, if you sign this paper, it will allow me to represent you in court. I've discovered some new evidence. Important new facts I'd like to present to the judge. I don't have to tell you that the legal process moves slowly. I don't know how long it will take before I get the hearing. And there are no guarantees."

Rosa remembered hearing those same words from the other lady and that didn't work out so well. Ever since one of the security guards had slipped her the rosary, she kept it out of sight in her pants pocket. She knew that at any time it could be confiscated by a stern, *follow the rules* guard, or swiped by another detainee in her dormitory. For now, just touching it through the jumpsuit comforted her. She closed her eyes and silently asked for divine guidance. *Am I making a mistake? Can I trust this man?* As she prayed, there was an awkward silence.

Many scenarios cluttered her mind. The fear of being sent back to El Salvador and possibly being killed by the military was not foremost in her thoughts. She no longer cared whether she lived or died. In her mind, what concerned her the most was Santiago. He needed her . . . and she needed him. In the end, her hands trembled. With the hunger for freedom in her eyes and great uncertainty, she said, "Yes, I sign."

After she shuffled out, he sat and pondered her situation. He planned to submit the form Rosa had just signed, giving him legal standing with the court. In addition, he planned to submit his motion for a new evidentiary hearing with a carefully written brief. Familiar with the procedures of the court—and anxious to get everything done before driving back to L.A.—he grabbed his briefcase and marched across the foyer to the other side of the courtrooms. He wanted to get on the court docket as quickly as possible.

As it turned out, Alex recognized Lisa in the Clerk's Office. Even though she had cut her sandy blonde hair short, the aura of softness remained. She was concentrating on some paperwork, unaware that he stood in the open doorway watching her. Manila file folders were neatly stacked on her desk and on the credenza behind her. Several years back, she worked in the Los Angeles Immigration Court on Olive Street. In their small legal circle, gossip ran rampant. Nothing was private. Alex knew her abusive husband had stalked her after their divorce. Just to taunt her, he would pop-up at the little diner where she often ate lunch or at the gym where she worked out. She had been forced to get a restraining order.

After her divorce, Lisa began dating Alex's handball partner. After a few years, that relationship fell apart. Alex remembered they had been to his home several times, once for his annual Fourth of July party and once at an open house on New Year's Day. Alex understood why she felt compelled to start fresh.

Finally, he rapped lightly on the open door.

Startled by the noise, Lisa raised her head. It took a few seconds to place him, but then she broke into a wide smile. "Well, well, well, look what the wind blew in. If it isn't Alex Villareal, himself. How've you been? How's that all-American family of yours?"

"Great. My wife's still working at Cedar-Sinai. The kids are growing up. Doug's almost as tall as me. Next year George will be a freshman and Sharon will be starting junior high school. How 'bout you. How've you been?"

"Not bad for an old broad. Have a seat."

"Thanks," he said, lowering himself into the standard metal chair. He rested his leather briefcase on the chair next to him. He crossed one leg over the other as they chit-chatted about mutual friends. Eventually the conversation got more personal. "How's life out here in the boonies?"

"Honestly, moving here's the best thing I ever did. My daughter got married and moved to Dallas. So, there's just me. I do my job and I'm out by five. Let me tell you, it's a helluva lot calmer than L.A. That's for sure. I bought a cute little condo in Apple Valley. It's got a nice community pool and a small gym."

While she talked, Alex scanned her sparse and impersonal office. No photographs, no mugs, no memorabilia of any kind. No little kids' drawings taped to the filing cabinet. "Truthfully, starting over would scare the *bejesus* out of me," he said honestly. "It can't be that easy. What about friends? Have you made new friends?"

"Yeah. No complaints. Trust me. No one here's a native. So, everyone's super friendly. I know some of the clerical staff plus a few judges. From time-to-time someone throws a party or a group of us go to dinner. I've also met my neighbors. Nice people. I had knee surgery awhile back, but I'm back playing tennis. But here's the nicest part. When I go home, I'm not looking over my shoulder, fearful my ex- might show up."

"It sounds like you're in a pretty good place in your life. Enjoying your freedom."

"You bet."

"Listen, speaking of freedom, I've taken on a case that involved a Hispanic woman who has been languishing here for about two years. Give or take. And I believe she's as innocent as Mary Poppins."

Lisa raised her eyebrows and chuckled. "Really . . . Mary Poppins? That's a stretch."

"Yep, as innocent as Mary Poppins." He uncrossed his legs and leaned in, looking serious. "Lisa, I'd really like you to do me a favor. I have a motion for an expedited hearing. I've got my client's case number and my brief, with facts that should exonerate her. Can you see to it that she gets on the docket sooner rather than later? And hey, a sympathetic judge wouldn't hurt."

"I won't do it for you. But I'm a sucker for Mary Poppins. For her, well, I'd tap dance down Main Street in Disneyland."

He laughed. "I'd like to see that."

"You've been at this game long enough to know that the judges can swing either way, depending on what cereal they ate for breakfast."

"Yeah, I know. But you've got to admit, some judges are more kind-hearted than others."

"I can't make any promises, but I'll see what I can do. Give me her case number."

He shuffled some papers. "Oh, here we go. Case A-10340795. Lisa, I can't stress enough how important this is."

After thanking her, he put his hands behind his head and stretched, thinking he had been sitting for too long. Then almost as an afterthought he said, "The system," and he bent two fingers up on each hand as quotation marks for emphasis, "owes my client a fair hearing. Her two previous hearings were shams. Disgraceful. And to add insult to injury, when she got picked up, her son was left alone. Nobody, and I mean no governmental agency, gave a rat's ass about him."

Chapter 52

Expedited Hearing

THREE WEEKS and three days passed before Alex Villareal got his expedited hearing in Judge C. J. Guerro's courtroom. Except for the American flag, a round wall clock, and a framed photo of the president, the courtroom was as plain as the inside of a cardboard box. Although Rosa was not present, she was aware of the hearing. As a detainee, she was not able to receive incoming calls. To find out the results, Alex Villareal left money in her account and instructed her to call him that evening.

Judge Guerro, with the face of a pugilist and a deep, sonorous voice, rapped his wooden gavel three times. "Court is now in session. In the matter of the U.S. Immigration and Naturalization Service (INS) vs. Rosa Lopez, Alien number A-10340795, the case will now be heard. Mr. Villareal, will you be representing the petitioner, Rosa Lopez?"

Alex Villareal stood. "Yes, Your Honor." As he sat down, he smiled inwardly. His friend Lisa did what he asked. She got the hearing in front of a more sympathetic judge. *He may or may not see things my way,* Mr. Villareal thought, *but at least it was a step in the right direction.*

"Mr. Carre, will you be representing the U.S. Immigration and Naturalization Service?"

Mr. Carre, a young lawyer with a mop of straight, brown hair and an exceptionally youthful face, replied, "Yes, Your Honor."

"Thank you. Be seated."

"Mr. Villareal, let's get on with it. Please state the reason for this expedited hearing."

Mr. Villareal relished the drama of the courtroom. He unbuttoned his suit jacket, put on his rimless glasses, and took a moment to glance at his notes. "Thank you, Your Honor. If I may, I'd like to review my client's unjust situation. On Wednesday evening, September 13, 1985, at approximately 6:00 pm, my client received a phone call from a man she had worked for on previous occasions, but never met. She only knew him as Armando. When her job was completed, she would receive a check in the mail from A. T. Transportation Company.

The judge interrupted. "You mentioned she had worked for this man on previous occasions. But you neglected to say what kind of work your client did."

"I was getting to that, Your Honor. Her task was always the same . . . to pick up temporary workers that had been driven by someone else from Tijuana to National City, in California. Her job was to transport them from National City to work in various fields in the San Diego area. On the evening of her arrest, she drove to National City to meet three passengers at 9:00 p.m. As they pulled away from the curb, the U.S. Border Patrol stopped her vehicle. The two agents that stopped her vehicle assumed the three passengers were illegals and being smuggled into the country. According to my review, Rosa Lopez was charged with not one but two sections under *U.S. Penal Code 1324: reckless disregard that aliens had entered the United States and attempted transport of illegal aliens.* In the eyes of the law, two very serious crimes. In researching her case, I discovered evidence that her arrest turned out to be a gross injustice. Each of her three passengers was in possession of an H-2A visa, which allows workers from Mexico to temporarily work in the fields."

"I know the laws, Mr. Villareal. No need to lecture me."

"I apologize, Your Honor. The two arresting agents were fluent in Spanish. Yet," and he paused to emphasis his point," in order to intimidate my client and her passengers, they deliberately chose to address them in English." Then with more than a little sarcasm, he added, "perhaps . . . if they had asked for their papers in Spanish, a language they understood, this whole fiasco would never have happened, saving the courts time and money. At any rate, when my client's three passengers were arraigned, the Spanish speaking public defender that represented them quickly discovered they were, in fact, carrying H-2A visas. In the eyes of the court, if you have an H-2A visa, you are *not* an illegal alien. The charges against my client's three passengers were dropped, and they were immediately released."

Mr. Villareal continued with all the flourishes of courtroom dialogue, knowing he was going in for the kill. "If justice was truly served, the presiding judge should have released my client as well. Since she was *not* transporting illegal immigrants, releasing her would have been the appropriate action. Instead, they tagged her. She remained in jail for three additional days until she could be interviewed by an agent from the Immigration and Naturalization Service. INS, dropped the ball as well. If they had done their job, and researched the situation, they would have known that her three passengers were *not* illegal and had been released, making the charges against my client moot. Instead of releasing her as they should have, they transferred an innocent woman to Apple Valley Detention Center where she has languished for well over two years. TWO YEARS, Your Honor, held for a crime she didn't commit. At the time of my client's preliminary hearing, she barely spoke English. Like so many others, she was intimidated by the formality of the courtroom, and did not have the benefit of an interpreter or an attorney."

The judge interrupted. "As an illegal immigrant, the court is under no obligation to provide an attorney or translator."

"That is true, Your Honor. Nevertheless, without a thorough understanding of the law, she was simply asked to affix her signature to legal documents admitting her guilt. And furthermore," Mr. Villareal said pointing a finger in the air for emphasis, "no one—and I mean no one—bothered to advise her that she was eligible to seek asylum.

"My client is from El Salvador. As you well know, it is a completely lawless country, involved in a brutal civil war. Her husband was tortured and murdered by the military. When they dumped his body in front of her house, she found three of his fingers in a plastic bag along with her name and the names of her boys. It was the crudest of warnings. The military in El Salvador plays for keeps. Rosa Lopez had every reason to fear for her life and that of her two boys. Is it so wrong to try and save yourself and your family?"

"Mr. Villareal, please stick to the facts."

"Yes, Your Honor. Only after months of incarceration did my client learn—and then only from another Spanish speaking detainee—that she had the right to seek asylum. A volunteer, a well-meaning young lady, but not a lawyer, assisted my client in filing the appropriate paperwork requesting an asylum hearing. She waited eleven months for that hearing and it was a travesty.

"Your Honor, my client is a hard-working mother whose young son was left alone to fend for himself. She is neither a criminal nor a danger to society. She could hardly be considered a risk to our national security. I pray that this court uses judicial discretion to protect Rosa Lopez. And that you will find it in your heart to provide justice and grant her asylum. Furthermore, I seek her immediate release on a bond which we are prepared to put up today."

After Mr. Villareal sat down, Judge Guerro turned his attention to the young attorney.

Mr. Carre rose and swiped a lock of hair from his forehead.

"Yes, Your Honor. As stipulated, I represent INS, the Immigration and Naturalization Service. On a personal level, I very much regret the unfortunate experiences Rosa Lopez has endured. But we deal with thousands of illegal aliens every day."

When Mr. Villareal heard the bogus term *illegal aliens,* he cringed but knew better than to interrupt.

Mr. Carre continued. "Each case is a story unto itself. And yes, some are more complicated than others. Nevertheless, I want to remind the court that no matter what happened, Rosa Lopez remains an illegal alien. Your Honor, as you well know, Immigration and Naturalization Service is charged with protecting our nation's borders. Plain and simple, it is our job to carry out the law of the land. It is also our job to apprehend and deport any-and-all illegal aliens. Despite the unfortunate circumstances of Mrs. Lopez's incarceration, she is here illegally." He paused, hoping that point would sink in with the judge. "The immigration courts have been more than fair. They have heard her case not once, but twice. And both times she has been ordered back to El Salvador, her country of origin. I am simply doing my job and I hope you see it in your heart to do yours."

Alex Villareal popped out of his seat. "Your Honor, may I address the issue of deportation?"

"You may," the judge said, glancing up at the clock," but please keep it short."

Reading the judge's growing impatience, Mr. Villareal responded. "This will be brief. Let's not pretend it is as simple as just sending her back to El Salvador. It is a death warrant. The civil war has not ended. For decades, the government has used death squads to terrorize their own people. They have killed thousands, nuns and priests, journalists, and teachers, along with other decent folks just going about their daily lives. Rosa Lopez is simply a woman who treasures life, a *refugee* who can no longer live in her own country. She is not asking anything more than to remain in the United States for her safety and that of her son. I rest my case."

"Thank you both. I will take this case under advisement," the judge said, in an even, noncommittal way. "You should be hearing from me within ninety days."

When he heard the judge say he would take Rosa Lopez's case under advisement, Mr. Villareal felt a glimmer of hope, a slight opening, but with no guarantees. He knew Rosa would be crushed that nothing had been decided. He understood Rosa's predicament. For her, life boiled down to endless tedium . . . another ninety days of waiting. From his experience as an immigration attorney, he understood that for those incarcerated, there often comes a time of deep despair . . . when endless prayers are forgotten, and dreams of freedom slip away. And he didn't want that to happen to his client. Most of all, he wanted to offer her hope.

The intensity of the hearing drained his concentration. By the time Mr. Villareal climbed into his four-year old Mercedes, his head felt as if it was stuffed with sand. Instead of returning to his office in Century City, he decided to drive back to Tarzana. That way he could avoid the brutal commute traffic. Ten minutes after he pulled into the garage, he traded his suit and tie for a shabby tee-shirt and baggy warm-up pants. He grabbed an icy beer from the refrigerator and plopped down in his new leather recliner in the family room. He opened the *L.A. Times* to the sports page, hoping to catch up on the Lakers.

After downing his Corona, he glanced at the clock by the television and figured he might be able to catch Stuart at work. He knew Rachel and Stuart were anxious to hear what happened in court. When Stuart got on the phone, Mr. Villareal gave him the run-down. "I'm not sure what it means, but the judge said he would take Rosa's case under advisement. And he'd let us know within ninety days."

"Is that good or bad?"

"It's hard to say. But here's the good thing. Sometimes it's a flat-out no, but he didn't say that."

"Did you speak to Rosa?"

"Not yet. On my last visit, I left fifty bucks in her account with instructions to call me tonight."

Chapter 53

Court Recommendation

Century City, California

SEVERAL MONTHS PASSED and Alex Villareal was onto other cases. One day he left the office early, too frustrated to continue working. He bought the *L. A. Times* outside his favorite little café run by a Greek couple, intending to grab some lunch and read the paper. Lately he had put on a few extra pounds but couldn't resist ordering their home-made lentil soup—the special of the day—along with a grilled cheese sandwich. While waiting to be served, he scanned the headlines on the front page:

Two Teenagers Dead in Drive-by Shooting

He found himself mumbling, *Jesus Christ, what's happening? L.A. is spinning out of control. Gangs shooting at each other all the time. Innocent kids being killed.*

He returned to his office. Stopping at his secretary's office, he asked, "Did the mail come in?"

"On your desk . . . and here's your call-back slips."

Thinking he needed to catch up, he wondered what was going on with his stomach. He pulled a roll of Tums from the center drawer of his desk and chewed one absent-mindedly as he scanned the stack of mail. When he caught sight of the envelope that read *U.S. Immigration Courts, Apple Valley Detention Center,* he immediately set it aside. He picked up the sterling silver letter opener—a gift from his wife when he passed the bar some twenty-one years earlier—and quickly sliced the top of the envelope open. He pulled out two printed sheets of paper and glanced over them.

The official letter read:

Immigration and Naturalization Service vs. Rosa Lopez, Alien # A-10340795

Before this case is adjudicated, it is recommended that your client, Rosa Lopez, complete the enclosed questionnaire.

Alex Villareal shook his head. Why on earth did it take two months to get this simple letter and questionnaire out? But then, he thought, there's no accounting for the bureaucracy of the court. At least it's positive news.

He skimmed the questionnaire.

1. Do you have any prior immigration violations?

2. Did you have any disciplinary infractions while in detention?

3. Do you have any criminal history?

4. Do you have any issues with mental health?

5. List your schooling.

6. List your job training and work experience.

7. Do you have close relatives residing legally in the U.S.?

8. Do you have a reference from a chaplain who can vouch for your good behavior while in detention?

9. Include any letters from family members, former employers, or friends.

10. Will you have a sponsor? List on business letterhead.

11. If released, will you have a job?

When Mr. Villareal read the last few questions, he was more than pleased. He laid the letter down on his desk and checked his watch. Then he thumbed through his Rolodex searching for Rachel or Stuart's home and work numbers. He liked this part of his job best, delivering hopeful news. He remembered that Rachel taught school and probably couldn't be reached. But with luck, he could catch Stuart at the resort.

Stuart was out of his office and couldn't be reached. A little disappointed, Mr. Villareal left a message with his secretary. "Call me. I've got some encouraging news."

When Stuart got back to his office and saw the message, he immediately returned the call. "What's up?"

"Listen, Stuart, I got promising news and want to run it by you. I just received a letter from the court. Judge Guerro hasn't made a definitive ruling, but things are looking encouraging. With his cover letter, he enclosed a questionnaire that Rosa Lopez needs to complete and return to the court."

Stuart immediately thought of all the bullshit surveys he received on the phone or in the mail. "What does he want to know?"

"Mostly routine stuff. About Rosa's education and work experience. Even about her behavior while in detention. But there are several parts she'll need help on. Most important, he wants to know if she'd have a job and a sponsor. That's very encouraging. It indicates he isn't making a snap decision one way or the other. In the back of his mind, he could be thinking about releasing her. Stuart, if she had a job waiting for her . . . and a sponsor, that would give her a lot of Brownie points."

"Really?" Stuart said, growing excited. "You really think he could release her?"

"It's a possibility, nothing more."

"If that happens, I'd say you're a miracle worker. No kidding."

"I won't jump for joy quite yet. You never can tell with these fickle judges. But a future job and a sponsor would put a few more chips in the positive column."

"Look, I can find a place for her here at the resort or at another little motel the company owns. No problem. But I can't sponsor her," Stuart explained. "I've got three kids."

"What about your boss, Mr. Banning? Maybe he'd be willing to sponsor her."

"Could be. But I can't answer for him. I'd need more details before asking him."

"Sure. It's easy enough to explain. Mr. Banning will have to fill out an I-864 form. It's a legally binding document that guarantees that Rosa won't become a financial burden to the government. And if she gets asylum, down the road she'll need a sponsor to apply for a *green card.*"

"Ah, yes. The *golden ticket.* But I'm confused. If I give her a job and Banning agrees to sponsor her, isn't that all she needs to get that green card.

"Well, not exactly. It's a long, complicated process. Plus, it takes money. There's an application fee. It isn't as if the government doles out green cards like library cards. If Rosa is granted asylum, she's got to wait a year before she can begin the application process.

"Well, what about Santiago?"

"When Rosa applies for a green card, Santiago, as a minor, is also eligible. Stuart, what do you know about the people who are caring for Santiago? Isn't one of them a relative of some sort?"

"If I've got the story straight, Nacho is Rosa's first or second cousin. Something like that."

"Is he in this country legally?"

"I don't know. But I'll find out. I know his wife Yolanda was born here."

"Great! That would make him legal. All good news. Have him write a letter of recommendation, too."

"Okay. Listen Alex, I've got to run. Someone's waiting for me. Send the form for Banning and I'll look it over. If I have any questions, I'll get back to you. Otherwise, I'll forward it to him. I'll get Nacho to write a letter. What about Rachel?"

"Yes, have her write a letter. You, too. Even her son. Collectively, it all helps."

"I can see why you've got such a great reputation. You're thorough as Hell."

Alex smiled when he hung up. At least he got the ball rolling.

As Alex drove back to Tarzana after work, he was stuck in slow-moving commute traffic on the 405. Wedged between a Southern Cal Edison van driven by a Hispanic man and a Chevy with an Asian driver, Alex thought about the diversity of the country and its immigration issues. *So long as there are nations at war, or people starving, or dreaming of a better life,* he mused, *people will take huge risks to get here. That's what keeps me in business.*

After catching up with his family at dinner, Alex settled down to watch the news. When he heard the words El Salvador, his ears perked up. Dan Rather, the CBS newscaster, reported six heavily armed men seized the eldest daughter of President Duarte as she arrived for classes at a private university.

"Jesus Christ, does the fighting ever end there?" Then he thought

about the judge's letter regarding Rosa and felt good about his day.

On a prior visit, he had arranged for Rosa to call him every Friday, in case there was any news. When Rosa called, she immediately sensed a happier inflection in his voice.

"I've got promising news."

There was stunned silence. In prison, one has a designated sentence and could count down the days. But in detention, there was no time frame at all. You were trapped. At the mercy of an impersonal system. Rosa had been disappointed so many times in the past, that she dared not hope for her release.

"The judge is asking for more information about you. He sent a questionnaire, a list of questions. Rosa, that's a very good sign. On Wednesday I'll come see you. We need to get the ball rolling." Then he chuckled to himself. *He was not sure she understood the idiom: Get the ball rolling.* He reworded his thoughts. "Next Wednesday I'll come and help you answer the questions." Alex tried to explain the conversation he had with Stuart and the possibility of getting a sponsor. But cautioned her not to get too excited since there were no guarantees.

Driving beyond Apple Valley was a real inconvenience, but he had no choice. *What was the government's strategy, building the detention center so far out of the way? Probably did it to keep the mainstream from knowing what was going on. Like the Japanese internment camps during World War II. Out of sight, out of mind.*

Alex groused to himself remembering that Apple Valley Detention Center was built by a private corporation alongside their privately-run prison. Land was dirt cheap in this God-forsaken place. They were by far the biggest employer in this blighted community and could hire guards—grateful to have a job—at minimum wage. It all made sense from their point of view. But not for their family and friends, and certainly not for the attorneys trying to visit the detainees.

Chapter 54

Promises

Apple Valley Detention Center

WHEN STUART CALLED Banning and asked him to be a sponsor, Banning thought for a second. Then quickly responded, "You mean all I've gotta do is sign some papers and put her to work at the hotel. What the Hell?" It was just that simple. Rosa had her job and sponsor. It took her attorney, Alex Villareal, precious time to collect all the forms, letters of recommendation, and complete the paperwork to submit to the judge. On pins and needles, Rosa tried not to get her hopes up too high. Yet, she couldn't help thinking about the life she was missing. And she hungered more than anything to be with Santiago.

Inevitably, the wheels of justice ran on a slow track. It took another six plus weeks before Judge Guerro ruled on her case.

At long last, Rosa Lopez finally got her due:

GRANTED ASYLUM, SHE WAS
FREE TO REMAIN IN THE UNITED STATES

When she heard the news, she broke down and sobbed from happiness and relief that her long nightmare was about to end. Under the terms of her release, she would be given a permit to work. Further down the road, she could apply for an adjustment of status. That meant she could take the final leap and apply for a *green card.*

But in a detention center, life was not that simple.

Before Rosa could obtain a release date, she had to wait for the bureaucratic paperwork between her attorney, the court and the corporation running the detention center to be finalized. The private detention center dithered for almost three additional months before finalizing her discharge papers. When she was finally notified of her release date, it seemed like a mirage.

Rosa began to count down the days.

On the day of her release, she awoke before dawn. Lying in bed, surrounded by a dorm full of women, she couldn't help hearing their whimpering, muffled cries, and loud snoring. But for once, it didn't bother her. At exactly six o'clock the clarion call of the morning wake-up buzzer—more like a horn playing a long note—filled the dorm. She offered a silent prayer of gratitude. *Today I'm going home. I'M GOING HOME!* Not that she didn't think of it before, but she was reminded once again, that she didn't really have a home. Neither in El Salvador, nor in California. If everything went as planned, she would go back to Yolanda and Nacho's apartment. But for the time being, none of that mattered, so long as she could be with Santiago.

Rosa's emotions zig-zagged from joy to fear and back to joy. She had been disappointed too many times to expect it to go smoothly. *Strange things happen around here,* she thought. *Suppose they trick me. I heard that sometimes the guards pull somebody out and fly 'em to Texas or wherever. Maybe they'll put me on a plane and send me back to El Salvador.*

With no word, Rosa reluctantly continued to follow the daily routine. She washed up, made her bed, and stood in line for the early morning head count. The women were just about to march to the mess hall for breakfast when Officer J.T. Vicente, a nasty female guard with rounded shoulders and a bloated stomach, walked through the double doors.

"Hold it a minute. Stay in line," the duty officer barked to the women.

For a moment Officer Vicente spoke quietly with the duty officer. Then she ordered Rosa to step out of the line.

Rosa did as she was told. Standing in silence, she waited for direction. She knew better than to ask the questions that swirled through her head. Unless giving orders, the more sadistic guards—including Officer Vicente—simply refused to engage in any meaningful conversation. Rosa always found their hostility disheartening, causing her to feel invisible and worthless.

In a snarky voice, Officer Vicente indicated she was bored and less than thrilled with her assignment. "Get back to your bunk and gather your things." There was no small talk. In fact, there was no talk at all as they walked back to Rosa's bed. With her arms folded across her ample bosom, Officer Vicente instructed Rosa to strip her bed and take everything from her plastic bucket beneath the bunk.

"Everything?"

Officer Vincent repeated herself. "Didn't I just say everything?"

Even though it was heavy, Rosa juggled all her bedding, plus an extra jumpsuit, her toothpaste, toothbrush, shampoo, and towel—all her worldly possessions. She kept her rosary hidden in her pants pocket. *Maybe it's happening. Maybe I'll be free.* But Rosa's trust in the system was nil.

In silence, Officer Vicente escorted her through the network of interconnecting corridors to the sterile locker room where it all began. Rosa's mind was ablaze with bad memories. She recalled the all-consuming fear and confusion of that first day. With the other humiliated women, she had stood bare-ass naked waiting for her allotment: jumpsuits, tee-shirts, clogs, and bedding. Then her mind drifted, remembering the kind, sympathetic Hispanic *detainee* who had been working the counter that day. As she allocated the clothing and bedding, she had gently patted Rosa's hand and tried to reassure her that everything would be okay.

Well, she was right, Rosa thought, feeling stronger. *Somehow, I've made it through.*

Today another detainee was working behind the supply room counter. Officer Vicente handed the woman Rosa's release papers.

Rosa didn't recognize the woman's dark face. *Probably from another pod.*

The tall, lanky Haitian woman with unusually thin arms handed Rosa a plastic bag.

Rosa looked puzzled.

"For your hairbrush, shampoo, and toothpaste. They're yours. You paid for 'em." The woman lifted a cardboard box onto the counter. "Remember, you put your things in this box the day you got here. It's been closed since then. Want me to open it . . . or would you like to do it?"

"You open, *es* okay."

Despite the musty smell, Rosa was overcome with joy to see her worn jeans, tee-shirt, and navy blue sweat jacket.

"Go change your clothes. What belongs here must be returned. Dump the clothes in the red bin," she said pointing over toward the benches. "Towels and sheets in the blue one. Leave the clogs next to the bins. When you're done, Officer Vincente will walk you over to the In-Take Offices. You'll sign some forms, and they'll write you a check."

Once again Rosa looked puzzled.

"They'll pay you for your work . . . and whatever's left in your account. It's not much, but, hey, it belongs to you. Lucky girl, you're on your way out."

When everything was exchanged and put away, Officer Vincente escorted Rosa through the corridors to the In-Take offices. At the designated counter for those departing, Officer Vicente demanded the attention of a stone-faced male clerk. "This here's Rosa Lopez. Here's her release papers."

Without looking up, the clerk replied, "Be with you in a minute."

Rosa never took her eyes off him as he finished writing something, then handed it to another clerk. Finally, he pulled a manila folder from the in-box on his desk and ambled over to the counter. He flipped open the file and carefully scrutinized Rosa, comparing her to the two mugshots stapled to the inside cover. When convinced it was the same person, he addressed her. "There's some papers to sign." After handing her a ballpoint pen, he said, "Where I've marked in yellow, write your name."

Rosa's hand quivered as she carefully printed her first and last name four separate times. The clerk slipped the signed papers back in her folder and handed her a check for $41.85—a dollar for each day she worked that month, plus the remainder of the money Rachel and the attorney had given her for incidentals and phone calls, minus what she had spent at the commissary.

"You're free to go," he said in a bland voice that contradicted the importance of the moment. He acted as if it were an everyday occurrence, as if Rosa had not lost two plus years of her life, had not endured daily humiliations, and the constant fear she would be sent back to El Salvador. "If you're waiting for your ride," he said, "take one of those gray chairs against the wall." As he returned to his desk, as an afterthought, he flung out the words *Good Luck*.

Officer Vicente, convinced her job was completed, slipped away without so much as a good-bye.

For the moment Rosa just froze. She had been institutionalized for so long, with someone constantly telling her what to do, that the transition seemed surreal. She could stand, she could sit, or she could just walk through the door. It felt odd realizing the choice was hers to make. Holding her plastic bag—filled with her worldly possessions—she sank into one of the plastic chairs against the wall, overcome with emotions.

That morning, on their way to the detention center, Rachel and Santiago alternated between animated conversation and long periods of silent reflection. For the most part, Rachel's husband Stuart concentrated on testing his new Ford Country Squire as they drove along the back roads, but occasionally he jumped into the conversation.

When they finally arrived at Apple Valley Detention Center, there were a few confusing moments. In the past, Rachel had always parked in the Visitors' Center parking lot. But now, according to the direction, they were told to drive to the In-Take building, located on the east side in a restricted area of the large compound. A high chain link fence topped off with concertina wire surrounded the courtyard. Several uniformed sentries stood at the electronic gate, checking everyone's credentials before allowing them to pass through.

Once inside the secured courtyard, Santiago could hardly contain his excitement. Rachel and Stuart had never seen him so upbeat. As they were buzzed through the double glass doors of the In-Take office. Santiago immediately spotted his mother sitting alone—without handcuffs or a plastic barrier. *"Mamá! Mamá!"* he screamed. Tears of joy rolled down his cheeks as he flew into her waiting arms.

For Rosa, the tenderness, the human touch, the overwhelming force of love—that had been held in abeyance for so long—felt mystical, transcending time and place. In that moment, all the frustration and angst, the misery and loneliness that they both felt for so long dissipated into thin air as they clutched each other, afraid to let go.

For the first ten minutes, Rosa and Santiago's effusive emotional responses were so powerful that Rachel and Stuart could do nothing but stand back like voyeurs and watch. She caught Stuart attempting to dab at the tears that pooled in the corner of his eyes. She turned and whispered to her husband, "You know, at heart you're a wimp. You'd probably cry if you watched *Bambi*."

"Stop it! Show some restraint."

Rachel pressed her hand into his and squeezed hard, as if to say it's okay to cry. She waited until Rosa and Santiago calmed down before introducing her husband to Rosa. *"Este es mi esposo, Stuart."*

Overcome with gratitude, Rosa couldn't stop smiling. In her broken English, she tried to thank Rachel and Stuart, but seeing the joy in her face was all the thanks they needed. Santiago thought his mother looked more beautiful than the Madonna. Being a young boy, he hadn't noticed the subtle changes. Her once round cheeks now had a hollowness and she had developed a few frown lines across her forehead. Though she wore her thick black hair pulled back in a ponytail, thin strands of gray poked out here and there. During Santiago's visitations, his mother was always wearing a baggy orange jumpsuit. He didn't realize that she had lost almost twenty pounds.

As she stood up, Rosa exclaimed, "My jeans, they be so baggy, maybe they fall down."

While his mother was incarcerated, Santiago learned to fend for himself. Out of necessity, he had acquired one of life's important skills: how to make-do and adapt. "Mamá," he said, "here, I'll give to you my belt."

Everyone laughed, puncturing the intensity of the moment.

Except for the sundries, the only additional item that Rosa brought out of the detention center was the rosary that Santiago had somehow managed to sneak in. But that one item made all the difference. Rosa truly believed her prayers had been answered. In her mind, it was just a few days later that Alex Villareal, the immigration attorney, had walked into her life, replacing her despair with a flame of hope.

Santiago remained at his mother's side as they strolled through the parking lot. He wouldn't let go of her hand for fear she might disappear again. At the same time, Rosa could hardly wait to put some distance between herself and the detention center. When the car pulled away, she had no reason to look back for one last view. For her, the nightmare had ended. Rosa believed

God had given her a whole new life. Reborn, she was more than ready to move forward.

Relieved that Santiago's situation finally worked out, Stuart concentrated on driving while Rachel—for once quiet—sat in the front passenger seat smiling like a jack-o-lantern.

That morning, before picking up Santiago, Stuart reminded Rachel not to overwhelm Rosa with questions, to let her and Santiago relish their time together. For the first ten minutes of their drive back to Desert Oasis, Rachel did what he recommended; she simply listened as Rosa and her son sat in the back seat conversing in Spanish. It didn't matter that Rachel couldn't understand; she sopped up the pure happiness in their voices.

Proud of himself, Santiago smiled as he addressed his mother. "Look, I saved the letter from Javier. Inside, *es* a picture of his baby."

Rosa wasted no time opening the envelope. Her joy was spontaneous. She laughed and laughed as she focused on the photo of the baby. "Oh, my granddaughter, she's so precious!"

Rachel couldn't ignore the blissful occasion. Although she had promised Stuart that she would be quiet, she turned around to congratulate Rosa. "Just think, you're a grandma now."

Rosa handed her the photo. "She looks just like Javier, my other son," she explained, half-laughing, half-crying.

"Oh, she's beautiful! Such big eyes!"

Although invisible, euphoria engulfed Rosa. Just breathing freedom was sheer bliss. But for the rest of her life, she would appreciate the things most people take for granted. The warmth of the sun. A cool, gentle breeze. Music. Laughter. Flowers. Birds. Bright splashes of color. The freedom to choose, to dress and eat when and what she wanted.

A brown shopping bag had been sitting on the floor in the back of the car. Santiago had one more surprise for his mother. He placed the bag in front of her. "Open it," he commanded like the Cheshire Cat in *Alice in Wonderland*.

She pulled out a Fanta orange soda and a giant bag of Doritos chili, limón flavored tortilla chips. Still giggling, she hugged him.

"Your favorites!" he said, excited to be giving his mom a present.

"*Mi hijo,* you are the light of my life. How did you remember? For so many months, I dreamed about all the things I missed. This was always there . . . on the top of the list." She hugged him again and showered his head with gentle kisses. "I have so many people to thank." She leaned forward, with her hands touching the shoulders of Rachel and Stuart. "I not know the words to thank you."

Chapter 55

Bad News

Reno, Nevada

AT FOUR-THIRTY in the morning, Stuart's eyes fluttered. He thought he was dreaming. Then it dawned on him. The phone was ringing. He flung his arm out, stabbing for it. *Shit. Who's calling? Only bad news comes this early.*

He growled, "Hello," and then tried to clear his throat.

"This is Pepper. Sorry I'm calling so early."

"Yeah . . ." Still in a fog, Stuart vaguely remembered him. Banning's hippie friend, the one that used to manage the kitchen at the resort. When Stuart took charge of the resort, he replaced him. The last he heard, Pepper moved back to Reno and joined the jolly band of "party-goers" within Banning's elite circle.

"I got bad news." Pepper's voice cracked. "Banning's dead."

"WHAT?" Suddenly more coherent, Stuart's mind began to reel. "What happened?"

Not willing to go into the details, Pepper spoke in generalities.

"It's a long story. But I thought you oughta know."

"Pepper, hold on." Stuart said, reaching for the lamp. "Where are you? Reno?"

"Yeah. St. Mary's Hospital."

"Banning. When . . . when did he die?"

"A few hours ago," Pepper's voice cracked as he tried to contain his raw emotions. "Ya know, we were partying, like we always do. He started acting weird. Said he felt like heaving. The next thing I knew, someone, I forget who, yelled that he was sprawled out on the bathroom floor. When nobody could rouse him, Arlene called 9-1-1. He must have died on the way to the hospital."

Stuart had always predicted that with Banning's constant partying, it was inevitable that someone in his entourage would wind up dead. But in his wildest dreams, he never imagined it would be him. Banning was always the lucky one. The one calling the shots. "Pepper, is there anything I can do? Want me to notify someone?"

"No. I'll take care of it."

"What about a funeral?"

"To early to tell. I'll get back to you on that."

By the time Stuart hung up, he was wide awake. He sat in the living room processing the news. With Banning dead, there would be in-fighting over his money. Family, lawyers, trustees, court battles. But his real concern was personal. *Who was going to take over the reins? Would the heirs sell the resort? Would he still have a job?* Different scenarios tumbled in his head like dust motes on a windy day.

That morning Pepper tried to get hold of someone to officiate at Banning's funeral. Banning was never a church goer. Nor were his friends. Not one of them could recommend a clergyman. In desperation, Pepper contacted the Rock of God's Word, a storefront church which happened to be across the street from the time-share hotel. He met with the middle-aged pastor, a non-descript man, who wouldn't stand out in a crowd.

Three days passed before everyone could fly in for Banning's funeral. At the mortuary, the pastor proffered a canned sermon heavy on platitudes and psalms. Afterwards a cortege of cars—including Willy chauffeuring Pepper and several of Banning's playmates in the black Rolls Royce—drove out to the cemetery. The temperature lingered in the low 40's and a frigid wind rolled down from Mt. Rose.

A year-and-a-half earlier, Dani had divorced Banning and moved to Los Angeles with Monique, their five-year-old daughter. She had been doing her own partying, and hooked-up with Friedrich, another wealthy playboy, who happened to be the single heir to a German industrialist. Monique—the daughter she shared with Banning—had always been Dani's annuity, her financial ace-in-the-hole. After their divorce, she had received an overly generous settlement—a Mercedes, an expensive house in Beverly Hills, tuition for Monique's private school, and substantial child support.

Seated on the artificial turf nearest the open grave, was Gretchen—ex-wife number *one*—plus Hanna, their nineteen-year-old daughter, along with Hannah's young husband. Next to them was Dani, ex-wife number *two*. This motley group, considered the *first-string* mourners, were bundled up in heavy black coats, scarves, gloves, and *de rigueur* sunglasses.

Other mourners segregated into familiar clusters. The closely-knit band of salesmen, who had worked for Banning since his early days in Los Angeles, positioned themselves behind *the family.* They were the nearest thing Banning had to real friends. A few of the bookkeepers and hotel staff came to pay their respects. A cadre of his playmates huddled together, whispering among themselves. This group included Jeanné and Marina, who thoughtfully left their babies at home.

Rachel and Stuart had flown in from the desert that morning. Stuart stood back and scanned the crowd. He recognized Arlene, Banning's lady friend to whom he had given the ten grand, Willy, his Jamaican chauffeur and jack-of-all-trades; and the two that piloted his jet. He spotted Tony Lugano, the bagman who made frequent trips to the Cayman Islands. Tony looked somber as he spoke quietly to Banning's personal attorney and the CPA, now the designated trustees of his estate.

Pastor Grayson, wearing a black vestment with a large embroidered white cross, stood alongside the highly polished, *top-of-the-line* mahogany casket. Taking his job seriously, he tried to offer comfort to the professed mourners. He had no idea that those closest to the grave were primarily concerned with their alimony checks, child support, and the provisions of Banning's will. The others who gathered around were concerned about their jobs and present lifestyles.

"Death is nothing more than a journey," Pastor Grayson droned, "like crossing the horizon into the unknown." He recited a common prayer unfamiliar to those gathered there.

Upset that she didn't have a warmer jacket, Rachel shivered as she stood alongside Stuart. Living in the desert, she had forgotten just how cold Reno could be. Stuart, too, only wore a medium-weight jacket that did nothing to protect him from the piercing wind.

Rachel whispered to Stuart, "You know, in death it all boils down to what kind of box they put you in."

Stuart gave her one of his looks.

But Rachel couldn't restrain herself. "It's either a plain pine box or fancy mahogany with silk lining."

"Would you please stop?"

Rachel just kept talking. "You know, in India they just burn your body and throw the ashes in the Ganges River. A native Hawaiian lady once told me that in the olden days, the natives just committed the body to sea on the out-going tide."

"For God's sake, Rachel," Stuart snapped, "be quiet."

But she continued. "None of it really matters. When you're dead, you're dead. It's what you do with your life that counts."

Stuart squeezed Rachel's hand tightly, as if to say *not now*. He nodded his head and rolled his eyes towards Banning's girlfriends, indicating they might overhear her. "Can we talk about this later?" Although he agreed with her observations, he pretended he was concentrating on the pastor's homily about God's will.

At the end of the funeral, Rachel and Stuart drove the rented SUV back to the Reno airport. As they waited for their return flight to Southern California, Rachel continued with her diatribe. "I think Banning wasted his life. With his money, he could've done great things."

"Such as . . .?"

"Well, he could have been a whole lot more charitable. Buy a yacht. Maybe collect art, not *el cheapo repros*. I don't know what. Something."

"You really think collecting art is important?"

"Yeah," Rachel said dismissively. "At least in the end, there'd be something beautiful and enduring left behind. Banning threw his life away. All that money went up his nose. During the funeral, I couldn't help thinking what a waste. Today when I looked around, all I saw were people that fed off him in one way or another."

"Rachel, do you remember the words to Sinatra's songs?"

"Sinatra," Rachel said, contorting her face. "You and your pathetic love affair with ol' blue eyes. What's he got to do with anything? I'm serious . . . and you're joking."

"Ever hear him sing *I Did It My Way*?" With that, Stuart, who played Sinatra's music every chance he could, burst into song:

> *. . . I've lived a life that's full,*
> *I've traveled each and every highway,*
> *but more, much more than this,*
> *I did it my way!*

"Stop it! I'm not in the mood for your singing." She changed the subject. "Do you remember his daughter's wedding reception . . . on the paddle boat at Lake Tahoe in the middle of winter?" Rachel had such a vivid memory of the hilarious event. "We were all there, on the paddle boat waiting for the father-of-the bride to show up. He rolled in forty minutes late. God, we were all freezing our asses off when Willy drove Banning up to the pier in the Rolls.

He hopped out of the car in his plush, full-length mink coat, complete with a hood, like Michael Jackson at a Hollywood premier."

Stuart chuckled. "With all his money, there wasn't even an open bar. We had to pay for our own drinks. But," Stuart said, raising his index finger to make his point, "you gotta remember one thing. He did help Santiago and his mother . . ."

"Yeah, he did do that." A multitude of thoughts swept through Rachel's head. She was quiet for a moment, and then settled on an appropriate adage:

> *"I guess there's a little bit of good in the worst of us,*
> *and a little bit of bad in the best of us."*

EPILOGUE

Over time, amazing, unplanned events can often change the course of one's life. Sometimes it's called fate or fortune, luck, or providence. And sometimes it is the simple belief that one's prayers have been answered.

Not long after Stuart joined TRB World Holdings, Banning insisted they fly down to southern California to show him his two new acquisitions. Their first stop had been the shabby twenty-unit motel up on Miracle Hill. Built in the twenties or thirties, Stuart thought it was a useless piece of property. But over time, he had second thoughts. On closer inspection, he figured it still had some worth.

As Stuart upgraded Twin Palms Resort and Spa—the larger property—he sent the outdated, but usable furniture to the run-down motel that he renamed Sleepy Hollow Inn. Working on a tight budget, the once shabby building had been transformed into a charming little inn. Since it was less than a mile from Twin

Palms Resort and Spa, some of the massage therapists and resort employees—free-spirits in the true sense of the word—rented the renovated rooms. After work and on their days off, they gathered around the peanut-sized pool and chatted about New Age trends: chakras, crystals, their astrology charts, and health foods while smoking a little grass. Jokingly, they referred to the inn as their *kibbutz* or *commune.*

Before Rosa was released from the detention center, Stuart had quietly arranged for her and Santiago to live in what was once the manager's quarters at Sleepy Hollow Inn. With a little ingenuity, the resort's maintenance man had converted the manager's tiny office that faced the pool into a second bedroom. Santiago thought his new home heaven on earth—with his very own bedroom with a desk, a lamp, and a king-size bed with lots of pillows.

As stipulated in the court documents, Rosa worked as a housekeeper at Twin Palms Resort and Spa. She hitched rides to work with the good-natured, hang-loose hotel employees that lived at Sleepy Hollow Inn until she had enough money to buy a seven-year-old Honda Civic from one of the massage therapists. With a steady salary and health benefits, she was determined to do the right thing. Although it took her quite some time, she managed to repay Nacho for the minivan that had been impounded the night of her arrest.

She and Santiago finally felt safe in California. In her eyes, she was living the American dream. To thank the therapists and staff who helped her, Rosa frequently prepared a traditional Salvadoran dish—*pupusas de queso*—thick corn tortillas stuffed with cheese and accompanied with *curtido,* a spicy cabbage slaw.

Stuart had asked the accounting office in Reno to put Santiago on the payroll to wash windows and keep the outside of the motel picked-up. Always tight-fisted, they refused. Nevertheless, Stuart managed to pay him a modest stipend out of the resort's petty cash. By the time Santiago got to high school, his English had improved, and he had grown more accustomed to his adopted country and its peculiarities. Never a scholar, he worked hard to maintain reasonable grades, a prerequisite for playing sports.

By the time he was a high school sophomore, Santiago landed on the varsity soccer team. As many athletes do, he dreamt that one day he would be offered a scholarship to play soccer in college. Estrella, the cousin of one of his teammates, invited him to be an escort at her *quinceañera,* a lavish 15th birthday celebration, allowing the girl to officially begin dating. Although he was still shy, that single invitation opened his eyes to girls.

When Rosa's older son Javier lost his job at the car wash in Tijuana, he was too embarrassed to face his girlfriend Maria and her parents. So, he concocted a quixotic plan to return to El Salvador to avenge his father's murder. He got as far as Mexicali, where a group of teenage boys and young men gathered, all hoping to ride the rails south on *La Bestia.* As the train slowed as it rounded a curve, the motley group rushed helter-skelter to grab hold of a boxcar ladder and hoist themselves up. In the chaos, one of the young men accidentally bumped into Javier. He lost his footing and landed close to the whooshing metal wheels of the train. Feeling the ground rumbling, he hesitated. Ultimately, he laid on the ground watching as the train roared by him.

Shame-faced, Javier returned to his girlfriend in Tijuana and their baby. Finding a new job wasn't easy. Eventually he landed a warehouse job at the truck driver's tire company. Almost a year later, he and Maria—his first and only love—were married in the Holy Spirit Parish and moved out of her parents' apartment. Over the next five years, they had two more children, two boys, Mauricio—named after his father—and Juan. Years later, when Rosa and Santiago finally obtained their *green cards,* they were able to travel to Mexico to reconnect with Javier and meet his family.

Upon Banning's death, his personal attorney and CPA became trustees of his estate, including Twin Palms Resort and Spa. Stuart continued to manage it and began to dabble in local politics. Despite the bureaucratic roadblocks, Rachel forged on, teaching 7th and 8th graders at the middle school.

Acknowledgments

No author writes in a vacuum.

To begin my journey, I spoke with Stacey Witte, a social worker extraordinaire. In my quest for specific information, she put me in touch with Alissa Baier, an attorney who provided valuable material related to undocumented immigrants and the privately-run detention centers. In addition, I met with Sarah Nolan, an immigration attorney who worked for the state of New York. I was fortunate that my dear friend, Janis Musante, a California attorney, who volunteered to assist undocumented workers, also set me straight.

With our country's inhospitable climate towards immigrants, I prefer to thank some people simply by their first names: Daniella, Maria, Margarita, Ofelia, and Benjamin. I will forever be grateful to Ruben Jaimes, who provided information and clarity. And to Norma and Ben Guitron for allowing me to walk a mile in their moccasins.

This would never have happened without the encouragement and help of multiple manuscript readers: Mary Tripiano, Cynthia and Irving Shapiro, Sandy Rencher, Fay Katlin, Jackie and Jay Benson, Eudice Taran, Elaine Franklin, Deborah Uri, Myrna Chariton, Marcia Uri, Jerri Schubert, and Leslie Conley. My appreciation knows no bounds. Your suggestions were always right on. Your willingness to dedicate so much time to reading one version or another—sometimes more than once—kept my passion alive.

A special curtsy to Kathy Schindel, a superior editor who painstakingly read word-for-word, comma-by-comma, and line-by-line. I am grateful for your keen eyes, photographic memory, and command of the English language. You were truly a gift from Heaven. I will forever be indebted to my mentor, Irene Tritel, who constantly pushed me to finish this novel. To Mark Anderson, I valued your patience and wisdom. And finally, to Sissy Kaplan who worked diligently on the cover.

With love and gratitude to my children: Mimi, David, and Sherri, who understood my obsession and rooted for me every step of the way. Most of all, buckets of love and appreciation to my husband who constantly endured my frustrations with the computer, saved the day more times than I could count, and when I handed him a red pen, never complained about painstakingly reading another version.

Questions for Discussion

1. After her husband's murder, Rosa had to make a tough decision. She could either stay in El Salvador or flee, neither a good option. Her father dreamt that her life would be better in California. Do you think her odyssey was worth it? Have you ever had to make a difficult or frightening decision that could change the course of your life?

2. Javier, Rosa's oldest son, fell in love with Maria and chose to remain in Mexico. Did he make the right choice?

3. What are the obstacles *undocumented immigrants* face each day as they try to live under the radar? Does this affect their children?

4. All children do not come to school with the same skill set, nor the same socio-economic background. Should teachers be allowed to deviate from the standard curriculum to suit the needs of their students? What do you think schools could do to improve the educational experience for non-English speaking children? Have you ever volunteered in a classroom?

5. Private corporations listed on the New York Stock Market operate detention centers for profit? Is there enough transparency? Would it be better if the federal government operated them?

6. Is it necessary to incarcerate undocumented immigrants? Would it ease the system if some were able to put up a monetary bond, allowing them to live outside of a detention center until their asylum hearing? What about an electronic monitoring device, such as an ankle bracelet?

7. Rachel discovered words have power. What is the difference between an *illegal immigrant, an undocumented worker* and *a refugee?*

8. Do you think in the future, Santiago would be scarred from his experience being left alone? Do you think in the future, Rosa would be scarred from her experience in the detention center? What hope is there for Santiago after high school graduation? What opportunities will be there for him?

9. Why do you suppose immigration has become such an issue in the United States? Are there any precedents for it?

10. Judging from your own experience, are there significant differences between first, second, and third generation immigrations?